The Arnold and Caroline Rose Monograph Series
of the American Sociological Association

Sociology, ethnomethodology, and experience

Other books in the series

Sociology, ethnomethodology, and experience

A phenomenological critique

Mary F. Rogers

The University of West Florida

Cambridge University Press

Cambridge
London   New York   New Rochelle
Melbourne   Sydney

Published by the Press Syndicate of the University of Cambridge
The Pitt Building, Trumpington Street, Cambridge CB2 1RP
32 East 57th Street, New York, NY 10022, USA
296 Beaconsfield Parade, Middle Park, Melbourne 3206, Australia

First published 1983

Printed in the United States of America

Library of Congress Cataloging in Publication Data
Rogers, Mary F. (Mary Frances), 1944–
Sociology, ethnomethodology, and experience.
(The Arnold and Caroline Rose monograph series of the
American Sociological Association)
Bibliography: p.
Includes index.
1. Phenomenological sociology.   2. Ethnomethodology.
I. Title.   II. Series.
HM24.R648   1983   301′.01   82–23579
ISBN 0 521 25389 6 hard covers
ISBN 0 521 27409 5 paperback

to
Donald Vincent Rogers
and
Genevieve Maire Rogers

Contents

Preface

> In my case to know the world has always been accompanied by the desire to alter it. . . . I have always denied that the things which the world presents to us are stable and final reality.
>
> Nicolai Berdyaev, *Slavery and Freedom*

A friend of mine with staunch ideals and sharp talents accepts failure as a given; he aims for progress. That spirit underlies my effort to show the potential fruitfulness of phenomenological sociology. Whatever progress I make here will assuredly deepen my own phenomenological beginnings, virtually issue an intellectual invitation to my colleagues, and probably tax my sense of intellectual responsibility.

I write as a phenomenological beginner. Phenomenology has won my commitment as a sociological theorist. Yet it is not, of course, without its shortcomings. Certainly, for example, solipsism lurks as a continuous danger for all philosophers, including phenomenologists. Yet rigorous adherence to phenomenological method short-circuits the problem of solipsism. Certainly, too, phenomenologists debate among themselves and criticize one another's methods, data, and analyses. Yet virtually all phenomenologists assign primacy to human consciousness. To that extent they consistently concern themselves, in one fashion or other, with meaning, experience, constitution, the self, and essentially related matters. The progress I aim for involves implicitly showing that phenomenology is no solipsistic enterprise and explicitly showing that phenomenologists are a community of scholars who have in common some central concerns and some challenging tasks. The space at hand precludes overtly criticizing phenomenology or airing the disagreements among phenomenologists. My intellectual responsibility – indeed, my progress – does demand, however, that I be honest about my intellectual position and that I be painstakingly methodical in defending it.

I also write as a sociologist. I am unqualified to augment the exegetical and critical literature on Husserl's work and am uninterested here in phenomenological literary criticism, psychology, and aesthetics. My broad purpose is to demonstrate the theoretical and methodological advantages phenomenological sociology holds. Thus I offer a selective exposition of phenomenology that leaves aside major portions of Husserl's work, such as transcendental logic and the theory of numbers. To date, no social scientist has offered an introductory exposition of phenomenology. I want to fill that gap with a detailed mapping of the phenomenological literature relevant to social scientists.

The possibilities that move me concern recovery and discovery. A phenomenological sociology might help us recover the spirit of our predecessors who refused narrow interpretations of social reality. At the same time it might revitalize our sense of discovery concerning social life and the human experiences that shape and are shaped by varieties of togetherness. A phenomenological stance heightens possibilities for actual methodological and theoretical advances. Phenomenological sociology means, above all, open-ended sociology, that is, sociology so rigorously self-conscious that it invites methodological and theoretical pluralism. Briefly put, phenomenology offers sociologists opportunities for widening and deepening "sociological consciousness,"[1] a level of consciousness our naivetés, both professional and nonprofessional, seek.

To date, phenomenological sociology has developed as a variety of "interpretive sociology." If I in fact make progress here, I will show that all sociology is interpretive and that phenomenological sociology lifts that insight out of the taken-for-granted sphere. By labeling one sociological approach "interpretive," we sociologists imply that other approaches somehow advance themselves without benefit of interpretive activities. Here our language snares us. The phenomenological approach to language, which I favor over ethnomethodological and structuralist approaches, alone shows how phenomenology stands to benefit sociologists. Phenomenologists treat language foremostly in relation to experience rather than in terms of speech, conversations, and texts. In the process they remind us that words can entrap as well as free us.

My intellectual and psychological indebtedness is far-flung. To my parents I owe more than words permit me to acknowledge. Their constant love and continuous confidence have advanced my spirit and given me the determination to persevere.

To Maurice Natanson I owe a turning point in my intellectual life. His encouragement and criticism have helped me burst some long-standing intellectual limits. Most of all, though, his careful scholarship, splendid writing, and dedicated teaching have provided me with boundless inspiration. Although William Julius Wilson played a less direct role in stimulating this work, his influence on my intellectual habits and self-confidence has made a crucial difference. To my colleagues Dallas A. Blanchard and Ramon A. Oldenburg I am grateful for unfailing support and encouragement. I bear the same indebtedness to Lucius F. Ellsworth, Dean of the College of Arts and Sciences at The University of West Florida.

I am grateful, too, to Bodil Gilliam and Hope Loper at the John C. Pace Library of The University of West Florida. Linda Longsworth, Claire Hoewt, and Nancy Moore typed sections of the first draft of the manuscript. Their careful work facilitated my progress. To Charlie Mae Steen, however, I am most indebted for excellent typing and, besides that, for strong support whenever I became discouraged. To my students, too, I am indebted. In my Contemporary Sociological Theory course they bore up well as I labored over the matters of phenomenological sociology and ethnomethodology. Paula Brush, Gilbert Schultz, and Sandy Wilkinson merit special mention.

Martha L. Rogers also merits a special thanks. She lived with the radical fluctuations of mood that accompanied my writing. Not once did she complain, and many times she outdid herself with words of encouragement and deeds of kindness.

I am also deeply indebted to the National Endowment for the Humanities. The Endowment provided me the opportunity to study with Professor Natanson at Yale University in 1977 in an NEH Summer Seminar. In addition, the National Endowment for the Humanities awarded me a Summer Research Grant in 1979 that enabled me to complete the first draft of this study. To the people at the National Endowment for the Humanities I owe opportunities to enhance my teaching as well as advance my scholarship.

Finally, I owe a great deal to my husband Mandrake. We married when my work on this manuscript was nearing an end. Thus his support during that final stage was, in a sense, blind. Mandrake's help was a leap of faith. Coupled with his extravagant love, that faith helped me complete this project.

I remain, in the final analysis, the sole person responsible for whatever shortcomings mark this study. Were it not, though, for the encouragement of people too numerous to name, no manuscript would have appeared. Without shirking my responsibilities, I reiterate my thanks to them with the hope that I can give others what has been given me.

Introduction

What is needed is not the insistence that one see with his own eyes; rather it is that he not explain away under the pressure of prejudice what has been seen.

Edmund Husserl, "Philosophy as a Rigorous Science"

Phenomenology strikes most sociologists as an enigma. Because their acquaintanceship with it derives from social scientists and neopositivistic philosophers, many sociologists view phenomenology as nonscientific or even antiscientific. In that vein also lie beliefs that phenomenology is subjectivistic, intuitive, or esoteric. I aim to undercut those misconceptions by illuminating the fruitfulness of phenomenology for sociologists. That is the first broad purpose of this study.

Edmund Husserl (1859–1938), who laid the foundations of phenomenology, worked during the early twentieth century when the grounds and limits of knowledge were becoming scholarly uncertainties. While he was developing phenomenology, epistemological crises impelled Marxists-Leninists toward the sociology of knowledge, John Dewey toward experimental logic, and Bertrand Russell and Alfred North Whitehead toward reconsiderations of the foundations of mathematics and symbolic logic.[1] Husserl's response to the crisis of knowledge represents *a* philosophy only in the loosest sense.[2] Initially, we grasp more by approaching phenomenology as a set of methods for disclosing our presuppositions about human experience, conceptualizing about human experience, and describing its invariant elements.

The phrase "human experience" hints at Husserl's ambition. He investigated the breadth it implies: thinking, doubting, imagining, remembering, anticipating, meaning, perceiving, verifying, willing. He also treated familiarity and strangeness, habit and taken-for-grantedness, time-consciousness, corporeality, intersubjectivity, the self, and common sense. Those activities, givens, and accomplishments presuppose human consciousness. Most fundamentally, Husserl's phenomenology proffers methods for studying

1

human consciousness and its consequences. His phenomenology "hinges upon the acknowledgment of an experiential order, born by consciousness, in which and through which objects, events, and relations achieve their status as features of awareness."[3] Generically, phenomenology emphasizes the primacy of consciousness.[4]

Phenomenology differs from a "philosophy of internal experience,"[5] since it rejects the dichotomies of interiority-exteriority and subjectivity-objectivity. It also contrasts with speculation, since it examines "things themselves" *only as* they present themselves to consciousness. Devices called "reductions" constitute the methods of phenomenology. Their disciplined use establishes a radical empiricism capable of describing human experience and its invariant features.

Phenomenology also stands distinct from existentialism. Yet the existentialism of Jean-Paul Sartre, Maurice Merleau-Ponty, and Paul Ricoeur is sometimes called the "second school of phenomenology."[6] Husserl's later studies stimulated the existentialism (or existential phenomenology) that derives from Martin Heidegger, one of Husserl's students and colleagues. Husserl's concept *Lebenswelt* ("life-world") links his phenomenology with existentialism.

In general, existentialists (or existential phenomenologists) emphasize the unique tension between "essence" and "existence" that marks the human condition. They address the conduct of life, particularly choice making, the exercise of responsibility and freedom, and the drive for authenticity. Their work also exhibits a hermeneutical bent.[7] Finally, existentialists are likelier than (other) phenomenologists to treat the moral and political dilemmas human beings inescapably face. Although the existentialist perspective is sociologically relevant,[8] limitations of space and time preclude my discussing it here. Thus I draw on existential phenomenologists only peripherally, focusing instead on Husserl's phenomenology and its post–World War II development by such scholars as Alfred Schutz, Aron Gurwitsch, Maurice Natanson, and Thomas Luckmann.

Phenomenology is no panacea for whatever philosophical poverty and ambiguity infect sociology. Yet it does offer superior philosophical advantages. The first is its open-endedness. Phenomenological results are not additive; each phenomenologist is a "downright beginner" who must reconstruct other phenomenologists' findings.[9] Moreover, phenomenology is more a flexible orienting frame than a fixed interpretive scheme. It imposes no specific worldview. "The things themselves" and one's own perpetual beginnings are the primary resources for arriving at phenomenology. The other principal advantage of phenomenology is its encompassing applicability. In principle, every aspect of human experience lies within its scope. Phenomenology can illuminate whatever individuals experience.

Alongside those advantages lie methodological challenges. Doing phenomenology requires taking as little as possible for granted. In fact, phenomenological methods aim at eliminating what the investigator takes for granted so that "things themselves" appear without the distorting influence of presuppositions. The use of phenomenological methods culminates, then, in suspending the presuppositions that make up the "pressure of prejudice" Husserl opposed.

I shall begin by sharing the observations and judgments that led me to phenomenology. In Chapter 1 I examine some classical and contemporary critiques of sociology. Those critiques converge on issues phenomenology clarifies. Thus some long-standing critical tensions within sociology imply that our discipline leans toward phenomenology as a helpful philosophical frame. Chapter 2 focuses on consciousness and constitution, activities at the heart of Husserl's concerns. Those processes necessitate attention to time-consciousness, identity, objectivity, horizon, typification, and givenness. In Chapter 3 I turn to meaning, experience, and the self in relation to human consciousness. Chapter 4 examines how phenomenologists mesh the ideas of sociality, typification, anonymity, and the "natural attitude." That chapter treats the *Lebenswelt* or world of everyday life. Of necessity that world is a collective buildup that we all presuppose in all our experiences.[10] In Chapter 5 I discuss phenomenological methods and show how phenomenology relates to empiricism.

On the preceding grounds I undertake a phenomenological critique of ethnomethodology in the second part of this study. Although sociologists often view ethnomethodology as a phenomenological sociology, it bears only a tenuous relationship to phenomenology. Some ethnomethodologists do, however, claim a phenomenological orientation as well as intellectual debts to phenomenologists. Thus a phenomenological critique of ethnomethodology makes sense. I undertake that critique to demonstrate that ethnomethodology departs from its (presumed) phenomenological beginnings and fails to illustrate the sociological application of the phenomenological frame.

In Chapter 6 I survey the origins of ethnomethodology as well as the constructs, major findings, and methodological strictures ethnomethodologists offer. Chapter 7 represents a critical application of the phenomenological frame to ethnomethodological methods, conceptualizations, and analyses.

In addition, I indicate phenomenological omissions in ethnomethodological interpretations of the common-sense world. Together, Chapters 6 and 7 accomplish the second broad aim of this study.

Chapter 8 gathers together the lessons implied in the preceding chapters. Using "social action" as a focal concept, I specify the necessary dimensions of a phenomenological sociology. I believe such a sociology has implicit roots in nineteenth- and early twentieth-century sociology. In fact, it captures the motives our predecessors repeatedly renewed in refusing narrow interpretations of social reality. The idea of a phenomenological sociology is, I maintain, part of our sociological heritage and its loss reflects crucial compromises.

1. The struggle toward
critical unity in sociology:
a phenomenological resolution?

There would remain for Sammler, while he lasted, that bad literal-
ness. . . . Endless literal hours in which one is internally eaten up.
Eaten because coherence is lacking. Perhaps as a punishment for having
failed to find coherence.

Saul Bellow, *Mr. Sammler's Planet*

It is simplistic to assume that once an enemy has been identified, those
who made the identification are liberated.

Maurice Natanson, *Phenomenology, Role, and Reason*

Philosophy and sociology have long lived under a segregated system
which has succeeded in concealing their rivalry only by refusing them
any meeting-ground, impeding their growth, making them incomprehensible to one another, and thus placing culture in a situation of per-
manent crisis.

Maurice Merleau-Ponty, *Signs*

Today Westerners experience a serious rift between knowledge and action.[1]
Their experiences commonly suggest that greater knowledge only aggravates
the desire for effective, satisfying action. Political knowledge finds few
effective outlets; a college education infrequently leads to professional opportunities; insights into institutionalized racism fail to eradicate it; knowledge
of the causes of chronic unemployment does not employ its victims. Under
such circumstances increased knowledge breeds skepticism, frustration,
and a sense of impotence. Vacuous private lives and impoverished public
life result.

Modern anti-intellectualism is but one expression of the commonplace
judgment that knowledge, after all, fails us. Common-sense experiences
imply that knowledge is no substitute for the close social bonds lost to
modern social organization and industrial technology. Rather, the knowledge
explosion intensifies the senses of finitude and powerlessness. Ultimately,

5

most individuals confront a peculiarly modern choice. They may bear the frustrations of knowledge with whatever grace they can muster or they may escape the shallowness of ignorance with whatever diversions they can afford.

Most individuals sidestep an irrevocable or self-conscious commitment to one of those alternatives. Since "dignity is as compelling a human need as food or sex" and knowledge in modern societies commands dignity,[2] acquiring and displaying knowledge remain important to most individuals. Thus whatever their attitudes toward knowledge, individuals pursue it, however unsystematically. Yet the experience of a gulf between knowledge and action persists. Its most acute manifestation is the crisis of legitimacy in Western societies today.[3]

That crisis shapes our self-conceptions, our perceptions of other human beings, and our institutional structures. It stamps our actions, interactions, and reactions. The twentieth-century crisis of legitimacy *rests on* skepticism about the value of reason and the possibility of truth; it *expresses* distrust of the bearers of authority. Our sociological predecessors foresaw the crisis we face. Twentieth-century sociologists have extended their insights, often citing social scientists' own contributions, whether by commission or omission, to the malaise of Western culture. Their criticisms imply that phenomenology can ease the divisive tensions within sociology and within the world it helps to shape.

Sociology and the Crises

The gulf people experience between knowledge and action concerns the divide between scientific knowledge and everyday action. The knowledge that disappoints people – the knowledge that strikes them as *practically futile* – is scientific knowledge. When their disenchantment with technical knowledge grows, people incline to question the rights of those whose authority rests on claims to superior (i.e., scientific) knowledge. No matter how inchoate, people's doubts about the worthwhileness of scientific knowledge exacerbate the difficulty of efficiently wielding authority. Authorities then face a crisis that raises their costs or reduces their options. Although "crisis of legitimacy" implies bureaucratic concerns with efficient control, its most serious ramifications are cultural rather than bureaucratic in nature. Specifically, the crisis of legitimacy implies a Crisis of Reason. To the extent that bearers of formal authority symbolize Reason in modern Western societies, doubts about their rights to dominate represent skepticism about Reason itself. Reason is threatened with disrepute. Every crisis of legitimacy carries that threat.

Significantly, the knowledge–action gulf also points to a Crisis of Common Sense in modern everyday life. That gulf rests on a pervasive, though subtle, denigration of nonscientific knowledge. It ignores the routine, sometimes striking successes common-sense knowledge generates. Indeed, in modern everyday life common-sense knowledge often goes unrecognized. At best, people assign it a grossly inferior status in relation to scientific or technical knowledge. As they cope with their disappointment in scientific knowledge, then, modern people tend also to repudiate their common-sense knowledge. Ironically, by its very nature that knowledge more often than not leads to effective action in everyday life. Trained to denigrate it, however, people who sense the divide between scientific knowledge and practical action cannot help but experience a woeful gulf between "knowledge" and action. Hand in hand with the Crisis of Reason, then, is a Crisis of Common Sense. At one and the same time people doubt the scientific knowledge our culture emphasizes as a cure-all and overlook or denigrate their common-sense knowledge.

More than a century ago some social scientists foresaw Crises of Common Sense and Reason as long-term consequences of rationalization. They concerned themselves with the effects of bureaucratization, science, and rational action on everyday life. Their analyses not only anticipated cultural crises but also implied the likely utility of phenomenology in reorienting scientific activity and thus alleviating those crises.

I begin with Karl Marx and Max Weber as spokespersons for nineteenth-century social scientists. The spread of Marx's notions concerning alienation and the social conditioning of knowledge stimulated the Crisis of Reason. His concepts also enabled people to describe the experiences that collectively constitute the Crisis of Common Sense. Here, however, my interest lies with Marx's observations about the separation of science from practical life, the status of reason, and the effects of bureaucracy on everyday cognition.

Marx held that all theoretical and practical consciousness has reason as its latent foundation. He advocated the "reform of consciousness," efforts to help individuals understand their own acts of consciousness.[4] Such efforts require recognition of the close but increasingly opaque relationship between science and practical activity. Fundamentally, both scientific and nonscientific activities aim toward rational solutions to life's mysteries through "human practice *and the comprehension of this practice*."[5] Marx argued that "one basis for life and another for science is *a priori* a falsehood."[6] When separated from practical activity, scientific inquiry is liable to misrepresent reality.

Its object must influence scientific inquiry: "Not only the result but also the route belong to truth."[7] Neglect of those principles leads to "mystical results."[8] Science must, then, prove itself practically. "In practice, man must prove the truth, that is, [the] actuality and power . . . of his thinking."[9] Marx understood the loss of credibility science risks when it contradicts (or appears to contradict) the logic of people's practical experiences. Yet he regarded such (apparent) contradictions as mere by-products of inappropriate methods of inquiry, not as inevitable consequences of scientific activity.

Marx also implied the likely consequences of the bureaucratization of science and knowledge. He stressed that a bureaucracy is a "hierarchy of information." Individuals' positions in a bureaucracy determine the quantity and quality of their information. In a bureaucracy the structure of authority shapes knowledge; bureaucratic rationality molds bureaucratic knowledge.[10] And Marx decried bureaucratic rationality. Stressing the need to distinguish what bureaucracy actually is from how it regards itself, he argued that bureaucracies are "web[s] of practical illusions." They confuse form with content and vice versa; transbureaucratic purposes become narrow bureaucratic ones.[11] Large-scale organizations create, in other terms, their own (ultimately false) forms of rationality and falsify the practical by spawning illusions about its limits. Marx's perspective suggests a long-term paradoxical trend: on the one hand a denigration of mundane knowledge, and on the other hand a disparagement of "rationalized" organizations and the knowledge they artificially separate from everyday life. In sum, the "rational" separation of bureaucrats (officials, experts, administrators) from practical people, whose lives largely contradict bureaucratic logic, leads to Crises of Common Sense and Reason.

Weber's findings about bureaucratization and disenchantment are well known. "Bureaucratic administration means fundamentally the exercise of control on the basis of knowledge" that is technical and continuously supplemented.[12] Bureaucratic knowledge is also "secret"[13] because of the "striving for power."[14] The conjunction of bureaucratic knowledge, power, and durability leads to disenchantment not only with bureaucracy but also with science and technical knowledge. Weber's scheme also treats the relationship between legal-rational and charismatic authority. His analyses of charismatic leaders exploiting widespread "distress," the formation of their discipleships, charismatic domination, and the routinization of charisma account for how social orders contain disenchantment, accommodating themselves to crises of legitimacy.[15] Thus Weber forecasted not only the problem of maintaining legitimacy but also bureaucratic "solutions" to that problem.[16]

Marx's and Weber's ideas converge on disenchantment as a bureaucratic by-product. In their discussions of bureaucracy, though, they diverge on the topic of rationality. For Weber "rational" meant maximal efficiency and the exercise of control through knowledge.[17] Marx took issue with that narrow a conception. In addition, the two thinkers disagree about the humanistic merits of science. Weber mildly chastised those who demand from science more than "artificial abstractions" and "analyses and statements of facts."[18] But Marx criticized sciences that artificially abstract from everyday life. In general, Weber viewed disenchantment and crises of legitimacy as consequences of frustrated needs and the structural divide between bureaucrats and other members of society. Although Marx agreed with that judgment, he also emphasized the biases of science that promote bureaucratic sluggishness in the face of Crises of Common Sense and Reason.

Twentieth-century sociologists have further detailed the problems that preoccupied Marx and Weber. During the 1930s, both Karl Mannheim and Robert Lynd propounded ideas reminiscent of Marx's and Weber's. Like Marx, Mannheim decried the tendency for exactness to supersede "knowledge of things," overshadowing the question of which method best suits a problem.[19] Concerned also about the weak philosophical foundations of American sociology, Mannheim stressed the dangers of aphilosophically formulating research problems. He hinted that a reflexive element minimizes the play of social factors in research. Lynd focused more on how sociology should enhance culture than on how culture shapes sociology. His concerns included the division of social scientists into scholars and technicians, their concentration in bureaucracies of higher learning, the ahistorical and aphilosophical character of American social science, and the loss of "the person" in social-scientific research. Most of all, Lynd's *Knowledge for What?* pleaded for responsible social science.[20] Lynd believed the social sciences should be "judged by their adequacy in helping man to resolve his difficulties."[21]

C. Wright Mills provided the most impassioned exposition of the shortcomings of contemporary sociology. In *The Sociological Imagination* he described "grand theory" unable to touch base with concrete reality and abstracted empiricism unable to advance a credible epistemology. Mills accounted for those faults by emphasizing bureaucracy and careerism. Stressing the cultural responsibilities of the social sciences, Mills underscored the importance of the "sociological imagination" in people's everyday lives.

What they need, *and what they feel they need*, is a quality of mind that will help them to use information *and to develop reason* in order to achieve lucid summations of what is going on in the world and of what may be happening within them.[22]

The promise of sociology, according to Mills, lies in honoring the "human variety" through interdisciplinary, historical, and comparative studies. Thereby social scientists fulfill their distinctive cultural tasks.

Finally, Mills addressed the perilous status of reason and freedom:

Great and rational organizations – in brief, bureaucracies – have indeed increased, but the substantive reason of the individual has not. Caught in the limited milieux of their everyday lives, ordinary men often cannot reason about the great structures – rational and irrational – of which their milieux are subordinate parts. Accordingly, they often carry out series of apparently rational actions without any idea of the ends they serve, and there is increasing suspicion that those at the top as well only pretend to know. The growth of such organizations, within an increasing division of labor, sets up more and more spheres of life, work, and leisure in which reasoning is difficult or impossible. . . .

Science, it turns out, is not a technological Second Coming. That its techniques and its rationality are given a central place in a society does not mean men live reasonably and without myth, fraud, and superstition. . . .

The increasing rationalization of society, the contradictions between such rationality and reason, the collapse of the assumed coincidence of reason and freedom – these developments lie back of the rise into view of the man who is "with" rationality but without reason.[23]

Thus Mills implied a Crisis of Common Sense and a Crisis of Reason. People feel the inadequacy of their knowledge as well as the need for a "quality of mind" capable of clarifying their worlds and their selves. Instead of promoting that quality of mind, sociologists now *function* within bureaucracies whose rationality stymies the sociological imagination. To that extent their *products* feed extant doubts about the worthiness of reason. Insofar as sociology compromises its promise, then, it aggravates the Crises of Common Sense and Reason.

Mills called for a sociology aware of its responsibilities; a sociology whose language is clear and vibrant; a sociology whose assumptions are explicit and soaked in historical, philosophical, and psychological knowledge; a sociology preoccupied with problems relevant to understanding the human condition rather than with problems easily studied; a sociology that "shuttles between levels of abstraction, with ease and with clarity";[24] a sociology that fulfills the visions of our predecessors and addresses the needs of our contemporaries.

During the past two decades, the issues Mills raised have continued to spark debate. Mills's concerns inform the "sociology of sociology," loosely identifiable by its critical focus on the social organization of sociology and the axiological dilemmas sociologists face.[25] During the 1960s, radical sociology and humanistic sociology rose to prominence. Both sociologies stressed commitments to explicit values and to epistemologies different from those of "establishmentarian" sociology.[26] That same period marked the emergence of dramaturgical sociology and ethnomethodology, both stressing micro-level investigation and distinctive methods. Finally, during the 1960s some sociologists, most notably Daniel Patrick Moynihan and James Coleman, tried to bridge the private troubles–public issues gap through involvements with the federal government, perhaps epitomizing the turn toward "applied sociology." In the 1960s sociology exhibited the turmoil, innovation, and hopefulness that then characterized large segments of American society. Like many other Americans during that period, however, sociologists often sidestepped programmatic attention to the roots of the problems they belabored. During the 1960s the Crises of Common Sense and Reason, for example, troubled few of us.[27]

Ironically, Alvin Gouldner wrote in 1970 of a *coming* crisis in sociology. Although he discussed matters that preoccupied Mills, such as the social organization of sociology and its misguided values, he failed to offer as comprehensive a vision. Gouldner shortchanged reason and common sense, although issues about their status underlie his treatise.

Also ironic is Gouldner's plea for a "reflexive sociology." Gouldner belittled ethnomethodology, though it expressly advocates reflexive scholarship. Gouldner demanded a more rigorous sociology of sociology. In that connection, he virtually called for a phenomenological sociology. In inveighing against buried presuppositions ("domain assumptions"); in assuming a connection between knowledge of self and knowledge of the world, and asserting the primacy of the former; and in rejecting the independence of science from common sense, Gouldner leaned toward a phenomenological sociology. Moreover, his sympathy for interpretive sociology and his conception of the social world as "constituted by men" also suggest a phenomenological orientation.[28]

In *For Sociology*, Gouldner vindicated himself by attending to reason and the need for a philosophically mature sociology. Sociology's first task is to disclose the "conditions required to sustain rational discourse about social worlds. . . ."[29] Gouldner urged that sociology elucidate daily life and vindicate reason.[30] But, says Gouldner, "the sociologist will tell you he is not a philosopher, almost as if he believed that ignorance of philosophy was the beginning of sociological wisdom." Similarly, sociologists often act as if their products are separable from their methods.[31] Gouldner advocated an integration of the social sciences based on philosophy, history, linguistics, and hermeneutics. That integration would, presumably, advance the understanding of social life on the level of practical reason. Again, Gouldner leans toward a phenomenological sociology.

Gouldner's critiques, like Mills's, have provoked considerable debate. His proposals have not, however, alleviated the axiological and epistemological dilemmas that plague sociologists. As president of the American Sociological Association, Lewis Coser indicted "present developments in American sociology which seem to foster the growth of both narrow, routine activities and of sect-like esoteric ruminations. . . . Together they are an expression of crisis and fatigue within the discipline and its theoretical underpinnings."[32] And Anthony Giddens has criticized the epistemological bases of social theory, arguing that we need fresh frameworks for analyzing the development of advanced societies.[33] Finally, as Alfred McClung Lee has recently shown, "Sociology for whom?" remains a central challenge that divides sociologists and impedes the development of a humanistic sociology.[34]

Phenomenology and sociology

Among the persistent criticisms of sociology, several themes stand out. First, critics doubt that neopositivistic methods alone can elucidate social life. In other terms, concern about the epistemological grounds of sociology is common. Meshed with that theme are demands for clear philosophical foundations that extend beyond a logic of inquiry. A second theme is that sociologists need to reflect more about their work, particularly its epistemological bases and its cultural consequences. That most sociologists work in bureaucracies has led many critics to insist, too, that sociologists clarify the relationship between their assumptions and the social organization of sociology. Finally, some critics advocate skepticism toward the invidious contrasts between science and folk knowledge. Those contrasts assume that in some sense science stands apart from the common-sense world. The question of how scientific rationality and practical rationality intermesh also raises questions about the nature of knowledge itself.

These themes represent a latent critical unity among sociologists concerned about the limits and possibilities of their discipline. At the same time, they represent the boundaries of the major sociological debates, for example, methodological individualism versus methodological holism, value-free versus value-committed sociology, and quantitative versus qualitative methods. All three themes relate to the nexus between sociology and philosophy. Each alludes to the necessity of disclosing and clarifying that nexus – in short, desegregating sociology and philosophy – so that sociologists might resolve the specific issues these themes encompass.

The themes imply the likely fruitfulness of a philosophical frame that addresses both epistemology and human experience. The philosophy likely to benefit sociology must also address the relationships between experience and knowledge, between the practical and the theoretical attitudes, and between common sense and reason. Further, it must provide methods for determining and controlling presuppositions and for becoming more rigorously reflective. In sum, sociology demands a philosophy that responds to the question of how human experience discloses realities. The philosophy best suited for all these tasks is phenomenology.

Phenomenology focuses on knowledge in the broadest sense. One of Husserl's goals was the radical clarification of knowledge. Although that radicalism does *not* equate "being" with "being-known," it does assert that the only access we have to being is its being-known. Phenomenologists describe the correlation between existents and acts of consciousness; namely, every existent presupposes acts of consciousness. "Existent" refers to that-which-is-taken-to-exist, where "is-taken-to" subsumes "is-perceived-to," "is-demonstrated-to," "is-felt-to," and other experiences that present the *possibility* of the idea of existence as a specific actuality. "Existent" refers to anything *given* as existing.

In the common-sense world existents occur as that-which-(is-taken-to-) exist; that is, the acts of consciousness that realize the *possibility* of the idea of existence are not themselves objects of awareness. In everyday life we take for granted the existence of all the objects we experience. In contrast, the phenomenologist methodically examines the "is-taken-to," which consists of acts of consciousness like believing and perceiving. The goal is to account for the initially given existent as an instance of a specific kind of possibility, for example, the possibility of imagining, perceiving, judging, or believing. Thus phenomenology describes how we constitute objects of knowledge through acts of consciousness.

Related to the phenomenological focus on knowledge is a concern with experience. All knowledge presupposes not only acts of consciousness but also experience. Husserl clarified the roots of experience by examining what is experientially given rather than what is built up on experiential grounds.[35] He showed that a primordial necessity governs experience. Moreover, Husserl explored the conditions that make experience possible. Following Husserl, phenomenologists try to describe experience without schematizing it. Since description itself is a schematizing activity, however, they can only approach that goal.[36] Nonetheless, they elucidate what the experience of objects entails and, conjointly, what essential features consciousness exhibits. Phenomenologists demonstrate that "experience is neither a substitute for reality nor a veil that falls between us and what there is, but rather a *reliable medium of disclosure* through which the real world is made manifest and comes to be apprehended by us."[37] Concerned with the essential structure of experience, phenomenology ultimately reconciles what we commonly call "reason" and "experience."[38]

Thus far, phenomenology presents itself as the methodical clarification of the conditions that make human experience possible. As such, phenomenology concerns

the descriptive delineation of what presents itself to consciousness as it presents itself and insofar as it presents itself. . . . [It] seeks in the most radical way to examine consciousness directly, to appreciate its contents and structures quite apart from prior scientific commitments or philosophical pre-judgments, and . . . strives, above all, to regain the immediate experiential world which we have forgotten, denied, or bartered away.[39]

Phenomenologists pursue these goals at the "level of essential interpretation"; namely, they treat an event or thing "as an exemplar of its class or type."[40]

Yet phenomenology is compatible with empirical methods. One can, for example, do phenomenology and do sociology simultaneously. The phenomenological and empiricist standpoints complement one another. Phenomenologists grant the indispensability of empirical methods for determining facts. They stress, though, that empiricists cannot clarify, let alone validate, their presuppositions using empirical methods. Empirical work sets aside skepticism about reality and adopts an implicit rather than a critical theory of knowledge. The empiricist theory of knowledge presupposes intersubjectivity that is accessible to analysis but for which empirical methods cannot account.[41] Husserl claimed that "no objective science can do justice to the subjectivity that achieves science."[42] Yet phenomenological analyses neither substitute for nor oppose empirical analyses. Rather, they clarify the structure of experience and disclose empiricists' presuppositions.[43] Phenomenology thus provides grounds for reflexive involvement in empirical work. In short, "empiricism begins where phenomenology leaves off."[44]

Husserl wanted to elucidate the grounds of science. He thought that their obscurity feeds modern intellectual and cultural crises. "There is, perhaps, in all modern life no more powerfully, more irresistibly progressing idea than that of science." Moreover, "our age wants to believe only in 'realities.' Now, its strongest reality is science, and thus what our age most needs is philosophical science."[45] Husserl aimed to correct naive objectivism (i.e.,

Scientism), which implies that physical objects are more "real" than ideal objects and that scientific knowledge is the paradigm for all knowledge.[46] He showed that common sense incorporates a logic that is neither unsophisticated nor misguided. Thus Husserl argued against a "double-world" perspective in hopes of restoring the dignity of mundane experience while respecting the contributions of science.[47]

Husserl concerned himself, then, with the Crises of Reason and Common Sense. Sensitive to their debilitating ramifications, he intended that phenomenology be no "less than man's whole occupation with himself in the service of universal reason."[48] Phenomenology represents "a defense of Reason. There is, Husserl insists, a teleology proper to human action: it must be directed toward its own completion within the larger network of the fulfillment of all consciousness in rational terms."[49]

The social-scientific relevance of phenomenology lies in its probing concern with knowledge. Phenomenology views knowledge as perspectival and open-ended, on the one hand, and invariantly grounded and directed toward evidence, on the other hand. For phenomenologists, Reason is an activity that discloses and reconciles those two aspects of knowledge. Phenomenologically, the fulfillment of reason lies in appreciating the universal grounds of all knowledge and continuing the quest for less and less incomplete knowledge. In sum, phenomenology invites beginners to deny an unbridgeable gulf between the abstract and the concrete, the theoretical and the practical, the scientific and the common-sensical. It reminds us that both science and common sense remain unconcerned with epistemology and metaphysics, that both "commence where philosophers end."[50]

Phenomenological sociology: a preliminary illustration

The phenomenological approach to knowledge holds methodological insights for social scientists, whose roles demand reflexive attention not only to social-scientific knowledge but also to the common-sense knowledge that underlies their subject matter. More generally, phenomenologists' attention to meaning, experience, selfhood, and the world of everyday life make their findings acutely relevant to social scientists. Yet phenomenology remains a bugaboo for many social scientists who assign it, at best, an ambiguous status.

Before surveying relevant phenomenological findings, then, I want to illustrate a virtually phenomenological stance at work in a sociological study. Thereby I aim to undercut the beliefs that phenomenological sociology is esoteric and that it offers only a fresh jargon that glosses over the problems sociologists face in their work. For those purposes I turn to one of Kai T. Erikson's studies. Although his *Wayward Puritans* is neither overtly nor fully phenomenological, it does resonate with phenomenology. His study shows, first of all, that the presence or absence of phenomenological terminology is not itself a reliable indicator of a study's phenomenological status. More importantly, since it was well received, Erikson's study illustrates the potential attractiveness of phenomenologically oriented works. Finally, Erikson's study offers a sound sociological reference point for the exposition of phenomenology that follows. Alongside Erikson's *Everything in Its Path*, which we will consider in Chapter 8, *Wayward Puritans* offers sociological access to the phenomenological perspective.

In *Wayward Puritans*, Erikson's point of view and overriding goals appear phenomenologically relevant. He presents himself as a disinterested observer methodically attempting to grasp the subjectively meaningful experiences that underlay the social constitution of deviance among the Puritans in seventeenth-century Massachusetts. That constitution, Erikson found, was a difficult process involving conflict between the religiously unorthodox and the politically powerful. Erikson aimed to detail that constitution by describing the objective social facts built up from subjectively trying events.

Early in his report, Erikson notes that "we sometimes give [the Puritans] credit for a kind of success they did not in the least want to achieve."[51] We fail, in other terms, to understand the Puritan world on its own terms. We overlook the motives, plans, and other subjectively meaningful experiences that moved them in common, distinctive directions. Erikson puts those concerns at the center of his analysis. That the Puritans themselves kept "useful records" provides a crucial basis for his study (p. viii). He relies as heavily as possible on them, since "they are the voices of the Puritans themselves speaking of the world in which they lived" (p. x). To grasp what their experiences meant to them, the researcher "must begin by looking at the world [the Puritans] claimed as their own rather than the world they happened to make" (p. 33). They themselves "supply our only view" of the way they regarded and made sense of their experiences (p. 109). More generally:

When the student is primarily concerned with learning how a given society developed or changed from one period to the next, he naturally looks at those pivotal events which seem to "make" history. . . . But when the student is primarily concerned with the underlying structures of society he must look for his data in the ordinary cycles of everyday life, in the habits and behavior of everyday people, for these point to a dimension of history which can only be learned by observing how often commonplace events reoccur. (pp. 164–165)

In phenomenological terms, Erikson's broad concern is the Puritan life-world; his specific focus is how the Puritans' constitution of deviance expressed, maintained, and changed their world over time.

Erikson approaches his subject matter aware of the differences between the theoretical and the common-sense attitudes. He stresses that "human events are neither general nor particular until some student arranges them to fit the logic of his own approach" (p. vii). Events have a logic of their own independent of whatever logical character they exhibit after an observer schematizes them using the logic of an academic discipline. Moreover, within the theoretical attitude any number of "logics" are available; the two most relevant to Erikson's study are those of the historian and of the sociologist. Yet each of those logics loses its "theoretical crispness" when a scholar is more interested in thoroughly examining the object of inquiry than in respecting the socially constructed boundaries defining academic territories (pp. vii–viii). "Perhaps all one can do about the problem," Erikson concludes, "is to state as clearly as possible where [one's] dependencies lie" (p. x). Erikson suggests that overly close attention to certain events can "blur rather than sharpen" the details of a human "story" (p. ix); the theoretical attitude, ideally, avoids both an unduly particularistic and an overly universalistic outlook. Simultaneously, it recognizes that the "distinct shape" of events is an ex post facto achievement foreign to individuals' immediate experiences of those events (pp. 43–44).

Within those general limits, Erikson hints at several additional features of the theoretical attitude. First, he suggests the crucial role the imagination plays in its fruitful application. In passing, Erikson indicates, for example, that "we may imagine that a hush spread quickly over the courtroom" (p. 96). When directed toward understanding the subjective meaning of human events, then, the finely honed theoretical attitude relies on imagination as a line of access to what people leave out of their accounts and records. In fact, imaginative reconstructions, such as the one alluded to above, validate the understanding the researcher develops about the subjective meaning of specific events. Erikson demonstrates the role of imagination in commenting on the trial of Anne Hutchinson:

When we wander across the pages of this transcript we are apt to get tangled in the underbrush of words, but if we read ahead without regard for the meaning of those words we soon begin to sense a rhythmic counterpoint in the sounds of the conversation – the smooth, seasoned tones of John Cotton, the crisp logic of Anne Hutchinson, the contributions of the clerical chorus in the background, and the whole punctuated by an occasional rattle of anger from John Wilson. . . . The examination, which continued through two sittings, never lost this metric quality. The various participants seemed to be moving in cadence, joined together in a kind of ceremonial chant; and while this effect may be more striking to modern readers who do not understand the arguments being exchanged, it is easy to imagine that the Boston congregation had a sense of sharing in a ritual inquisition. (p. 104)

Here Erikson not only underscores the centrality of imagination to the theoretical attitude but also reminds us that imagination comprises so sharp a sensitivity to words that it discloses the forms words themselves presuppose. Second, although he uses statistics, Erikson largely overcomes the temptation to treat statistical data apart from the individuals they report about. Erikson prefaces his statistical considerations accordingly: "In the following pages . . . we will be dealing with hundreds of unknown settlers who appeared in the courtrooms of Essex County just long enough to become a statistic in the colony's records" (pp. 164–165). Throughout the survey that follows, Erikson persists in referring to categories or types of concrete individuals. He knows well the utility and pitfalls of statistical data. Finally, Erikson understands that the theoretical attitude aims at superseding the uniqueness of the particular cases it treats; specific cases are, for the theoretically inclined observer, exemplars of universal structures. Thus Erikson approaches the Puritan experience "as an example of human life everywhere" (p. viii).

In *Wayward Puritans* Erikson's specific focus is deviance, defined as "conduct which the people of a group consider so dangerous or embarrassing or irritating that they bring special sanctions to bear against the persons who exhibit it"; thus deviance is "a property *conferred upon* that behavior by the people who come into direct or indirect contact with it" (p. 6). Erikson's definition is phenomenologically relevant in several respects. First, it stresses that a group does not define and punish deviance; *individuals* do. Second, it implies that individuals' interpretive schemes lead them to perceive danger, feel embarrassment, or experience irritation in reaction to specific types of behavior. Third, they apply sanctions not to behavior but to other individuals whose behavior they perceive and interpret, either directly or indirectly. People constitute deviance, then, not only in face-to-face relationships but also in anonymous or mediate relations. The net of perceptions, interpretations, and negative reactions that constitutes deviance is far-flung in any social world. Moreover, Erikson indicates that the "conformist" and the "deviant" are products of the same culture, "inventions of the same imagination" (p. 21). Thus deviance presupposes socially constituted and socially shared interpretive schemes that condition consciousness so as to constitute the social categories defining deviance as a discernible reality.

Interpretive schemes consist of the types or categories that people routinely apply in ordering and making sense of their experiences. Erikson alludes repeatedly to the relationship between deviance and the use of such socially shared categories. The constitution of deviance involves "sifting a few *important* details out of the stream of behavior [an individual] has emitted and . . . in effect declaring that these details reflect the *kind* of person he 'really' is" (p. 7; my italics). In the constitution of deviance, then, people apply types that enable them to make sense *together* of events and behaviors that jar their attention; "important" details surface in that shared effort at establishing sense. The constitution of deviance involves "filtering out" or abstracting and then "coding" or typifying the details of behavior that individuals perceive (p. 7). Deviants thus mirror the types and values that distinguish a specific, socially conditioned worldview. Thus it comes as no surprise that the form and shape of "persistent troublers" are only the forms and shapes of a distinctive social world (p. 23).

Sometimes, as in the Puritan case, the categories that permit perceptions of and reactions to deviance are themselves being constituted as "reliable" elements of a shared interpretive scheme. As the source of widely shared categories, language best indicates that collective situation. Erikson sensed, for example, that in Anne Hutchinson's trial the courtroom exchanges are scarcely comprehensible unless one appreciates that "the two principals were trying to speak a language which had not yet been invented, to argue an issue which had not yet been defined. In a sense, the trial was an attempt to develop such a language" (p. 93). In other terms, "the court *did* know why Mrs. Hutchinson had to be banished, but it did not know how to express that feeling in any language then known in New England"; the Puritan world was changing, but its members "had no vocabulary to explain to themselves or anyone else what the nature of these changes were [*sic*]. The purpose of the trial was to invent that language, to find a name for the nameless offense which Mrs. Hutchinson had committed" (p. 101). Thus the Puritans faced the problem of establishing the means to "register" their experiences (p. 104). Alert to the relationship between language and a shared world, Erikson implies that the constitution of deviance is, originally, the constitution of a language that makes shared perceptions possible. He suggests, further, that the emotions of powerful Puritans keyed their emergent knowledge, conditioning the language they were creating to make their experiences intelligible.

In grappling after the language necessary for the constitution of clear-cut deviance, the Puritans were constituting a world. For the most part, Erikson discusses that process in terms of group boundaries. Those boundaries, he argues, are meaningful reference points "only so long as they are repeatedly tested by persons on the fringes of the group and repeatedly defended by persons chosen to represent the group's inner morality" (p. 13). In other terms, the constitution of a taken-for-granted, shared world presupposes categories that distinguish that world from other worlds and *at the same time* indicate those types of members whose behavior is felt to jeopardize the distinctiveness of that world. Common-sense knowledge governs the simultaneous constitution of a world and the forms of deviance that signal its distinctive character. Even though that knowledge is fraught with contradictions and inconsistencies, a potent logic directs it. Erikson points out that the Puritans

> never saw the contradictions in their theory (nor would they have worried about it if they had) and continued to feel that their position was derived from the soundest logic. . . . The essential strength of that logic lay in the conviction that the truth had been forever discovered in its entirety. . . . The twentieth-century reader . . . may sooner or later decide that it is nothing more than a versatile display of sophistry, but he then must remind himself that men who already *know* the truth have scant need for the niceties of inductive reasoning (p. 48).

For the Puritans, the Bible catalogued knowledge; it conditioned their memories and anticipations (p. 49). The religious enthusiasm Anne Hutchinson advocated was simply not possible in the resultant (i.e., constituted) "orthodox company of saints" (p. 85). Thus her trial necessitates examining the "larger situation" that occasioned it. The details of the arguments themselves – the words spoken – only partially disclose the common-sense logic and social forms that led to her condemnation (p. 82). Her trial was "a tribal ceremony, a morality play, a ritual encounter between two traditional adversaries . . ." (pp. 100–101). Although her personal biography and her own behavior are not unimportant to an understanding of her outcome, "it is far more important to understand the shifts of mood that made the settlers responsive to her arguments . . ." (p. 106). Nonetheless "Mrs. Hutchinson was a full partner in the transactions which led to her banishment and did as much as anyone else to set its basic tone and character. We do not know whether she got what she *wanted* from the court, of course, but it is fairly clear that she got what she *expected*, and in fact played an active role in realizing that prediction" (p. 100).

For Erikson, then, common-sense knowledge, a naive logic, and the aim to create and sustain a world interplay to constitute the types of people "known" to be deviants. His delineation of that complex process pays attention to language, mundane logic, social forms, biography and history, motives, interaction, taken-for-grantedness, meaning, and the social constitution of knowledge. From a phenomenological viewpoint, his study is masterful. Yet, as we will see, his analysis could be fruitfully extended by explicitly exploiting the phenomenological frame. Erikson might, for example, have focused more attention on how a social world *originates*, since the Puritans were mindful of establishing a *new* world. Such attention would have brought him closer to the a priori conditions of any social world and, therefore, put him in closer touch with the connection he supposes between the constitution of a world and the constitution of deviance. Further, at some points Erikson's analysis might have benefited from Schutz's concept of finite province of meaning, since many of the conflicts he delineates rested on incompatibilities between a world of (unorthodox) religion and a world of politics. The boundaries separating those two provinces of meaning were fluid and ambiguous, as Puritan language itself showed. By considering finite provinces of meaning Erikson might have equipped himself to treat the complexities built into *a* world that comprises diverse sets of meaning-compatible experiences. The Puritans themselves, it seems, lacked the wherewithal to recognize and then enact the principle that *a* world is not only "common" but also partitioned into distinct provinces of meaning. Had Erikson approached the Puritans' constitution of a world in those terms, his analysis might have been deeper as well as wider in its applicability. Finally, phenomenological grounds would have steered Erikson away from the reification his formulations sometimes suggest. Occasionally, Erikson says things like a "community . . . feels jeopardized" or a "group expresses its concern" rather than referring to acting individuals (p. 20). Sometimes, too, he refers to forces rather than human acts and their consequences (p. 92). Such references contradict the principles his analysis discloses. A phenomenological orientation would have eliminated such departures from the overall tone and substance of his study.

In the main, however, Erikson's study stands as a phenomenologically sensitive, sociologically sound analysis. In implicit fashion, *Wayward Puritans* illustrates that phenomenology and sociology are compatible. At the same time, it implies the likely usefulness of phenomenological findings about consciousness and constitution. Those matters provide our starting points in delineating the phenomenological results most relevant to the social sciences.

2. Consciousness and constitution

> One keeps on playing year by year,
> Concerning the nature of things as they are.
>> Wallace Stevens, "The Man with the Blue Guitar"

> Philosophy is not a particular body of knowledge; it is the vigilance which does not let us forget the source of all knowledge.
>> Maurice Merleau-Ponty, *Signs*

Husserl insisted that phenomenology must show what consciousness "is," what it "means" through its acts, and how it "intends" the objective.[1] He initially assumed and later demonstrated that all particular acts of consciousness exhibit an invariant, universal structure. Thus Husserl's investigations reveal the laws of conscious life.[2]

For Husserl, consciousness is essentially contact with things. It is contact with *transcendent objects*, which are given as incompletely subsumed by consciousness and independent of its acts. Consciousness is also contact with *immanent objects*, which are given as completely subsumed by consciousness and entirely dependent on its acts. Consciousness is always directed toward things, whether the "thing" be the book I am reading or my friend Helen with whom I am laughing (transcendent objects) or my aim to write a book or my memory of having laughed with Helen (immanent objects). To imply, then, that things somehow enter into or are otherwise "in" consciousness is inaccurate.

Although they distinguish between the "real" and the "meant-as-real," phenomenologists do hold that consciousness is our sole medium of access to whatever "really" exists.[3] The range of consciousness is coextensive with the world, not the "real" world but *our* world. And our world encompasses not only the meant-as-real but also the meant-as-unreal, meant-as-possible, meant-as-impossible, and whatever else is conceivable.[4] What is real for us becomes so by acts of consciousness. In short,

we cannot know reality independently of consciousness, and we cannot know consciousness independently of reality – to do so would be to meet the one and the

22

other in isolation, which is an impossibility. We meet consciousness only as consciousness of something; and we meet reality only as a reality of which we are conscious.[5]

Thus phenomenology illuminates the common-sense world *as it is known and experienced*. It does not investigate Reality; it treats reality "only insofar as it is intended, represented, intuited or conceptually thought."[6]

Phenomenological findings reveal that consciousness is acts of contact with specific objects. Phenomenologists examine those acts and their objects only as they present themselves. They refuse to infer anything about an act of consciousness using what is presented in another act of consciousness.[7] Phenomenologically, investigators prejudice themselves when they draw conclusions about an act of consciousness on the basis of other distinct, though related, intentional acts. In general, phenomenological approaches to consciousness incorporate two of Husserl's principles. First, acts of consciousness are never entirely arbitrary; an invariant structure governs them. Second, acts of consciousness cannot be completely isolated from other such acts;[8] acts of consciousness interconnect closely, though each is unique. These principles imply the interrelationship among intentionality, givenness, and horizon.

Intentionality, givenness, and horizon: the structure of consciousness

Husserl indicated that the principal subject matter of phenomenology is intentionality, which refers to the essential (or "eidetic") structure of consciousness.[9] "Intentionality" means that all consciousness is "consciousness of"; namely, consciousness is always directed toward objects.[10] Intentionality concerns the essential functioning of consciousness, not a static feature of conscious life.[11] It refers to the multiplicity of acts whereby consciousness establishes our world as a series of mutually implicated objects. Thus the concept of intentionality underscores the necessary interrelatedness of all objects, both transcendent and immanent, that make up a shared world.

Intentionality implies both "consciousness of objects" and "objects of consciousness." Both aspects concern phenomenologists when they describe consciousness. When they focus on *consciousness of* a given object, their interest is the *noesis* of an act of consciousness; when they focus on the given *object of* consciousness, their interest is the *noema* of the act. The noesis is the acting-toward (the intending) and the noema is the acted-toward (the intended) which together form every intentional act. Noetically, every act "gives" a sense; noematically, every act "contains" a sense.[12] The noesis bestows meaning; the noema is the meaning established by the noesis of a given act(s) of consciousness. For example, when I look at the candle on my coffee table, I see misshapen wax built up from many burnings. The noesis is perceiving; the noema is the candle-as-perceived. I might begin to recall the way that candle looked before I burned it. Then the noesis is remembering and, as long as my object of consciousness remains the candle itself, the noema is candle-as-remembered. I might then recall the friend I invited to dinner when I first lit the candle. The noesis remains remembering; the noema becomes friend-as-remembered. Later I might think about inviting my friend to dinner again. Now the noesis is anticipating and the noema is dinner-party-as-anticipated.

Every act of consciousness is a noetic-noematic unity. For every intentional act that unity is distinctive and ascertainable. Phenomenological investigations of acts of consciousness thus incorporate noematic description and noetic description. In noematic descriptions, phenomenologists examine an intentional object as a set of determinations established by a specific mode(s) of consciousness. In noetic descriptions, they focus on the modes whereby consciousness determines its given object.[13]

The noetic-noematic structure of acts of consciousness raises the question of givenness. Husserl's stricture about "the things themselves" bound phenomenology to the descriptive investigation of nothing more and nothing less than what is given in immediate experience. Phenomenologists clarify givenness by examining *phenomena*, that is, things as they themselves immediately *appear* in the absence of existential presuppositions and interpretive schemes. Phenomena are given, then, in unadulterated intentional experiences. Their investigation enables the phenomenologist to disclose what human experience itself is, pretheoretically and prereflectively. Properly understood, noesis and noema refer to the essential structure of intentional experiences within the phenomenological sphere.

The noetic-noematic correlation implies that "givenness" involves a great deal more than a phenomenon's "simply being there." Givenness comprises specific acts of consciousness that present an object. Givenness means that in this or that way (noematically) the thing (phenomenon) is presented through acts of consciousness (noetically). Consciousness can contact a given object with a variety of noeses. Those noetic modifications typically extend the determinations of the *selfsame* noema. Thus givenness fluctuates. Adequate or fulfilled givenness rests on a variety of acts of consciousness; the interconnections of those acts concern the horizonal quality of intentionality.

A noema such as photograph-as-perceived appears one-sidedly; that is, it is given in one of many possible manners of appearance ("adumbrations").

A photograph-as-perceived stands a specific distance from me, at a specific angle, on a specific desk, and so on. The idea of a perception apart from a perspective, like the idea of a perception in all possible adumbrations at once, contradicts both phenomenological and common-sense experience. Our experiences reveal that any object can be perceived under other profiles or aspects. Usually a sense of inadequacy conveys that lesson.[14] To some degree we know, then, that every perception has its horizon, a fringe of indeterminacy or incompleteness.[15]

All intentionality involves a horizon consisting of all the intentional possibilities "predelineated" at the moment by an incomplete sense of the intentional object.[16] The horizon of any object of consciousness is a set of possibilities for more precise determination of that object. Those possibilities involve an inner (or internal) horizon and outer (or external) horizon.[17] The inner horizon is what can yet be determined about a noema; those possible determinations rest on the potential for noetic modifications. The outer horizon is what can yet be determined about the objects associated with a noema; those possible determinations rest on the potential for intending those objects.[18] For example, I can look at a photograph from many angles. My determinations of the photograph-as-perceived thus expand, as I push its inner horizon forward in a sense. Part of the outer horizon of the photograph-as-perceived might be the peeling wall where it hangs. I may direct my consciousness toward that wall, remembering when I last painted it. Then my noema is the wall-as-remembered; the photograph becomes part of the outer horizon of my intended object.

Thus givenness includes determinable as well as determinate aspects of objects of consciousness. It necessarily includes anticipation as an unfulfilled or empty intention. Every horizon functions as a fluid but inescapable boundary of the meaning any act of consciousness bears. Together horizon, givenness, and intentionality constitute the roots of meaningful experience.

Time-consciousness, typification, and identity

The notions of intentionality, givenness, and horizon imply temporality and time-consciousness. That intentionality involves an anticipatory quality, that givenness fluctuates, and that experience is horizonal suggest the impossibility of atemporal, absolutely new experience. Human experience reiterates, enriches, recovers, modifies, and extends itself. Never, though, does it confront the thoroughly new.

The flow of inner time or time-consciousness makes possible the unities of conscious life. When individuals experience an object, they intend it within a "horizon of expectation"[19] built up from the totality of their experiences. Individuals intend objects not as extractions from a wealth of other experiences but as filaments of a stream of experience. Their intended objects appear within a system of expectations sedimented from prior experiences and directed toward future experiences. *Retentions* are the expectations sedimented from past intentional acts; *protentions* are the expectations preshaping imminent intentional acts. Both types of expectations inform all intentionality. Thus retentions and protentions do not establish distinctive intentional acts separate from other acts of consciousness. Their presence is continuous in human consciousness.

Together, retentions and protentions constitute the temporal horizon of every act of consciousness.[20] Since a temporal horizon governs the present, experience exhibits only relative discontinuities, not absolute breaks. As Husserl indicated,

every lived experience, every consciousness, is subject to the original law of flow. . . . *Every concrete lived experience is a unity of becoming and is constituted as an object in internal consciousness in the form of temporality.*[21]

In other terms, a now-retention-protention structure orders consciousness and the flow of experience. "Things themselves," therefore, are not first "given" and then intentionally "apprehended." Immanent temporality disallows that duality.[22] Moreover, without time-consciousness no object would be identifiable. The "agent" of time-consciousness in that regard is typification. In a sense, typification conjoins time-consciousness and intentionality.

When human beings experience an object, they necessarily assign its determinations to other objects perceived as similar. If the progress of actual experience confirms that assignment, the content of the original type is extended. The givenness of an object thus implies types built up through earlier analogous experiences. It always involves types that prescribe a preliminary familiarity and specify expected attributes. Thus human beings intend objects within horizons of typical familiarity and precognizance.[23]

Thus intentionality involves familiarity mediated by types that more or less determine the object. The objects we intend are in a sense already known; *"unfamiliarity* is at the same time always a *mode of familiarity."*[24] For example,

the apprehension "object in general" – still completely indeterminate and unknown – already entails an element of familiarity, namely as a something that "somehow or other is," that is explicable and can be known in conformity with what is; i.e., as something which is situated within the horizon of the world considered as the totality of existents, something which itself is already familiar *insofar* as it is a being "in the world" and, correlatively, a being which must enter into the unity of our flowing experience.[25]

Individuals establish familiarity through *typification*, the continuous assignment of coordinates to the "empty horizon of familiar unfamiliarity"[26] that borders all experience. Through typification, human beings demonstrate that "all determination is enacted in descent from an encompassing whole."[27] Determination issues forth, then, from something broader than the given object; it begins with types.

Typification is vital to conscious life. For human beings, acts of typification mediate between an intentionality that is absolutely focused and one that approaches aimlessness. Through typification, consciousness "normalizes" its field "by freeing itself from extreme specificity and overpowering generality."[28] Thus acts of typification establish the possibility of transcending the particular in favor of essential forms.[29] Although typification does not guarantee such outcomes, it is a condition of them. Typification does, however, guarantee identity and lead toward objectivity. As an essential feature of intentionality rooted in the now-retention-protention structure of consciousness, typification also leads to the matter of constitution.

Constitution

Husserl concerned himself with the grounds of knowledge, with reason and common sense, and with the conditions that make the actualities of *our* world possible. Intentionality, givenness, horizon, and time-consciousness provide insufficient bases for treating those ultimate problems Husserl addressed. We "know," for example, that beliefs, stereotypes, facts, opinions, and decisions pervade the world we share. How do we "know"? What kinds of "knowing" underlie those "realities" of daily life? Thus far, I have mentioned some elements necessary for our "knowing" and for "realities." But I have only alluded to how those elements interplay to establish the possibility of completed realities-for-us. Husserl's concept of constitution addresses the problem of how human beings "complete" judgments about reality, whether qualified (e.g., hypothesis) or not (e.g., fact).

Although Husserl used "constitution" ambiguously,[30] a decided consistency underlies his conceptualization. Tapping that consistency necessitates juxtaposing Husserl's conceptions of intentionality and inner time-consciousness with his concept of process. Then his processual approach to constitution becomes clear.

For Husserl,

"process" is . . . a concept which presupposes persistence. Persistence, however, is a unity which is constituted in the flux, and it pertains to the essence of flux that there can be nothing persistent in it.[31]

Thereby Husserl pinpointed the difficulties not only in understanding constitution but also in distinguishing between structure (persistences) and process (flux). He found that in the flux of consciousness are phases of lived experience that lack an essential characteristic of persistence, namely alterability. The phases of consciousness are identifiable; namely, we can intend them again and again as *that* part of the flux. Because we cannot alter them, however, they are not persistences. Husserl went on to indicate how persistences and flux relate:

But in a certain sense is there not . . . something abiding about the flux, even though no part of the flux can change into a not flux? What is abiding, above all, is the formal structure of the flux, the form of the flux. . . . The form consists in this, that a now is constituted through an impression and that to the impression is joined a train of retentions and a horizon of protentions. This abiding form . . . supports the consciousness of a continuous change. . . . [32]

Here Husserl implied two aspects of intentionality, consciousness of continuous change and consciousness of a current impression.

In fact, Husserl discussed the "double intentionality of the stream of consciousness" in terms implied by the above passage. "Double intentionality" refers to two aspects of a single stream of consciousness. *Transverse intentionality*, the one aspect, is consciousness of the unity of an intentional object through discrete retentions; *longitudinal intentionality*, the other aspect, is consciousness of the past experiences that generate an intentional unity.[33] Thus at one and the same time intentionality encompasses consciousness of an object's identity and consciousness of the past experiences that established its identity. Intentionality involves, then, consciousness of *this* object and consciousness of *those* experiences that enable the individual to intend this (type of) object. In other terms, intentionality is consciousness of the sense of an object and consciousness of the past acts whose cumulative consequence is that sense.

The structure of the stream of consciousness is thus a double intentionality where consciousness of continuity intersects consciousness of the present.[34] That structure correlates with time-consciousness and the noetic-noematic structure of intentional acts as well as with givenness, horizon, type, and identity. Thus far I have treated only transverse intentionality. My neglect of longitudinal intentionality has impeded discussion of Husserl's ultimate concerns. In other terms, attention to constitution was lacking.

Constitution is the process whereby longitudinal intentionality achieves its results, foremostly identity and objectivity. "An object is 'constituted' within certain connections of consciousness which bear . . . a transparent unity so far as they carry with them essentially the consciousness of an identical X."[35] Thus constitution is the becoming-present-of-an-object.[36] The limits of any object's constitution are a "totality of possible experiences, perceptions of one and the same thing."[37] Objects of consciousness are constituted, then, in the sense that any "known" object is a correlate of a *group* of intentional acts.

More generally, conscious life is unified into an encompassing "cogito," "a synthesis that, as a unitary consciousness embracing . . . separated processes, gives rise to the consciousness of identity and thereby makes any knowing of identity possible."[38] Yet the *appearances* of an object and the *object itself* do not represent sense-perceptions versus some concealed reality. The difference is between determinate presentations of the object, on the one hand, and all the possible modes of givenness of that same object, on the other hand.[39] "Simply being there" always points, then, toward further noemata. Givenness points toward some unfulfilled idea.

The phenomenological investigation of constitution begins with a focus on the longitudinal intentionality taken for granted in daily life. The goal of constitutional analyses is to account for the identity and objectivity of a transversely intended object by examining how longitudinal intentionality functions. Thus the phenomenologist takes a given object as an index to the synthetic processes that intend it. The investigator traces the syntheses[40] presupposed by the object's givenness as *this* objective thing. The logic of constitutional analyses incorporates a whole-parts standpoint.[41] In general, the whole is this-object-taken-as-objectively-existing, for example, a fact, human being, a judgment, evil, love. Constitutional analyses begin with an "objectivated" sense or sedimented meaning and show how that meaning originates in more fundamental acts of consciousness.[42] Each act of consciousness examined in such analyses contributes some *part* to the *whole* objectivated sense of an object. The phenomenologist discloses each act's function in syntheses of identification.

Constitutional analyses disclose the "layers"[43] of experience that establish identity and objectivity. Their ultimate goal is to reveal the grounds of sense and meaning. Thus the endpoint of full-fledged constitutional analyses is the formally indivisible "wholes" that in some sense constitute themselves rather than derive from a synthesizing succession of intentional acts. Those wholes are the noetic-noematic structure of consciousness and inner time-consciousness. In short, constitutional analyses begin with accomplished wholes and reveal their origins in the primordial wholes that make intentional acts possible.

Constitutional analyses examine active and passive constitution, differentiated in terms of active and passive genesis.

In active genesis the Ego functions as productively constitutive, by means of subjective processes that are specifically acts of the ego. Here belong all the works of *practical reason*, in a maximally broad sense. . . . Ego-acts, pooled in a sociality, . . . become combined in a manifold, specifically active synthesis and . . . *constitute new objects originally*. These then present themselves for consciousness *as products*.[44]

Logic, mathematics, and the exact sciences exemplify active constitution. Strictly speaking, consciousness is actively constitutive only on higher levels, that is, those more removed from primordial grounds. Yet active constitution presupposes passive constitution. Specifically,

anything built by activity necessarily presupposes . . . a passivity that gives something beforehand; and when we trace anything built actively, we run into constitution by passive generation.[45]

Passive constitution involves prereflective syntheses of intentional experiences. In other terms, individuals commonly intermesh their acts of consciousness without awareness of their intentional activities. Such experiences nonetheless presuppose the intentionality and inner time-consciousness that structure the stream of consciousness and make constitution possible.

Constitutional analyses force attention to the bond between intentionality and meaning. Every intentional act *means* something. Constitutional analyses disclose "on the noetic side, the openly endless life of pure consciousness, and as its correlate on the noematic side, the meant world purely as meant."[46] Phenomenological inquiry into consciousness reveals its two inseparable sides, synthesis and a variety of appearances. Synthesis is a function of transverse intentionality; the multiple modes of appearance belong to longitudinal intentionality. Together they *constitute* objective identities from a "passing flow of multiplicities."[47] Constitutional analyses demonstrate how "facts of synthetic structure" build up through multiple modes of appearance that presuppose the "passively flowing synthesis" of inner time-consciousness. They reveal that intentional acts "mean" more than is explicit at any moment, that consciousness necessarily "intends beyond itself."[48] Constitutional analyses thus uncover horizons.

Constitution necessarily involves a "coming-into-appearance-of-meaning"; it is the way meanings come to be.[49] It concerns how intentionality creates the more meaningful from the less meaningful. But meaning implies a subject or Ego who experiences sense both as a goal and as an accomplishment.

"Ultimately the ego, too, is a certain meaning that needs to be explained. The constitution-problem thus includes the ego itself."[50]

Progress in knowledge . . . involves more than the accumulation of objectively valid cognitions; it means the growth of a subject progressively better equipped to know and to be the validating source of the knowledge it has or acquires.[51]

From this perspective, the self is constituted in and with its experiences.[52] Thus the notion of constitution also raises questions about the essential structure of experience as well as the self.

3. Experience, meaning, and the self

There in the unexalted chronicle of the familiar is disclosed the image of what we may still become.

Maurice Natanson, *Phenomenology, Role, and Reason*

I am installed on a pyramid of time which has been me.

Maurice Merleau-Ponty, *Signs*

Experience and consciousness

Human beings routinely expect that their experiences will reveal the nature of human existence. Phenomenology affirms that expectation by refusing to deny the givens of human experience. It also radicalizes that expectation by insisting that only experience can account for *our* world. Phenomenologically, every known object is experienceable. Presuppositions are, therefore, unnecessary. Abandoning them, phenomenologists pose the questions of what and how experience is. The phenomenological approach to experience necessitates exploring its relationship to consciousness. That exploration exposes experience as a line of access to all varieties of human knowledge.

Like consciousness, experience apparently involves both acts and a unitary stream. Everyday language expresses both those senses. Often we refer to *an* experience. Sometimes, too, we question the amount of relevant experience others have as prospective employees, trainees, and volunteers. In both instances "experience" refers to acts, taken singularly or collectively, that we abstract from an individual's total experiences. Everyday language also expresses the idea of experience as a stream. For example, people sometimes say, "Experience has taught me . . . ," where "experience" means one's whole conscious life, undifferentiated by types of acts and periods of time. Seemingly, consciousness and experience coincide.

32

Experience, like consciousness, is always *of* something. We can examine it noetically-noematically; that is, we can divide our attention between experience of an object (noetic focus) and an object of experience (noematic focus) in order to understand the structure of experience. Experience also shares with consciousness a constitutive layering. Husserl found that the theoretical attitude presupposes and builds on the pretheoretical attitude of everyday life. The ordering of terms in his *Experience and Judgment* assigns primacy to (prereflective) experience.[1] Thus Husserl's starting point in investigating experience was the pretheoretical awareness whereby the ego "lives its experiences" without articulating about or reflecting on them.

Experience in the first and most pregnant sense is . . . defined as a direct relation to the individual. . . . [Judgments of experience] are preceded by the self-evident givenness of individual objects of experience, i.e., their pre-predicative givenness. The self-evidence of experience, therefore, should be that ultimately original self-evidence which we seek, and therewith the point of departure for the elucidation of the origin of the predicative judgment.[2]

In their daily lives, people live prepredicatively in the "certainty of being." Their experiences involve a "simple believing consciousness" whose objects are pregiven. All other kinds of experience are modifications of everyday prepredicative experience that point back to it as the original mode of givenness. In other terms, the predicative activities occasioned by problematic experiences are modalizations of prepredicative experience; they presuppose the objects that are "simply there" prepredicatively. Predicative activities like conjecture, phantasy, and doubt are examples of such modalizations.[3] Predicative experience, which involves a subject and a predicate, rests on the unpolarized structure of prepredicative experience. In general, then, experience comprises receptive, spontaneous processes that lay the grounds for active phases where individuals approach the "predicative stage of articulated knowledge."[4]

Another feature of experience that suggests its coincidence with consciousness is its provisional character. Like consciousness, experience is perspectival. It only *tends* toward completeness. Although intentions can be fulfilled, their fulfillment lies in the *adequacy* of the individual's determinations, not in their absolute completeness. Phenomenologically, experience thus exhibits an "if-then style,"[5] both prepredicatively and predicatively.

Despite the similarities between experience and consciousness, Husserl did not regard them as fully coextensive. He sometimes used the phrase "conscious experience," implying that not all the elements of experience involve intentionality. Experiences occur within a *stream of experience* that encompasses unintended sensory data and feelings.[6] Husserl implied that at any moment experience necessarily exceeds what consciousness can disclose, even though experience demands consciousness. Husserl's conception of experience alludes to the embodiment of consciousness; that is, "experience" broadly refers to concrete participation in a world known only through an intentionality that reduces its richness even while affirming it through its now-retention-protention structure and its horizonal quality. At any moment, then, experience always involves consciousness but comprises more than consciousness can disclose noetically-noematically. I am breathing; I sit on a hard chair; my hand grasps this pen; the air conditioner hums and the sunlight changes intensity; I feel happily content; and on and on. Although all those features are part of my current experience, I do not intend them. Moreover, I have only a remote awareness of my capacity to intend any of them if the course of experience demands it. For example, if my breathing falters, I will surely direct my attention to breathing-(taken)-as-a-problem. Ordinarily, though, I am conscious while breathing rather than conscious of breathing. Nonetheless respiration, a spatial location, a body posture, and so forth are essential ingredients of my experiencing the present. Are these elements only potential determinations within the horizon of my intentional acts? The response to that query must be both positive and negative: Temporal perspective determines whether or not experience and consciousness are coextensive.

The experience of the present encompasses this thinking as well as this room, this mood, this physical state, these smells, these sounds, and much else. Without doubt every experience has *an* object, but it has its object less exclusively than consciousness intends its object. The experiencing "I" is embodied, spatially located and sensorily stimulated; the intending "I," though ontologically embodied, is foremostly cognitive. The experiencing I is intentional in the broad sense; it presupposes sensory data that are not intentionally accessible. The intending I is intentional in the narrow sense, particularly in its predicative activities. My current experience, for example, is *of* thinking; predicative acts of consciousness constitute its core. Yet this experience would be a different one were I thinking elsewhere, feeling less happy, or enduring a headache. But these acts of consciousness – these thoughts – can remain the same regardless of location, physical state, and mood. My experience can change, then, while its narrow intentionality remains constant.

It is helpful to think of experience as only partially anonymous because of its embodiment and to think of consciousness as ultimately anonymous because of the invariant structure that governs its functioning. At its roots, intentionality represents an expression of Everyperson rather any specific individual. Phenomenology reveals a universal structure of consciousness that transcends the consciousness of ontologically unique individuals. Consciousness is, in other terms, transpersonal in its primitive functioning. Although it provides the grounds for uniqueness, consciousness first expresses what is universally human. On the other hand, from the outset experience expresses the singularity of the individual. Considered primordially and moment by moment, then, consciousness and experience relate closely but do not coincide fully. That the two are distinct can be seen in the ease of referring to an *act* of consciousness. But we deny the richness of experience by referring to its moments as "acts." Rather, experience presents itself as a flow comprising the simultaneity of breathing, hearing, seeing, feeling, and all else that currently situates an individual in a world.

Considered over time, however, the streams of consciousness and of experience do coincide. The double intentionality of the stream of consciousness makes the stream of experience a coherent flux. Intending the stream of experience virtually transforms it into the stream of consciousness. For example, if we think about or otherwise intend our academic or sexual or political experiences, we tap the retentions built up from past intentional acts. We intend, then, elements of the stream of consciousness when we direct attention to the stream of experience. Thus from a longitudinal perspective consciousness and experience are coextensive; from an atemporal or cross-sectional perspective they connect closely but overlap incompletely. In short, the edge of consciousness is experience and the nucleus of experience is intentionality.

Husserl described two types of experiences. *Simple (or unfounded) experience* is the straightforward apprehension of objects by virtue of their obvious sense; it is the prereflective experience of properties given at the corporeal level. *Founded experience* presupposes simple experience but involves a theme and reflection.[7] Phenomenologically, then, the first question is not "*What* do we experience?" but "What *is* experience?"[8] The former question biases investigators in favor of founded experience. The latter question concerns the roots of simple experience, intentionality and time-consciousness.

Husserl's distinctions concerning experience and consciousness serve several purposes. First, his use of "experience" complements his virtual emphasis on the cognitive aspects of intentionality. "Lived experience" turns his scheme toward the sensuous and emotional qualities of human experience alongside its cognitive features. Second, Husserl's conception of simple experience closes the door to the possibility of infinite regress in his investigations. "Constitutive layers" implies no more than the possibility of a final or ground layer. The notion of simple experience points to the final foundations of conscious life. Restricted to the givens of human experience, phenomenology ventures no deeper than that level.

Lived experience and meaning

Experientially, the given is immediately present(ed) to the individual; it is the blunt aspect of experience.[9] In everyday life, givenness has a "with-in" structure. Lived experience is *in* the world, which is taken as unquestionably real, yet it is *with* or alongside that world, which is given as its horizon.[10] Thus experience, like consciousness, exhibits no absolute boundary between interiority and exteriority. A general description of experience must consider its with-in structure in order to account for its intrinsic meaning.

Many scholars, including phenomenologists, approach the structure of experience by treating situations as its fundamental units.[11] Two phenomenological principles make "situation" a useful concept. The first principle is that every lived situation incorporates elements derived from biographical events that belong exclusively to the individual as individual.[12] One's situation fluctuates as past experiences alter the bases for apprehending the present. This first principle suggests that the span of an individual's situation is determined, in part, by the stream of experiences that led to "this (immediate) situation." An individual's situation depends, then, on biographically conditioned predispositions to cast the net of awareness widely or narrowly. The second principle is that situations occur within finite provinces of meaning that transcend the immediacy and uniqueness of the present moment. *Finite provinces of meaning* are "meaning-compatible experiences" or experiences unified by a "cognitive style" that stamps them as belonging together.[13] The present is always a *type* of lived reality that rests on and expresses the invariant structures of consciousness. Thus every situation has unique immediate elements and boundaries yet expresses the universal by its relation to a finite province of meaning, such as the world of daily life, of science, of religion, or of dreams. Understood as an expression of universal provinces of meaning and of unique retentions of past experiences, situation is *the* basic unit of experience. "Situation," in short, does justice to the with-in structure of experience.

Phenomenologically, every situation exhibits a characteristic "cognitive style" and distinctive "accent of reality" that mark it as this or that *type* of situation. Fundamentally, "types of situation" refers to varieties of "more or less complicated meaning-contexts."[14] To delineate types of situations requires examining the stream of consciousness and the intentional styles that actualize its possibilities. A fruitful insight for beginning such a delineation is that no experience is without meaning.[15] Every experience is *structured*; every experience is oriented toward that *of which* it is an experience.[16] Beginning with the minimal meaning inherent in all experiencing, we can move toward describing the constitution of whatever additional meaning individuals build up on its basis.

Phenomenologists investigate "lived experience." With that phrase they emphasize that everyday, practical experience is active and evaluative, not narrowly cognitive and judicative.[17] Although the phrase is redundant, its "lived" stresses that human experience is richer than empiricist conceptions admit. The phenomenological viewpoint thus stresses concepts and descriptions that refer to experienc*ing*. Phenomenologists regard examinations of *what* is said as "experiential refusal"; they investigate what "occasioned the saying."[18] "Lived experience" alerts us, then, to the prepredicative processes in everyday life that make predicative experience possible. Finally, the phrase suggests a subject and subjectively meaningful processes. For these reasons, phenomenologists often use "lived experience."

Phenomenologists have shown that lived experience is temporal, horizonal, interpretive, and familiar. Those features account for the complexity of lived experience. They also imply the boundaries of the problem of meaning.

Everyday experiences universally reveal that objects occur simultaneously or successively. Thus experiencing itself points to temporality as its form.[19] Together with intentionality, the flow of inner time organizes lived experience. Because it occurs in temporal phases, at any moment experience is basically incomplete.[20] In a sense, experience is a flow of interruptions resting on inner time-consciousness.[21] Yet the capacity to return again and again to an intentional object guarantees a continuity that overrides whatever discontinuities and incompleteness an experience presents. Each moment of experience has a unique temporal position that can never be recaptured. Yet the present acquires permanence through retentions and protentions. An experiential moment never exists, then, apart from intentionally related moments.

Retentions and protentions shape all lived experience. For phenomenologists, the process of retention and the association of "partial intentions" with time phases make meaningful experience possible.[22] And retentions imply protentions, since the immediate just-past (a retention) is no more easily separable from the immediate future than it is from the present. Now, shading off into the past through retentions, just as surely leans toward the future through protentions. Every past experience, in fact, prescribes various future experiences. In that sense, every experience is future-oriented.

That no experiences are isolated or self-contained means that experience has a "beyond,"[23] a horizon of unfulfilled components. Experience involves expectant as well as attendant meanings.[24] Thus it is essentially open. "Horizon" concerns the experiential absence of full unity; namely, it refers to the incompleteness inherent in lived experience.

Although every experience has a horizon of possible other experiences of the same object without limit, those possibilities do have boundaries, since a horizon is prescriptive. Through types, which are elements of the familiar,[25] the individual anticipates further determinations of an object. The horizon of any experience thus consists of limitless but not fully indeterminate intentional possibilities. In our experiences, then,

the context of any event is open and undecided in any strict way. The notion of "world" remains constant, my believing in the world remains fixed in its essential certitude, but the givenness of experience is permeated with undefined possibilities.[26]

Our situations "point to what is not, to what may be, to the coherent world our fragmented existence recognizes as potentially realizable."[27] In other terms, the horizonal structure of experience makes all knowledge perspectival and open-ended. At the same time, it implies the interpretive dimension of all experience.

Lived experiences are interpreted realities. This does *not* mean that all experience involves reflection. Every lived experience is, at root, interpretive since it fixes a sense that is prereflective and uniquely constituted. That any lived experience, uniquely constituted out of past experiences, gives rise to a recognizable or familiar situation is what the interpretive quality of experience concerns. Interpretation thus refers to constitution. Specifically, the interpretive dimension of experience involves the constitution, whether passive or active, of meaning. Every experience implies a description.[28] Whether or not an individual adopts that description as a predicative task, the sense of its possibility indicates the passive constitution of meaning at the prepredicative level. Attention itself is thus interpretive. As the object of receptive or simple experience appears less imprecisely, determinations often contradict the expectations passively constituted out of past experiences of that object.[29] Attention then cancels those expectations. Thus prepredicative experience is interpretive in two broad senses: It is selective and self-correcting.

Lived experience is also interpretive in another sense. In various ways, experiences reach an end or "breakoff point."[30] At that point, the individual enjoys relative fulfillment of the empty intentions that marked the beginning of the experience. Although the horizons of experience cannot be eliminated, lived experience usually fulfills prior empty intentions *adequately*. The development of that adequacy – arrival at a breakoff point – represents an exercise in interpretation. Acts of interpretive striving, organized by the individual's interests, underlie both prepredicative senses of and predicative judgments about such adequacy. Interests infuse all lived experience with an interpretive bent aimed toward tentative closure. Thus every breakoff point is an interpretive accomplishment.

The interpretive quality of lived experience varies profoundly. Sometimes we "surrender" ourselves to the stream of experience; at other times we "stop" to reflect on it. *Reflective* attention establishes discrete experiences. The reflective glance makes the prereflective unity of identity a unity of meaning.[31] All intentionality involves a "scheme of experience" or

a meaning-context which is a configuration of our past experiences embracing *conceptually* the experiential objects to be found in the latter but not the process by which they were constituted. The constituting process itself is entirely ignored, while the objectivity constituted by it is taken for granted.[32]

When individuals direct reflective attention toward their experiences, the scheme of experience becomes an *interpretive scheme* based on "what one knows" or "already knew." An interpretive scheme is the known to which we refer the unknown in active interpretation.[33]

Since it concerns what is known, an interpretive scheme delineates the boundaries of the familiar. It is a frame people use to assign meaning to the unknown or the unfamiliar. Through interpretive schemes people ease the discomfort associated with unfamiliar or insufficiently known objects. Interpretive schemes are conceptual configurations based on typification. The translation of singular lived experiences into objective meaning-contexts through typification endows lived experience with both coherence and anonymity. Thus individuals modify their lived experiences through the process of typification that transposes those experiences into their "stocks of knowledge."[34]

Interpretive activity is a condition of the familiarity that pervades daily life.

A pattern of intention and attitude, merged with memorial notes and sly expectancies, underlies even the most casual elements of experience. Nothing is presented to me which is pristinely stripped of association and implication, nor is anything received by me which enters my perceptual doors without ringing a bell that reverberates throughout my being.[35]

Every object of experience presents itself, then, as "an object in its horizon of typical familiarity and precognizance."[36] No experience is pretypical: Type and experience originate together.[37]

As that segment of our lived experience *presently* needing no further investigation,[38] the familiar presupposes identity and type. It rests on continuous syntheses of recognition, either of selfsameness (identity) or of similarity (type).[39] Although every experience encompasses the atypical by virtue of its uniqueness, the individual suppresses its atypical elements in generating familiarity. The application of types necessarily suppresses "irrelevant" features of the objects we experience.[40] Common-sensically and prereflectively, we expect the typical to recur. And the typical does recur because of types constituted in the past, appropriate to the present, and prescriptive of the future. Thus

typification is the generic term for an abstractive process one of whose central accomplishments is the experience of the familiar. . . . In the results of typification I am able to recognize the boundaries of my world: even the strange is typically constituted and appropriated as a limit of the familiar.[41]

The world of lived experience is, in sum, necessarily typified.[42] As Schutz and others have shown, the typical is essential to the organization of experience, not a mere consequence of translating experience into knowledge.[43]

Like consciousness, experience is always "of (something)." The "of _____" that infuses experience is from the first a "*type* of _____," for example, a type of object, a type of feeling, a type of person. Thus every experience not only determines what *this* object is but also prescribes a type. Determinative contact with an object implies similar objects as empty intentions associated with the horizon of the given object.[44] The type thus constituted is a monothetic grasping of the polythetic determinations sedimented from prior experiences.

Typification is possible because the time designations which are bound to the *individual steps in the polythetic constitution* of meaning may be set aside in attending to the *monothetic result*. . . . Thus, typification proves to be . . . the product of the abstractive capacity of inner time-consciousness.[45]

Typification thus reduces multiple determinations (polythetic constitution) to a single grasp (monothetic result) of similar objects. As such, typification establishes lived experience as our line of access to knowledge.

Every individual's stock of knowledge rests on experientially derived types. Yet types are more or less anonymous. Their degree of anonymity determines the degree of familiarity individuals experience. The more anonymous the type, the less detailed its content and the wider the span of similar objects it encompasses. But the more anonymous a type is, the less interpretive relevance it tends to have.[46] Thus in our daily experiences we often need to reconstruct types to some extent as we face atypicality. To be "sufficiently familiar" means "to have established a type of such a degree of anonymity or concreteness so as to satisfy the interpretational requirements necessary to determine the topic at hand."[47] Types thus permit the transcendence of the immediate by letting us act *as if* similar objects are essentially the same. At the same time types "bind us elastically to the past."[48] Typification also establishes the anticipations that pervade everyday life.[49] Types imply anticipated similar experiences. They represent not only interpretations but also *expectations* as to future experiences of *this* type.[50]

At root, types are problem-oriented. Every type represents "a situationally adequate solution to a problematic situation through the new determination of an experience which could not be mastered with the aid of the stock of knowledge already on hand."[51] What emerges as problematic not only implies specific gaps in the stock of knowledge but also the individual's interests.[52] Those interests, both immediate and projected, set the limits to which types are determined and familiarity is established. Any process of type construction or reconstruction is "broken off" when the individual has constituted sufficient knowledge for mastering the situation and anticipated similar situations.[53]

The breakoff point is not, however, a commitment to closure. It is a turn toward the taken-for-grantedness that presupposes idealized, implicit expectations in the form of "and so forth and so on" and "again and again." The first idealization is that my world exhibits a stability that indefinitely validates my determinations and guarantees the fundamental familiarity of my experiences; the latter, more basic idealization is that I can repeat my successful actions as long as the former idealization remains tenable.[54] These idealized expectations undergird all common-sense thinking and typification. They might best be labeled the expectations of "continuity" and "repeatability," respectively.[55]

The idealization of continuity comes into play when it becomes "a matter of indifference what, in addition, I might be given to apprehend in the consciousness that 'I could continue in this way.' "[56] That idealization presupposes the continued relevance of a type of object that need not, though, be acted on at present.[57] The idealization of repeatability concerns the likely progression of experience;[58] it presumes that I could indefinitely repeat my determinative contacts with a given (type of) object.

Together the idealized expectations of continuity and repeatability make possible a coherent stream of lived experience. They shape the "interruption" of taken-for-granted experiences when the individual's interests demand further determination of that type of situation. They condition such determination in the form of expectations that the given situation is *essentially* as it was (continuity) and that one can again succeed, though from a somewhat different perspective, in determining its nature (repeatability). The resumption of taken-for-granted experience also involves the two idealizations as a condition of turning to "something else." Both the interruption and resumption of taken-for-granted experiences, then, rest on these idealized expectations.[59] The meaning of lived experience also presupposes these idealizations that prevent immobilization by orienting unique experiences toward a future pregiven as meaningful.

Meaning and the self

Phenomenological findings about experience emphasize consciousness as the source of meaning and the stream of consciousness as a continuous conferral of meaning. Moreover, phenomenologists have found that all experience occurs within a "field of sense" that rests on inner time-consciousness.[60] At root, the sense underlying human experience presupposes not a simple "there is" but rather "it is possible *a priori* that there is."[61] Building on that basic sense, "each conscious process . . . '*means something or other*' and bears in itself, in this manner peculiar to the *meant*, its particular *cogitatum*."[62] Thus intentionality implies meaning, since all "consciousness of" necessarily specifies the nature of its object and that specification is a meaning.

Husserl's studies show that human beings endow their experiences with meaning by fulfilling empty intentions through acts of consciousness. But since consciousness and experience are horizonal, meaning always remains an open-ended accomplishment. The fulfillment of empty intentions always exposes additional intentional possibilities ("and so forth and so on" and "again and again"). Phenomenologists find, then, that any *actual* meaning escapes exhaustive analysis,[63] even though they have accounted for *possibility* of meaning by describing the structures of consciousness and experience. In broad terms, meanings are modes of givenness, passively or actively constituted through acts of consciousness. Meaning is the basic "whatness" of experience or the noematic result of various noeses. Thus meaning transcends specific contacts with an object of experience; it presupposes inner time-consciousness.

The problem of meaning is, above all, a time problem. As the idealizations of continuity and repeatability imply, the formation of meaning involves senses of both the past and the present and anticipations of the future. Meaning refers beyond what is immediately given.[64] The now-retention-protention structure of consciousness makes meaning an accomplishment that, in a sense, favors time rather than any specific moment. "The first meaning-context of any experience is therefore that which connects it with past experiences and the anticipated future ones."[65]

When human beings actively constitute it, meaning derives from the way they regard their experiences, specifically those that have already occurred. *In the fulfilled sense* only past experiences are meaningful.

We must contrast those experiences which in their running-off are undifferentiated and shade into one another, on the one hand, with those that are discrete, already past, and elapsed, on the other. The latter we apprehend not by living through them but by an act of attention. . . . Because the concept of meaningful experience always presupposes that the experience of which meaning is predicated is a discrete one, it now becomes quite clear that only a past experience can be called meaningful, that is, one that is present to the retrospective glance as already finished and done with.[66]

Present experiences are not, then, fully meaningful. For example, when we reflect on our selves, we capture its earlier phases.[67] Yet reflection on past experiences does occur in a meaningful present, as does "rehearsal in the imagination" of possible future conduct and its outcome(s). We base our reflections on *currently* operative interests and typifications.

Each Act of attention to one's own stream of duration may be compared to a cone of light. . . . The Acts of the cogito in which the Ego lives, the living present in which the Ego is borne along from each Here and Now to the next – these are never caught in the cone of light. . . . The actual Here and Now of the living Ego *is the very source of the light*. . . . "[68]

Thus current experiences involve passive constitution or *meaning-intention* of a monothetically grasped meaning. The active constitution of their meaning requires referring that monothetic grasping to the polythetic steps that established it. *Meaning-fulfillment* thus demands polythetic reconstruction. As a consequence, understanding and meaning are correlative.[69]

The self establishes both understanding and meaning. Meaning does not inhere in immanent or transcendent things; it is a dynamic relationship between self and its experiences. Meaning is thus reflexive. Fulfilled meaning derives from a reflexive self turned toward its past experiences. The self can also be an object of predicative experience. Most of the time, however, everyday experiences fail to actualize that possibility.

In the natural attitude of everyday life,

we simply *carry out* all the acts through which the world is there for us. We live naively unreflective in our perceiving and experiencing, in those thetic acts in which the unities of things appear to us, and not only appear but are given with the stamp of "presentation" and "reality."[70]

A self or Ego is among the objects given in everyday life as present and real. "I exist for myself and am continually given to myself, by experiential evidence, as '*I myself.*' This is true . . . with respect to any sense of the word ego. . . . "[71] As an object of lived experience, the self is given as a changing unity known through a stream of intentional acts. Unlike other objects of experience, though, the self presents a unique possibility crucial to knowledge and understanding.

The stream of experience which is mine, namely, of the one who is thinking, may be to ever so great an extent uncomprehended, unknown in its past and future reaches, yet so soon as I glance towards the flowing life and into the real present it flows through, and in so doing grasp myself as the pure subject of this life. . . . , I say forthwith and because I must: *I am*, this life is, I live: *cogito*.

To every stream of experience, and to every Ego as such, there belongs in principle, the possibility of securing this self-evidence: each of us bears in himself the warrant of his absolute existence . . . as a fundamental possibility.[72]

Thus the self is given absolutely; nothing else is as certain as the Ego and its stream of experience. Phenomenology systematically exploits the absolute givenness of every Ego. It emphasizes the possibilities the self holds for certainty and clarity. From a phenomenological viewpoint the self, dynamic and complex as it is, is fundamentally describable and ultimately comprehensible.

The "I" is the unity of a unique stream of consciousness or an "individual experiential structure."[73] The self uniquely actualizes the universal features of lived experience. It remains inseparable from its conscious activity (cogito), which is always contact with some object (cogitatum). Throughout phenomenological studies lies the theme of the Ego constituting its unique world of experience. As Husserl indicated, "the ego does not live in the positing of values and in the desirous striving grounded therein; rather, it lives in the activity of objectivation."[74] The self lives, more concretely, in its continuous reflections, memories, phantasies, and other intentional acts. It determines its selfsameness through different modes of intentionality.[75] Lived experiences, then, are not only "mine" but quite literally "me."[76]

Like other objects of experience, the self emerges through some mix of passive and active constitution. Every act of consciousness "leaves behind the ego which performed the act, and which by virtue of that act is rendered capable of a subsequent act it was not really capable of before."[77] The self is progressively and, for the most part, passively constituted in its achievement of valid cognitions. Like other objects, however, it is never finally given or thoroughly known. Its internal and external horizons remain, no matter how intensely the individual intends his or her self.

When is the stock of knowledge about one's self adequate? As with other objects of experience, the idealizations of continuity and repeatability govern the judgment that one's self is sufficiently familiar. Furthermore, individuals apply types to their selves, just as they do to other objects of experience.[78] Yet the problem of a breakoff point regarding the self raises questions not only of familiarity or adequate knowledge but also of consistency and certainty. In this one respect, the breakoff point for the self illuminates all breakoff points as well as the interruptions and resumptions of taken-for-granted activity in everyday life.

As an object of experience, the self is sufficiently known when the individual senses its significant consistency and, relative to past experiences, its certainty. The self is sufficiently grasped when those conditions obtain; it is preserved through attempts to sustain those conditions.

Striving for consistency of judgment and for certainty is thus a characteristic which is part of the general striving of the ego for self-preservation. The ego preserves itself when it can abide by its acts of position-taking, its "validations", its "This is actually so", "That is valuable, good." The ego reacts to everything which disturbs this self-preservation by a striving which is ultimately a striving toward unmodalized certainties, among which are certainties of judgment.[79]

Through such striving the individual aims to achieve a unique identity for the self, which executes a series of intentional acts but is experienced as transcending those acts. Through the constitution of an identity the individual continuously, though never absolutely, fulfills the unity of his or her stream of consciousness. The constitution of identity establishes the self as the paramount, certain meaning of *this* conscious life and all that it did, does, and will encompass.

Thus the establishment of all breakoff points involves judgments about one's self. When the individual considers resuming taken-for-granted activity at a given point, to some extent he or she looks at its implications about the consistency and certainty of his or her self. Although breakoff points involve pragmatic, situational considerations, above all they attempt to validate a self as the core meaning of human experiences.

The striving toward consistency and certainty represents intentionality put to the task of appropriating an intelligible, unified self. No human being ever completes that task. "The self is aimed at rather than experienced"; it is "never guaranteed, and . . . the demand in which it searches for itself is in a certain sense without end."[80] Yet the self that creates constructs, opinions, objectivities, images, and all else that constitutes our world is "not a secret, not an essential hiddenness."[81] Historically and culturally situated, individuals recognize and transform themselves through interpretive activity. Significantly, their experiences include not only interpretation and occasional reflection but also working. *Together*, those ingredients of everyday life make the open-ended self a taken-for-granted condition rather than a cause for obsessive contemplation.

    The abrupt turn to work prevents us from creating

the fiction of a subject that behaves in a purely contemplative way and which is not aroused to any practical activity by the existent by which it is affected environmentally.[82]

The topic of work merits attention, then, because of the phenomenological commitment to "things themselves" as we experience them. Unlike reflection, which sometimes undercuts the experienced unity of the self by presenting "partial selves," working continuously presents an "undivided total self."[83] "The working self, . . . experiencing itself as the author of this ongoing working, . . . realizes itself as a unity."[84]

The wide-awake self integrates in its working and by its working its present, past, and future into a specific dimension of time; it realizes itself as a totality in its working acts; it communicates with others through working acts; it organizes the different spatial perspectives of the work of daily life through working acts.[85]

I leave for the reader's further, perhaps phenomenological, consideration Schutz's finding about the tension between life and thought: "This is the very tension that is presupposed in all talk about meaning."[86]

4. The life-world

"Taking for granted" . . . would be morally legitimate if we realized that this is really a "grant," an unearned gift.

Herbert Spiegelberg, *Doing Phenomenology*

Out of ten fingers nine are different.

Chinese adage; W. S. Merwin, *Asian Figures*

Husserl's concern with twentieth-century cultural crises led him to the concept of life-world, or *Lebenswelt*. Husserl sensed that modern cultural crises derive from the radical separation of two finite provinces of meaning, the world of science and the world of daily life. Yet Husserl had found that all praxis, scientific and otherwise, includes "universal passive belief" that is certain of itself.[1] All human activity, in other terms, rests on the same invariant, unrecognized grounds. Husserl developed the concept of life-world to designate those grounds. For him, the concept pinpoints what is common to human undertakings as different as science and everyday life. The concept of life-world refers to a profound commonality whose recognition would, in Husserl's view, short-circuit the sense of fragmentation resulting from the modern emphasis on science as a nearly autonomous, immeasurably superior human activity.

For Husserl, the life-world was the "forgotten meaning-fundament" of science.[2] He aimed to demonstrate that "objective science itself belongs to the life-world."[3] Science does exploit "an ingenious theoretical technique, but [in the scientific sphere] the intentional performances from which everything ultimately originates remain ultimately unexplicated."[4] That science rests on the same ultimate foundation as all other human activities thus gets overlooked. In the process, human beings in modern cultures lose the sense of fundamental unity that might take the edge off their real and serious differences.

Although he stressed the grounds common to everyday life and science, Husserl in no manner regarded scientific achievements as reducible to common sense.

Objective knowledge must remain the ideal for all theoretico-scientific thought. Husserl does not for a moment question this ideal. What has occasioned the [cultural] crisis is not the appeal of objectivity in the methodological designs of contemporary science, but rather the failure to recognize that the scientific-objective explanation of the world has its origin in a concrete life-world [*Lebenswelt*] of perceptual, social, and praxis-oriented experience.[5]

Husserl did believe, however, that contemporary cultural malaise also derives from treating science as the cure-all for human problems. He believed that

the exclusiveness with which the total world-view of modern man, in the second half of the nineteenth century, let itself be determined by the positive sciences . . . meant an indifferent turning-away from the questions which are decisive for a genuine humanity. Merely fact-minded sciences make merely fact-minded people. . . . [Positivistic science] excludes in principle the questions which man . . . finds the most burning: questions of the meaning or meaninglessness of the whole of this human existence. Do not these questions, universal and necessary for all men, demand universal reflections and answers based on rational insight? . . . What does science have to say about reason and unreason or about us men as subjects of this freedom? The mere science of bodies clearly has nothing to say; it abstracts from everything subjective. As for the humanistic sciences, . . . their rigorous scientific character requires, we are told, that the scholar carefully avoid all valuative positions, all questions of the reason or unreason of their human subject matter and its cultural configuration. . . . But can the world, and human existence in it, truthfully have a meaning if the sciences recognize as true only what is objectively established in this fashion, and if history has nothing more to teach us than that all the shapes of the spiritual world, all the conditions of life, ideals, norms upon which man relies, form and dissolve themselves like fleeting waves, that it always was and ever will be so, that again and again reason must turn into nonsense, and well-being into misery?[6]

Unlike Lynd and Mills, Husserl did not emphasize the social responsibility of the sciences, even though he shared some of their concerns. Rather, he stressed the need for a conception of rationality that underscores its fundamental continuity from one finite province of meaning to another.

Husserl decried conceptions of rationality that repudiate both Reason and Common Sense. "The reason for the downfall of a rational culture does not lie in the essence of rationalism itself but only in . . . its absorption in 'naturalism' and 'objectivism.' "[7] Contemporary cultural crises originate in Scientism, the commonplace belief that only theoretical and scientific knowledge is valid and all else is *merely* speculation and common sense.

In Husserl's view, the cultural crises of the twentieth century infect the world of immediate experience or the life-world.[8] Although they cannot articulate it, individuals vaguely sense that "there can be a division of the sciences but not a corresponding division of man."[9] Husserl believed that we need to disclose the origins of our common world "in order to provide . . . for a radical self-understanding."[10] Phenomenology leads toward such understanding through methodical attention to the life-world where human beings originate meaning.

Elements of the life-world

"Life-world" or *Lebenswelt* refers to *the* surrounding world that provides the grounds of conscious existence. With-in[11] that world human beings exist

in the plain certainty of experience, before anything that is established scientifically, whether in physiology, psychology, or sociology. . . . We are subjects for this world, namely, as ego-subjects experiencing it, contemplating it, valuing it, related to it purposefully; . . . To be sure, all this undergoes manifold alteration, whereas "the" world, . . . persists throughout, being corrected only in its content.[12]

Thus the life-world is "the world in which we are always already living."[13] Although we may predicatively intend its meaning, we prepredicatively presume that the world is "simply there." As we will see, the life-world is the "thatness" human beings presume in their lived experiences of "whatness." As such, it

is the frame within which possibilities are open to us, the locus of realization of all our open possibilities, *the sum total of all circumstances to be selected and defined by our autobiographical situation.* Our belief in its existence is the unquestioned foundation for all possible questions, the unproblematic ground for the emergence of all possible problems, the prerequisite for transforming any unclarified situation into warranted ascertainability.[14]

Three features of the life-world suggest its sociological significance. First, human beings take the life-world for granted. Indeed, one of its most provocative features is its taken-for-grantedness.[15] Although human beings are inexhaustibly interested in their world, they remain unaware of themselves as "creative perspectives" on that world.[16] Second, the life-world is social, even though it is prescientific and prereflective. Husserl stressed that

to live as a person is to live in a social framework. . . . Here the word "live" is not to be taken in a physiological sense but rather as signifying purposeful living, manifesting spiritual creativity – in the broadest sense, creating culture within historical continuity.[17]

Socially, the life-world derives from the innumerable "and so on and so forths" and "again and agains" that underlie cultural objects like language, institutions, and standards of behavior. Such achievements are prepredicative ones that both science and common sense presuppose as elements of the real world. Finally, the life-world is a "paramount reality"; it is necessary for all human experience, communication, and activity. In the form of fundamental, implicit presuppositions, the life-world shapes all that is human.

The notion of life-world first concerns the "thatness"[18] of lived experience based on the invariant limits of human consciousness. "Life-world" does not stress actual "whatness" at all. The notion of life-world emphasizes the continuity and coherence at the roots of all lived experience. The life-world represents the nonteleological grounds for the teleologies built up in any particular worlds or finite provinces of meaning.[19]

Among phenomenologists, the life-world remains a principal interest that leads them to be concerned with common sense, language, and action. The universal "thatness" of lived experience unifies those concerns. "Life-world" refers to essentially unchanging, probably unchangeable, forms or structures of the biographical course of lived experience.

It is a constant of human being that each of us is born into a world already inhabited by Others, fellow-men like ourselves. It is a constant of mundane reality that each of us is born into a historical and cultural order, that we have language, that we experience the limits of existence in terms of the religious or magical, that we grow old together, and that we are destined to die. But it is also true that each of us can say "we," that we are able to share selected aspects of reality – appreciate the same poem, respond to the same music – without reducing them to idiosyncratic expressions or private contents of consciousness. And it is a prime fact of daily life that we take communication with fellow-men for granted, that is, we perceive the world and act in it on the unstated, completely immanent assumption, that Others see the world essentially as we do, that the one umbrella of reality serves us all.[20]

The world of immediate experience universally subsumes such forms of "thatness." *That* I shall die does not specify, though, *what* my death will involve – whether my body will be buried or cremated, whether it will be laid out or hidden away. Similarly, *that* I have a language fails to specify *what* my language is, for example, its intonations and its grammar. Thus every world of immediate experience presupposes the "thatness" of birth, intersubjectivity, language, and other universal elements of human existence. That human beings take for granted all those fundamentals is itself a universal feature of human existence. A phenomenology of the life-world discloses and clarifies such matters. Yet phenomenologists also attend to the culturally specific features of any actual life-world that instantiates the universal forms of lived experience. They recognize that the life-world, like consciousness and constitution, is a "unity in multiplicity."[21]

Any actual life-world is soundly cultural. People apprehend and interpret a life-world in a culturally specific way. Any life-world belongs, in other terms, to a specific group of human beings. Thus "life-world" essentially implies society and history as well as universality and invariance. Any actual life-world is a historically conditioned, changeable "whatness" within an invariant "thatness." It comprises culturally specific contents whose most basic structure is universally fixed. In studying an actual life-world, phenomenologists try "to find and to lay bare the acts of consciousness which . . . make this specific world possible as their correlate."[22] In Husserl's view, uncovering the source of all worlds involves two stages.[23] First, investigators must systematically trace back from cultural and scientific determinations to the original life-world; this is the task of mundane phenomenology. Second, beginning with the life-world, they must reveal the subjective operations it presupposes; this is the task of transcendental phenomenology. Together, mundane phenomenology and transcendental phenomenology specify the conditions of the possibility (or the a priori forms) of any actual or conceivable life-world. Yet the life-world itself cannot be directly experienced: "It is only as capable of taking on many appearances."[24]

Husserl understood that the world is whatever it is whether or not anyone is conscious of it. But once it appears as *the* world, it becomes intentionally certain but "incompletely intelligible."[25] Mundane phenomenology accounts for the universal certitude concerning *the* world and its taken-for-granted, though incomplete, intelligibility. Mundane phenomenologists study a specific world as an example that partially elucidates lived experience in any world. Involving no scientific or cultural presuppositions, mundane phenomenologists accept Husserl's invitation to "vary our actual world and transmute it to any other we can imagine," while imaginatively "varying ourselves" within the limits subjectivity itself prescribes.[26]

Mundane phenomenologists have found that the principal elements that structure the life-world include the natural attitude, the stock of knowledge, and social action. All the structuring of mundane experience emanates from the interplay of those elements. In short, the natural attitude, the stock of knowledge, and social action are the givens through which everyday life is continuously structured.[27]

Alfred Schutz (1899–1959) provided a mundane phenomenology remarkable for its findings about the invariant and constitutive features of the life-world as a social world. Schutz disclosed those features of social worlds that derive essentially from the human condition. Moreover, he showed how individuals constitute the commonness of the life-world, what its structure is, and what significance it has for social action. Maurice Natanson and Thomas Luckmann, who were students and close associates of Schutz, have each extended his studies of the life-world. Like Schutz's, their findings are indispensable to a phenomenological understanding of sociality.

The natural attitude

All of us are prereflectively acquainted with the natural attitude. It is the standpoint of all conscious activity except phenomenological reflection. The natural attitude undergirds all human experience as the belief in the existence of whatever concerns us, yet we never posit that belief. Rather, it pervades lived experience in an implicit way that we cannot articulate in daily life. In the natural attitude, the life-world is the "*unexamined* ground" or "the taken-for-granted frame in which all the problems which I must overcome are placed. This world appears to me in coherent arrangements of well-circumscribed objects which have determinate properties."[28]

In the natural attitude, we filter out the determinable indeterminacy of the objects we experience and intend. We "overlook" the dynamic quality of givenness and "deny" the constitutive powers of consciousness. Moreover,

in the natural attitude, there is at first (prior to reflection) no predicate "actual," no genus "actuality." It is only when we imagine, . . . and when, in addition, going beyond the occasional isolated act of imagination and its objects, we take them as examples of possible imagination in general and of fictions in general that there arise for us the concept of fiction (or of imagination) and, on the other hand, the concepts of "possible experience in general" and "actuality."[29]

Even then, the natural attutide persists as the "general thesis of the natural standpoint."

"The" world is a fact-world always there; at the most it is at odd points "other" than I supposed, this or that under such names as "illusion," "hallucination," and the like, must be struck *out of it*, so to speak; but the "it" remains ever, in the sense of the general thesis, a world that has its being out there.[30]

At its core, then, the natural attitude means standing-within-the-belief-in-the-world.[31] In the natural attitude, human beings suspend doubts about the existence of the outer world and its objects. Also suspended are doubts about the fundamental accuracy of their perceptions. "Suspended," however, does not imply intent here. The commitment not to doubt "the" world is not conscious; the very idea of such "wholesale doubt" does not occur to common-sense individuals.[32]

The phenomenon of the natural attitude implies other essential features of the life-world. First, it underscores the taken-for-grantedness of any life-world. In the natural attitude what individuals take for granted, above all, is the reality-status of the objects they experience.[33] *Until further notice* they assume the world will remain substantially the same (continuity) and that they can repeat their successful actions with substantially the same results (repeatability).[34] In connection with every problem is a "zone of things taken for granted" or a sector of the world that demands no further inquiry, even though its nature is not entirely clear.[35] Thus taking for granted means accepting one's knowledge as unquestionably plausible for the time being.[36] It also means acting as if objects *are* something rather than *are seen* as something.[37]

Much that people take for granted in the natural attitude concerns the social dimension of the life-world. Husserl emphasized that "believing in the world means holding fast to the immediacy of fellow men, the constructions *they* place upon experience, the vital glance whose source is not an eye but an intelligence."[38] Thus individuals prereflectively assume

(a) the corporeal existence of other men; (b) that these bodies are endowed with consciousness essentially similar to my own; (c) that the things in the outer world included in my environs and that of my fellow-men are the same for us and have fundamentally the same meanings; (d) that I can enter into interrelations and reciprocal actions with my fellow-men; (e) that I can make myself understood to them; . . . (f) that a stratified social and cultural world is historically pregiven as a frame of reference for me and my fellow-men, indeed in a manner as taken for granted as the "natural world"; (g) that therefore the situation in which I find myself at any moment is only to a small extent purely created by me.[39]

In fact, a *social, natural attitude* governs daily life. It comprises two fundamental axioms, the existence of conscious Others and a similarity between Others' and my experiences of the same objects. In the fully social, natural attitude individuals disregard their intuitive awareness that the same object presents itself to each individual in different adumbrations. In daily life, two idealizations subvert that awareness. One is the *interchangeability of standpoints*, the implicit belief that if I and Other changed places, each would experience a given object in the same overall fashion as the other experienced it in that place. The other idealization is the *congruence of relevance systems*, the implicit belief that I and Other, though biographically conditioned to differ in our understandings, can and do override those differences in pursuing our practical goals. Together these idealizations make up the *general thesis of the reciprocity of perspectives*, an idealization that structures every life-world as an essential element of its social character.[40]

Together with the idealizations of continuity and repeatability, these idealizations make possible the *relative-natural world view* that undergirds all
experience. That world view comprises "a system of typifications of the
life-world as such, socially objectivated, and established in sign systems,
above all in the mother tongue."[41] Thus the social dimension of the life-
world essentially rests not only on idealizations but also on a relative-
natural world view that presupposes typification, objectivation, and sym-
bolization. The natural attitude itself also presupposes those processes insofar
as they make it possible for individuals to regard objects as "there" rather
than as constituted.

Finally, the natural attitude suggests that for the common-sense person
action is more important than contemplation. Husserl himself emphasized
the priority of practical-evaluative activity in the world of daily life. Similarly,
Schutz and Luckmann determined that a pragmatic motive informs the natural
attitude.[42] The natural attitude and action essentially belong together.

The taken-for-grantedness, sociality, and action-orientation inherent in
every life-world are closely interrelated. Among the phenomena mediating
their interrelationship is common-sense knowledge, which is shaped by but
simultaneously   shapes   taken-for-grantedness,   sociality,   and   action-
orientation. Originally, however, the natural attitude provides the fundamental
presuppositions of everyday knowledge. To that extent the natural attitude
implies the phenomenon of common sense.

The stock of knowledge and common sense

In the natural attitude, individuals take for granted the possibility of cognition.[43] In the life-world the possibility of knowledge goes unquestioned,
then. Although individuals in the world of science tend not to take their
scientific knowledge for granted, they nonetheless take for granted, like all
common-sense individuals, the possibility of knowledge and the grounds
of its development. In short, the outermost limit of lived experience is the
problem of the possibility of knowledge, a problem outside the realm of
the natural attitude.

Individuals can take the possibility of knowledge for granted because
they have a stock of knowledge *on hand* and a stock of knowledge *at hand*.
On hand are the implicit presuppositions that make human experience possible, together with the knowledge the individual constitutes as the subject
of a unique biography and as a participant in a social world. At hand are
the specific intentions that constitute the individual's current experiences.
At its roots knowledge on hand involves, then, the unquestionable elements

necessary for a coherent stream of experience, while knowledge at hand involves the questionable elements necessary for any specific experience. In other terms, knowledge on hand transcends the individual's multiple situations; knowledge at hand concerns the types brought to bear in a specific situation.

Considered transculturally, the stock of knowledge on hand consists of fundamental elements and routine knowledge. The *fundamental elements* include the unchangeable spatial, temporal, and social structures of experience. My descriptions of the essential structure of experience and the natural attitude specified those elements that are a condition of the possibility of all human experience. The fundamental elements cannot be questioned, modified, or even articulated; they cannot become problematic. That they are permanently present to lived experience means that they are the inescapable grounds of conscious existence. In sum, the fundamental elements of any stock of knowledge are *given* absolutely. Their givenness provides a virtual standard for assessing the givenness of other objects of experience.[44]

Routine or habitual knowledge consists of skills, useful knowledge, and knowledge of recipes. Individuals acquire some routine knowledge with considerable facility (e.g., walking) and other routine knowledge with relative difficulty (e.g., learning Chinese). Once habitualized, though, such knowledge is *on hand* in all situations the individual experiences. Its elements become taken-for-granted know-hows that the individual applies prereflectively. Since it involves the transformation of capacities into standard, automatically applicable knowledge, routine knowledge offers the individual effective responses to recurrent situations that were once problematic. Although problematic situations can still arise for the individual, his or her routine knowledge as a whole goes unquestioned. Routine knowledge is given, then, as a trustworthy, unquestioned basis for achieving one's ends.

Considered culturally, the stock of knowledge consists of the fundamental elements necessarily on hand and *specific component contents* habitualized for the typical member of a society (e.g., speaking English, eating with forks) or the typical member of a subsocietal grouping (e.g., using a douche, giving a baby shower). Culturally, the stock of knowledge on hand is the system of know-hows directly tied to a specific relative-natural world.[45]

Considered situationally, the stock of knowledge comprises not only the stock of knowledge on hand but also the knowledge *at hand*. At any moment, the individual's stock of knowledge encompasses specific knowledge of *this* situation as a unique instance of its type.[46] *At hand* in a test-taking situation, for example, is a student's knowledge of *these* specific ideas and *this* teacher's mode of testing as well as relevant habitual knowledge (e.g., writing, reading, and analytical skills) and the fundamental elements that are always on hand. Every individual's stock of knowledge consists, in sum, of the fundamental elements common to all human beings, the habitual knowledge common to members of a given society and subsocieties, and the specific knowledge of a unique biography, all always *on hand*, along with the immediate knowledge the individual has *at hand* in the current situation.

As the individual's stream of experience progresses, knowledge *at hand* passes over into knowledge on hand. Knowledge at hand necessarily involves types whose utility is confirmed or questioned to some degree after experiencing any specific situation. Generally, any experience involves either routine activity and implicit confirmation of its relevant types or a problematic interruption of a routine activity and reconstruction of the types previously undergirding it. In one fashion or other, then, knowledge at hand is continuously absorbed into knowledge on hand, usually prereflectively. Thus descriptions of the stock of knowledge appropriately focus on the stock of knowledge on hand, specifically on the fundamental elements and the habitual knowledge the individual uses in encountering and comprehending the world. Thus "stock of knowledge," except where noted, will refer to the stock of knowledge on hand of the wide-awake, physically normal adult.

Every stock of knowledge includes "relevance-conditioned meaning-contexts between more or less familiar and more or less credible typical determinations, which are in more or less contradictory relations with one another."[47] At no time is the stock of knowledge fully integrated or consistent. Its elements include various "modalizations" of opinion as well as straight-forward certainties. Thus knowledge in and of the life-world "means not only explicit, clarified, well-formulated insights but also all forms of opinion and acceptance relating to a state of affairs as taken for granted."[48] The stock of knowledge is like a map. It provides means for determining one's location, both current and future, within the life-world. It maps out all that concerns or is likely to concern common-sense individuals; its variable details reflect their interests. Built on the invariants of experience and developed through typification, a stock of knowledge hints that, at root, knowledge derives from the stream of experience as a whole.

That experience and type originate together implies that knowledge and sociality necessarily correlate. Every stock of knowledge comprises determinations derived in part from individual problem solving and in part from socially objectivated solutions to commonplace problems.[49] The specific component contents of a stock of knowledge are, for the most part, socially derived. For those contents, individuals draw from a social stock of knowledge that comprises "the socially objectivated results of Others' experiences and explications."[50] Every stock of knowledge thus ties into a relative-natural world view governed by the logic of the natural attitude. That world view is part of the social a priori that shapes the taken-for-granted unities of subjective experience.[51] The logic of meaning-formation presupposes such a world view that manifests itself, above all, in language.[52]

Language is so central to common-sense knowledge, meaning, and understanding[53] that human beings "must talk about themselves until they know themselves."[54] Everyday language offers a veritable "treasure house of ready made pre-constituted types and characteristics, all socially derived and carrying along an open horizon of unexplored content."[55] The typifying medium par excellence, language is "the sedimentation of typical experiential schemata which are typically relevant in a society."[56] It makes objective "the customary attentional advertences and interpretational schemata for nature, society, and conduct in general . . . [which] are more or less firmly institutionalized in the social structure."[57]

Through language, subjective knowledge becomes objective and to that extent idealized and anonymous. In a sense, the translation of subjective knowledge into anonymous linguistic categories falsifies that knowledge. Specifically, the polythetic constitution of meaning and the essential temporality of subjective knowledge recede into the background as individuals constitute objective knowledge.[58] Objectivation thus involves an essential, though inadvertent, forgetfulness that consigns the subjective to a fugitive status. On the one hand, language provides the roots of intersubjective, anonymous knowledge that we take for granted in common, as we transcend biographical limitations. On the other hand, language provides the first hints of a "them"[59] that jeopardizes our sense of community.

A foregone sense of community underlies the Crisis of Common Sense currently infecting mundane experience. That crisis emanates from invidious distinctions between common-sense knowledge and scientific knowledge. Today people routinely regard the former as subjective and *ours* and the latter as objective and *theirs*. That common sense stands in need of defense itself suggests the degree of loss objectivation can generate. Since common sense informs all sociality and action, examining it illuminates the path ahead as well as further integrates phenomenological findings about the natural attitude and the stock of knowledge. At the same time the roots of the contemporary Crisis of Common Sense will be clarified.

Husserl wrote that

daily practical living is naive. It is immersion in the already-given world, whether it be experiencing, or thinking, or valuing, or acting. Meanwhile all those productive intentional functions of experiencing, because of which physical things are simply there, go on anonymously. The experiencer knows nothing about them, and likewise nothing about his productive thinking.[60]

For Husserl, the core of naiveté is the continuous, full-fledged unawareness of intentional achievements, both prereflective and reflective. Naiveté means, first of all, that individuals fail to see that they themselves constitute the objects of their experiences.[61] In the natural attitude, consciousness not only forgets its constitutive functioning but also provides no status for epistemology and metaphysics; they are unrecognized and unadmitted.[62]

"Naiveté" also infuses the more specific elements of individuals' common-sense knowledge. Viewed from "above" or "outside," that knowledge reliably appears as confused, inconsistent, and relatively incoherent.

Clear and distinct experiences are intermingled with vague conjectures; suppositions and prejudices cross well-proven evidences; motives, means and ends, as well as causes and effects, are strung together without clear understanding of their real connections. There are everywhere gaps, intermissions, discontinuities. Apparently there is a kind of organization by habits, rules, and principles which we regularly apply with success.[63]

Such knowledge takes likelihood, not certainty, as its ideal. "Naiveté" thus means that common-sense knowledge contrasts with technical knowledge involving formal logic, precision, attentiveness to all relevant details, and continually increasing sophistication of technique. Moreover, naive consciousness has a narrow rather than a wide set of concerns. Finally, it is personal and subjective rather than public and objective.[64] In sum, "the naive realism of the *Lebenswelt* consists in the way in which its taken for granted structures are *lived* rather than rendered objects of inspection."[65]

Common-sense individuals are all those human beings acting in the world rather than disinterestedly observing it.[66] Naive as they may be in some senses, such individuals base their activities on an "infinitely rich logic" that establishes a shared reality.[67] The naiveté that pervades the common-sense world is not, then, simplistic or uninformed. Rather, common sense succeeds without sensing its achievements. Nonetheless an elemental philosophy is implicit in everyday life, what Natanson calls "naive realism."[68]

As Natanson observes, ordinary language alone suggests that common sense is always "good." He further notes that common sense refers not to a cognitive faculty but to the character of social order. Common sense is "a mark of sociality, an emblem of man's involvement in the public world."[69] Thus it first concerns "the *structure* of man's action in daily life, not . . . the quality of his judgment."[70] Resting on the detailed logic of mundane naiveté, common sense structures the "experiential density" of everyday life.[71] In other terms, since they fix the essential structure of mundane action, the natural attitude and habitual knowledge make a *common-sense* world possible.

Because they can typify, intend and fulfill meaning, and focus on what is immediately relevant, human beings successfully deal with the world they simultaneously constitute as *our* world. Above all, daily life concerns the mastery of typical, recurrent situations. Beneath all its shortcomings, interruptions, and false starts is an unflappable success that far exceeds mere coping. Yet the common-sense person "will not cross the bridge before he reaches it and takes it for granted that he will find a bridge when he needs it and that it will be strong enough to carry him."[72] The individual is always in a situation demanding mastery and has on hand a stock of knowledge more or less tried and true. To that extent the common-sense person routinely integrates a present and a past that, together, reasonably assure a future of sufficiently strong bridges, as needed. Although it is future-oriented, common-sense is not crisis-oriented. Nor does it concern itself with what is essentially unforeseeable. Common-sense reasoning is oriented toward action, not truth or assertions.[73] It aims at successful action within a

structure of incompatibilities that is lived through as obvious. . . . Thus the purely conceivable hierarchies of plans confront specific and partially unalterable spheres of incompatibilities; the result is a system of motivations for *practicable* goals.[74]

To build a bridge is not practicable. The individual's retentions and protentions, sedimented in the stock of knowledge on hand, make it reasonable to aim only at mastering what can be anticipated and to assume arrival at a bridge when it might be needed. In large measure this is how common sense succeeds.

Social action

Phenomenologists examine the meaningfulness of conscious existence by studying finite provinces of meanings, sets of meaning-compatible experiences. Every finite province of meaning exhibits a distinctive tension of consciousness. It also has characteristic forms of spontaneity, sociality, and self-experience. Finally, within every finite province of meaning individuals adopt a specific time perspective and suspend specific types of doubts. In short, every finite province of meaning encompasses experiences that have a distinctive cognitive style.[75]

Thus finite provinces of meaning, such as the worlds of daily life, of science, of dreams, and of religion, do not divide the life-world into macro- and micro-level realities. Finite provinces of meaning are experiential spheres distinguished by the styles intentionality exhibits in various domains of taken-for-grantedness. Each spans a wide range of objects that belong together because of the characteristic way individuals intend and act upon them. In the world of daily life, for example, individuals ordinarily experience their own actions and those of others around them as meaningful. But institutionalized actions in social settings, the human intentions objectified in language, and the objective results of human acts (e.g., books, tools) are also meaningful without a shift in the style of consciousness.[76] These diverse objects make up a single world of meaningful experience. Similarly, in the world of science individuals find not only their own actions (e.g., designing experiments) meaningful but also the actions of others around them in that world who are pursuing their own projects. They also find meaningful the models and theories of their predecessors and their vaguely known contemporaries. Also meaningful are the technical vocabulary they take for granted together, the instruments they use, and the social organization of the establishment that employs them. In every finite province of meaning what is meaningful spans what is immediate and remote, both temporally and spatially. At the highest levels of anonymity and objectivity individuals constitute a world that they assume is accessible to anyone who is "willing, fit, and able."[77] They manifest that world in the actions each of them undertakes and routinely coordinates with others' actions in various zones of operation.

The Schutzian theory of action insists that human action is necessarily social. Action is always implicitly social inasmuch as it rests on the natural attitude and language. With profound frequency, action is explicitly social. Schutz's theory subsumes both senses of "social action." In fact, the findings he integrated systematically mesh those two senses in which lived experience and the life-world itself are thoroughly social.

Schutz's conceptions of action and act presuppose phenomenological findings about consciousness, constitution, and experience. On those grounds, Schutz defined action within a framework concerning human conduct or behavior.[78] *Conduct* is "subjectively meaningful experiences emanating from our spontaneous life."[79] Its broad intentionality and nonreflective activity rest on habit, tradition, and/or affect. Overt conduct is *mere* doing, covert conduct is *mere* thinking. When the individual has an Other-orientation, social conduct emerges. An Other-orientation rests on the general thesis of the Other as a conscious, experiencing being and experiences of the Other that uphold that thesis. *Social behavior* or social conduct is experiencing the Other through spontaneous activity. It includes various "feeling-activities" such as sympathy and erotic attraction.[80] Like all conduct, social behavior can be covert or overt. For example, I may feel antagonistic toward an Other (covert social behavior) or I may feel antagonistic toward her and spontaneously destroy the gift she gave me (overt social behavior).

Action is conduct devised in advance on the basis of a preconceived project. It is spontaneous activity *directed toward the future through projecting*, that is, anticipating future conduct by phantasizing. Not all projected conduct is purposive, however; therefore not all action is purposive. Overt action is by definition purposive, since it incorporates a "Let it be" that translates project into purpose and gears the individual into the outer world.[81] Covert action, however, comprises purposive and nonpurposive varieties, since an individual can project conduct without any intent to actualize the state of affairs being projected. An individual may, for example, daydream about how his or her conduct *might* manifest itself in a recurrent situation. In the absence of any intent to actualize the phantasized conduct the individual's daydreaming involves, by definition, action but not purpose. Similarly, the individual might project conduct in that recurrent situation, plan to realize it, and then dismiss that project. Again his or her conduct is covert action, but it is not purposive. Some covert action involves, then, relatively nondeliberative projecting of conduct.[82] In those cases habitual knowledge, knowledge of recipes, and other formulalike elements of the stock of knowledge at hand condition the individual to truncate action short of purposiveness.

Covert action is often purposive, however. Schutz labeled such action a *performance*. For example, an individual may summate mentally the grams of protein eaten during the course of the day for the purpose of determining whether he or she ingested sufficient protein. Significantly, some performances involve actualizing a projected state of affairs through noninterference.[83] An individual may, for example, deliberate as to whether or not to ever marry and project, in effect, two states of affairs for the purpose of choosing between them, one to be accomplished by one type of projected conduct and the other by an opposed type of projected conduct. If the individual chooses singlehood, his or her projected abstention from certain kinds of conduct is a covert action that involves purposiveness and projecting; it is a performance. The individual may, for example, decide to forego dating and related activities, avoid matchmaking friends, or severely limit the time spent dating any one person. This type of purposive covert action might be called "negative action."[84] Such performances exhibit deliberative, decisional features[85] as well as the projecting of abstention from specific types of conduct in order to bring about a given state of affairs.

An *act* is accomplished action, the outcome of action.[86] It is what action anticipates in its projecting. Since it is fundamental to his theory, Schutz's discussion of action and act merits detailed attention.

What is projected is the act, which is the goal of the action and which is brought into being by the action. . . . Indeed, only the completed act can be pictured in phantasy. For if the act is the goal of the action, and if the act were not projected, then the picturing of the action . . . would be an empty protention without any specific content, without any intuitive "filling-in." To be sure, it is proper to speak in ordinary language of my imagining my own action. But what is it which is really imagined here? Suppose I imagine myself getting out of my chair and going over to the window. What I really picture to myself is not a series of muscle contractions and relaxations, not a series of specific steps . . . from chair to window. No, the picture that I have in mind is a picture of the completed act of having gone over to the window. To this might be raised the objection that this is an illusion and that if we pictured our trip to the window with proper attentiveness we would count the steps and picture them. But to this objection there is a ready answer. If we do concentrate on each step or on each stretching of the leg, it will then turn out that what we are picturing is in each case a completed act: the act of having taken step one, the act of having taken step two, and so on. And the same will hold true of the parts of these steps in case we carry our analytic inclinations any further.

   The separate motions which constitute the execution of an action cannot therefore be pictured apart from the intended act which is constituted in the action. . . . What is visible to the mind is the completed act, not the ongoing process that constitutes it.

   Now we are in a position to state that . . . *action is the execution of a projected act*. And we can immediately proceed to our next step: *the meaning* of any action is its corresponding projected act.[87]

Schutz's conceptualizations of act and action imply that the meaning of an action and the meaning of an act differ. The first concerns the meaning-context of a future state of affairs phantasized as accomplished; its meaning-context or motivational context is an "in-order-to motive." From the actor's viewpoint the in-order-to motive for carrying out the action is the state of affairs being phantasized as completed in a project. The meaning-context of an act is a "because-motive" comprising, from the actor's retrospective viewpoint, the past experiences that led to the act. For example, in joining a health spa, a woman's in-order-to motive may be to reduce her dress size from average to petite. Her because-motives might include her participation in a youth- and fashion-oriented culture, her acceptance of the sexist double standard of aging, and her frustration at the prospect of recurrent taunts from her husband, who dubs her "chubby." More generally, while engaging in purposeful actions and resultant acts, the individual experiences in-order-to motives. The search for because-motives occurs only when the individual engages in self-explication that involves retrospection.[88] The two types of motives represent, in other terms, the subjective and the objective meaning-contexts of human activity. The differences between the two are crucial to our understanding of action. Confusing them distorts our understanding of how individuals determine their future conduct and experience their outcomes.

The preceding distinctions and principles underlie Schutz's conceptualization of *social action* as conscious experiences projected by the individual and intentionally related to an Other. Social action can be overt or covert. An individual might, for example, read a book in order to satisfy a colleague's expectations or might refrain from reading a book in order to avoid a friend's criticisms for wasting time on popular fiction. When the in-order-to motive of overt social action is to generate a certain conscious experience in the other person(s), social action becomes *social affecting*, which includes all communication.[89]

Two additional concepts are central to Schutz's delineation of the life-world as a social world whose structure emanates from action based on the stock of knowledge. An *orientation-relationship* is a social relationship involving only intentional acts of Other-orientation. Schutz emphasized that although they are common and socially significant, we cannot reliably observe orientation-relationships since they involve only an attitude toward another individual. The other concept central to his scheme is *social inter-action*, any social relationship that involves affecting-the-Other and intending for the Other to know that such affecting is meant. Social interaction is an "intersubjective motivational context" where "the in-order-to motive of the one becomes the because-motive of the other, the two motives complementing and validating each other as objects of reciprocal attention."[90]

The structure of the life-world

Schutz's approach to the structure of the social life-world begins with the face-to-face situation. As a theoretical construct specifying the limits of that situation, *thou-orientation* refers to the prepredicative, face-to-face experience of another human being purely as person, that is, not as a specific individual. In everyday life, however, the thou-orientation does involve degrees of apprehension and typification of the thou as a particular individual. When the thou-orientation is reciprocal, a *we-relation* emerges. In pure form a we-relation involves mutual awareness and sympathetic participation in one another's lives for some period of time, whether long or short. Empirically, we-relations involve various stages of apprehension and typification of other individuals. A barber and her customer, a father and his daughter, a tutor and his student, a shopper and a store clerk, a taxi driver and her passenger are all instances of we-relations. Such relations comprise enormous differences in the amounts of time the individuals spend together and in the amounts of physical distance that ordinarily separate them. Moreover, we-relations vary widely in how much their participants recognize them as such; that is, they vary in anonymity. Thus they differ, too, in the levels of mutual familiarity their participants achieve. Schutz introduced such a sweeping concept for one principal reason. He understood that any scheme concerning the social world must provide grounds for describing the constitution of intersubjectivity in everyday life. The "general thesis of the reciprocity of perspectives" specifies the idealizations that make intersubjectivity possible in everyday life; "we-relations" specifies the variety of social experiences that actualize the possibility of intersubjectivity. In other terms, the scope of the latter concept provides, at the most general level, grounds for describing how individuals constitute their world of common experiences. A dense configuration of we-relations, in sum, underlies the confirmation of the life-world's intersubjectivity.[91]

We-relations involve consociates, individuals who share relationships that rest on a community of space and time. But consociates represent only a tiny fraction of individuals' contemporaries, those with whom they coexist in world or standard time. Clearly, individuals do not directly observe their contemporaries or immediately share meaning-contexts with them. Yet lived experience draws no sharp line between consociates and contemporaries. In everyday life, meaning-contexts that are independent of any one individual's immediate situation relate one's own experiences to those of others. Specifically, every individual's stock of knowledge, which necessarily includes the idealizations of the social, natural attitude, guarantees that he or she experiences situations within wider, more lasting meaning-contexts than the present immediately encompasses. The transition from we-relations to *social relations* with contemporaries – from immediate experiences of the Other to mediate experiences of the social world – involves a considerable gray area where immediacy recedes and anonymity heightens.

Social relations with contemporaries rest on a they-orientation inferred from one's own experiences of the social world and involving an Objective meaning-context. The *they-orientation* is an orientation not to other persons as such but to types of individuals; one's partners in they-relations are types. Yet the difference between the "we" and the "they" in lived experience is not sharply given. The world of contemporaries is a "variant function" of face-to-faceness. Thus a continuous series of experiences joins the "we" and the "they."[92] Specifically,

I also use my typical knowledge in situations involving fellow-men. I grasp fellow-men as "people like . . ." and they are "thou's." On the basis of this double character of fellow-men there then occurs a third transposition: the mere contemporary, experienced by me as a type, is endowed with a conscious life like a fellow-man. But it must be established that I do not immediately experience the conscious life of the contemporary, but as it were "breathe" consciousness into the reference point of the they-orientation, into the type through an act of explication of mine. As a result, this consciousness remains just a typical, anonymous consciousness. It is clear that we have here touched on an important problem of the social sciences, that of the life-worldly basis of the so-called ideal type.[93]

Individuals experience contemporaries predicatively through interpretive judgments based on their stock of knowledge. As an Other-orientation, the they-orientation is constituted through typifications that provide bases for apprehending the conscious experiences of contemporaries as anonymous processes. Out of such inferential, discursive knowledge of contemporaries emerge *personal ideal types* that constitute the Other as an object of my experience lacking specific individuality.[94]

Similar principles govern our social relations to the world of *predecessors*, those in the past whose experiences do not temporally overlap with any of mine. Although the Other-orientation toward predecessors is passive, between the world of present social reality (contemporaries and consociates) and the world of predecessors lies a fluid boundary. "Simply by looking at them in a different light, I can interpret my memories of people I have known directly and indirectly as if these memories belonged to the world of my predecessors."[95] In fact, in every society individuals necessarily exhibit a "disposition toward the experience of generations and thereby a disposition toward a naive insight into the historicality of the social world."[96] And the temporal horizon of that insight is the indeterminate and indeterminable world of our successors: We can "know" no more than that there will be one.[97] In sum,

between the understanding of subjective meaning and the understanding of pure objective meaning there is a whole series of intermediate steps based on the fact that the social world has its own unique structure derived, as it is, from the world of direct social experience, of contemporaries, of predecessors, and of successors.[98]

Thus the structure of the life-world derives from human intentionality shaped by the temporal and spatial arrangements necessary for a shared world. Intentionality universally guarantees that the life-world itself transcends finitude yet exhibits temporal patterns built on the common-sense principle of "first things first." Also because of intentionality the life-world integrates the historical and situational features of human experience. Partitioned into worlds within actual reach and within potential reach,[99] the life-world expresses, too, the perspectival quality of all intentionality. In turn, the essential fluidity of human knowledge, together with the essential certitude of the Ego, provides the grounds for the human actions and acts that constitute any life-world as a social, structured field that is thoroughly *ours*.[100]

5. Phenomenological methods

Man knows nothing that is not in some way self-knowledge.
Ralph Harper, "Concerning Self-Knowledge"

"In the beginning" is also the language of phenomenological genesis;
it is the cry of origin.
Maurice Natanson, *Edmund Husserl*

As Lauer indicates, "one can be interested in the world or in the experience of the world. If one chooses the first, one can go wrong; if one chooses the second, one cannot."[1] Insistent on certitude, Husserl chose the second focus because of his commitment to clarifying experience. Broadly, phenomenologists investigate experience and its objects or, in phenomenological terms, the "ego cogito" (the noetic aspect) *and* the "cogitata" (the noematic aspect) of intentional experience. The translation from "experience and its objects" to the "ego cogito cogitata" suggests the phenomenological shift, accomplished methodically, from the common-sense experience of objects to the phenomenological experience of phenomena. That methodical shift, essential to all phenomenological practice, reflects Husserl's stricture that "the true method follows the nature of the things to be investigated and not our prejudices and preconceptions."[2]

Thus the clarification of experience demands methods that eliminate the preconceptions that obfuscate objects in the first place.[3] If we know an object adequately, no inquiry is necessary; if we do not, that inadequacy derives from the content of our knowledge (current determinations of the object) as well as its scope (current determinations of the object's horizon). In any case, an effective method of inquiry – a true method – demands freedom from preconceptions (extant determinations). If we carry those preconceptions into the inquiry, our results bear their weight. If, though, we dismiss our preconceptions as invalid or naive, we only create another presupposition about the object, namely, that it is not what we had thought it to be. An effective method demands that we neither introduce our preconceptions into inquiry nor dismiss them. Rather, we must *suspend* or *bracket* those presuppositions by foregoing any judgment whatsoever about them. And making no judgment about them means we make no use of them.

But what is left then? If we undertake an inquiry without any operative preconceptions, the problem of establishing a starting point emerges. The problem is false, however, for under these conditions a clear, absolutely given starting point presents itself, namely, the immediate experience of the object of inquiry. Yet to assume the existence or nonexistence of the object is a preconception. Thus what absolutely remains is actually, in the case of apparently transcendent objects, the *experience* of an object's *appearance*, which the investigator accepts as neither real nor unreal. The investigator *irrealizes* the object by suspending all preconceptions about it. In the case of immanent objects – a memory, for example, or a belief – what remains is the initial object *minus* the other immanent objects associated with it. In short, the starting point is a *phenomenon*. By its nature a phenomenon is certain. Phenomenologists focus on phenomena by using specific methods for making determinations of them.

Phenomenology permits no use of the results and methods of science, analytical reflection, or common sense. Phenomenological methods exclude the investigator's stock of knowledge at hand. They begin with only the immanent object being investigated (the noema) and the particular mode through which it is given (the noesis). In other terms, "to the things themselves" is a procedural admonition to study an object of experience as an object-of-*my*-experience and to exclude everything that does not belong immediately to that object as directly given. Or, alternatively, phenomenological methods require the suspension of all belief in a reality beyond intentionality.[4] In short, phenomenological methods are reflexive.[5] They involve the certainty of "seeing my seeing" inasmuch as a phenomenon is known as an object-of-*my*-knowing. In these respects, phenomenologists break from the natural attitude. They separate "the intentional lines between us and the world in order to uncover the umbilical cord that ties us to the world."[6]

For phenomenologists, that task involves commitment to Husserl's "principle of all principles": "*Whatever presents itself . . . is simply to be accepted as it gives itself out to be*, though *only* within the limits in which it then presents itself."[7] Within the phenomenological sphere adherence to that principle has two immediate corollaries, including the refusal to infer anything about an act of consciousness on the basis of another act of consciousness and the refusal to accept anything that is not itself directly given.[8] In other terms, phenomenological observation must be "original."[9] Thus getting to the things themselves requires considerably more than a methodological decision, however resolute. It requires persistent effort, perhaps even acceptance of phenomenology as a "philosophy of toil."[10]

A strictly descriptive orientation governs phenomenological methodology. Because it focuses on what is believed, imagined, or otherwise intended, phenomenological description inescapably incorporates a reflexive element. Furthermore, phenomenological description contrasts with scientific description based on idealizing procedures inasmuch as its descriptive claims are meant as definitive, not tentative.[11] Phenomenologists deal with essential rather than empirical determinations. They make no attempt to interpret the essence disclosed through phenomenological methods. Their sole purpose is to investigate what is given, not to relate the phenomenon to anything else and thus go beyond the phenomenon as absolutely given.

Phenomenologists rely on an experience-oriented methodology. By advocating the investigation of phenomena, Husserl sought to disclose the roots of reason in experience. He regarded the phenomenological attitude as "that form of reason which sets itself the task of converting the understanding into reason."[12] That our understanding exceeds reason is comprehensible in view of Husserl's findings regarding the natural attitude, the naiveté of daily life, the "forgetfulness" of the sciences, and the prepredicative bases of all knowledge and understanding. In the life-world, individuals understand within experiential matrices that necessarily remain unexamined. A methodical departure from that field represents a step toward reason, which we always assume is "there" but which we cannot fully disclose in daily life where its achievements rest on unrecognized presuppositions.

Within the phenomenological frame, *all* conscious life reveals itself as directed toward reason. But outside that frame the essential, universal grounds of reason – that is, the essential structure of consciousness – remain unclarified. To that extent, reason itself remains as much a matter of faith as of knowledge within the life-world. Nonetheless reason, which ultimately concerns possibilities of verification, continuously "makes evidence" and grasps the evident.[13] Those accomplishments belong to consciousness in all its modalities; that is, evidence has "a universal and teleological function in conscious life."[14] As the means of systematically disclosing the essential structures that make evidence possible, phenomenology establishes itself in the "service of universal reason."[15]

Epochē and eidetic reduction

The procedures phenomenologists use begin with the epochē and terminate with the transcendental-phenomenological reduction.[16] For purposes at hand, I need not detail each step of the progression to transcendental consciousness. Instead, I focus on three procedures central to the phenomenological treatment of phenomena. These include the epochē, the eidetic reduction, and the phenomenological reduction. These methods provide the simplest possible grounds for critically examining knowledge, specifically the immediate, presuppositionless experience of individual objects by a single knower. Thus phenomenological methods establish grounds for a counterpoint to natural-scientific theories of knowledge. They enable an investigator to get at the "things themselves" by confronting his or her self strictly as knower of this thing itself (the noetic focus) and confronting this thing itself solely as it is known (the noematic focus). Thus a phenomenologist transforms *the* world into *my* world or "world-taken-as-*the*-world" by me.[17]

Husserl insisted that phenomenological practice requires inhibiting all preconceived notions about one's object of inquiry and about the world.[18] That inhibition makes the given object a such-and-such-perceived, remembered, thought, valued, or otherwise intended. Phenomenological inquiry also requires abandoning assumptions about the existence of objects of experience and their horizons, because such beliefs are ungrounded.[19] Thus the existential status of the world and its objects shifts as one enters the phenomenological sphere. The phenomenologist remains conscious of his or her existence, grasping it immediately, but no longer experiences "the" world *as such* because he or she no longer assumes its existence.

The beginning of phenomenological inquiry is the epochē. "Epochē" is a Greek term meaning abstention. The epochē involves "putting out of action" the general thesis of the natural attitude.[20] It means "bracketing"

this entire natural world . . . which is continually "there for us". . . .
    If I do this, . . . I do *not* then *deny* this "world", . . . *I do not doubt that it is there*; . . . I use the "phenomenological" epochē, which *comletely bars me from using any judgment that concerns spatio-temporal existence.*[21]

But the epochē

is not a transformation of the thesis into its antithesis, of positive into negative; it is also not a transformation into presumption, suggestion, indecision, doubt; . . . *We do not abandon the thesis we have adopted, we make no change in our conviction. . . .* And yet the thesis undergoes a modification – whilst remaining in itself what it is, *we set it as it were "out of action", we "disconnect it," "bracket it."* The thesis is experienced as lived *but we make "no use" of it.*[22]

The epochē eliminates the grounds of doubt by suspending those "factual" matters that establish contingency and therefore the possibility of doubt. "When the epochē is in operation, whatever is known is known as essential and necessary."[23] The epochē thus opens up a rich sphere of experience different from common-sense experience. It provides for apprehending one's self purely as ego with a conscious life in and through which "the world" exists for the investigator only as he or she accepts it through acts of consciousness. In short, the epochē is a condition of the insight that "I can enter no other world than the one that obtains its meaning and acceptance in and from me."[24]

Although the epochē suspends the phenomenologist's complicity in experience, it is not a denial. The phenomenologist's "suspension" is an abstention from the validities presupposed in the natural attitude.[25] It involves "placing in abeyance" or "withholding assent."[26] Phenomenologists do not oppose or reject the validities of everyday life; they merely refrain from the subjectively meaningful, spontaneously renewed beliefs connected with the natural attitude. Paradoxically, in the very suspension of the general thesis of the natural attitude phenomenologists fully discover it.

As the disconnecting of the belief in the world the epochē is not a refusal to hold a belief which is already known to be a belief but in truth the first authentic *discovery of the belief in the world*: the discovery of the world as a transcendental dogma.[27]

The epochē is a negative achievement in the sense that it

functions as a *condition* for a knowledge of essence, not as a positive factor in grasping essences as they are; it simply assures that no foreign elements shall be admitted into the analysis; it says nothing positive with regard to what is there. If the phenomenological investigation is to be fruitful, the epochē must have its positive counterpart.[28]

The epochē represents "the methodological *commencement* of an unremitting assault on the peak of certitude."[29] As such, it brings one to the edge of the phenomenological sphere. Thus "epochē signifies at one extreme a narrowly construed act of restraint and at the other extreme is almost synonymous with phenomenological reduction,"[30] which is ultimately its positive counterpart.

Mediating between the epochē, whose effects remain operative in the phenomenological sphere, and the phenomenological reduction is the eidetic reduction. The eidetic reduction complements the epochē by making something of what remains after suspending the general thesis of the natural standpoint. Since the epochē does not establish anything, at the moment of epochē the status of the given object is unclear. Having put the factual out of play, the investigator faces "something" as an object of consciousness. Under such circumstances, it seems the investigator would ask a frustrating "So what?" after having arrived at the point of knowing only that "I" am and that "I" am aware of this "something." The eidetic reduction bursts that potential dead end by applying the phenomenological principle that *"every fact can be thought of merely as exemplifying a pure possibility."*[31] Thus what was *given* before the epochē as a fact can be *taken* after the epochē as an exemplar of some undetermined but pure possibility. The pure possibility that the object exemplifies is its essence. The eidetic reduction means simply intending an object of consciousness as an exemplar of an essence (or "eidos").

In effect, another "So what?" lurks as a possibility here. Phenomenologists circumvent it, though, by the method of free variation for investigating essences. Starting with an existent-for-me (object of consciousness), the investigator considers it as an example or exemplar, that is, as a mere possibility incidentally actualized. The logic of free variation presupposes that every existent is necessarily possible and imaginable and therefore exemplifies a class of possibilities. In other terms, free variation assumes a domain of "inexplicit typicality"[32] that sets the limits wherein the investigator can freely vary the object without losing its imaginability as an example of this *kind* of thing. Free variation involves, then, "running through" variations to determine which of them exclude, permit, and demand each other.[33] It does not, though, respect the "identity" of the initial object of consciousness, for that object is treated only as an example of something else. Thus variation and alteration differ.[34] If variation involved the perceptual rather than the imaginative mode, the results would be empirical generalities, which phenomenologists do not seek. Instead, phenomenologists operate at the level of eidetic necessity.

In free variation, each imagined variant is arbitrary, since it is only one particular instance of the eidos being determined.[35] It is not absolutely arbitrary, however, since every variant must leave the original intentional object still imaginable. When that object is not imaginable as a variant of the variant being imagined, the investigator has exceeded an eidetic limit. He or she must then exclude some feature(s) of the current variant from the determination of the eidos. The essence or eidos is what remains invariant throughout the imaginative variation of the original object. The essence is those elements without which an object of this kind cannot be conceived of or imagined. It is those conditions every variant must meet as an example or manifestation of a specific class of possibilities.

Eidetic assertions neither state nor imply factual matters. They entirely concern evidence of essential possibility and impossibility, not evidence of actuality. Although eidetic statements provide no bases for inferring about actual instances of an eidos or the specific properties those instances *in fact* manifest, they do specify the limits within which actual instances of a type of object must occur, that is, be experienced.

The phenomenological reduction

The eidetic reduction involves a noematic shift from object-as-factual to object-as-exemplar and the major eidetic method, free variation, involves varying the noema while holding constant the noesis of imagining. The phenomenological reduction changes the investigator's way of intending (the noetic aspect) the objects of consciousness that remain taken as exemplars. Most generally, the phenomenological reduction involves shifting from the mundane experience of acts of consciousness to acts of consciousness strictly in terms of their presentational functions.[36]

Earlier, we saw that because of its fundamental certitude every ego carries a crucial possibility concerning knowledge, evidence, and understanding. Further examination of that possibility demonstrates why the phenomenological reduction is necessary and what it accomplishes. Husserl emphasized that

each human being bears within himself a transcendental "I" . . . insofar as he is the *self-objectification*, as *exhibited through phenomenological self-reflection*, of the corresponding transcendental "I" . . . Every human being who carried out the [second] epochē could certainly recognize his ultimate "I," *which functions in all his human activity*. The naiveté of the first epochē had the result . . . that I . . . proceeded in one leap and without grounding . . . *to attribute to the mankind in which I find myself the same transformation into functioning transcendental subjectivity* which I had carried out alone by myself. *In spite of the methodical illegitimacy, this contained a truth*. At all events . . . we must . . . do justice to the *absolute singularity of the ego* and its central position in all constitution.[37]

Here Husserl indicates that the epochē and the eidetic reduction leave intact the "I" implicated in mundane activities. As long as an "I" functions in inquiry, the lived experiences whose synthesis is an identity affect the inquiry, mostly in the form of idealizations and typifications. The active presence of an "I" means that consciousness still has common-sense elements. Though reduced, it remains significantly mundane.

Specifically, the empirically objectified "I" with its unique identity "proceeded in one leap" and remained after the epochē and eidetic reduction.

Having suspended the general thesis and therefore recourse to the factual, "I" assumed that its methodical determinations would, of necessity, be made by any other human being who had performed the same operations. The naiveté of that assumption is that "I" am clearly not *any* other human being than a uniquely constituted self. Such naiveté has its roots in the life-world, for the truth Husserl alludes to undergirds that world as the general thesis of the reciprocity of perspectives. That thesis is what "I" assume, even after executing the eidetic reduction. Significantly, under conditions of phenomenologically reduced consciousness that thesis is no longer an assumption but a truth. Given reduced consciousness, standpoints do become interchangeable and relevance systems do become congruent. As Husserl indicated, the problem is not that the assumption is false but that it has not been demonstrated as a "true assumption" or principle.

Disclosing the truth inherent in the general thesis of the reciprocity of perspectives demands an "ultimate I" that functions in all human activity. That "ultimate I" cannot be temporally constituted, since at some point an "I" might then have acted without benefit of that "ultimate I." Nor is it unique to any "I," since it is a "transcendent I." What *functions* in all human activity is whatever constitutes *human activity*, whatever is essentially human in terms of activity as opposed, for example, to corporeality. Thus the pure possibilities of which "I" and "you" and "he" and "she" are particular actualizations still need to be phenomenologically disclosed in order to demonstrate the truth of the general thesis at hand. "Accordingly, . . . a second reduction is required, . . . a reduction to the absolute ego as the ultimately unique center of all constitution."[38] The necessity of that reduction attests to the "absolute singularity" of each actual ego while it opens the way to disclosing the pure possibilities each ego uniquely actualizes.

The phenomenological reduction strips consciousness of its mundane quality,[39] permitting observation of consciousness itself in its essential functioning. It brackets the general thesis of the reciprocity of perspectives and everything that thesis presupposes, most importantly objectified others and a self-objectified "I." Putting that thesis and its presuppositions out of play is the condition of entry into the realm of pure consciousness or "finally reduced consciousness"; "ego cogito" becomes "Ego cogito." The realm of pure consciousness reveals consciousness as the medium of access to whatever-(is-taken-to-)exist. It is the realm of "originally achieving" consciousness.[40]

Tersely put, in phenomenological reduction what we know about the world and what we take for granted about experience are scrutinized in terms of a purely egological standpoint whose own origin and becoming are thematic problems for self-analysis. . . . The phenomenologist stands in relationship to the field he surveys in reduction no longer an empirical self in touch with the world but as a phenomenological observer concerned with the "world" as the intentional correlate of transcendental subjectivity.

It is . . . complicity of the self in history and, more subtly, the tacit but intersubjective intent of what is usually called *personal* life which phenomenological reduction strives to undercut.[41]

The transcendental ego is, in other terms, the attainment of phenomenological reduction. The transcendental ego *is* (intentionally) its experiences. It has (is given) no "being" apart from what is immediately perceived and thus encompasses no "mine" as such. The transcendental ego is, then, anonymous consciousness belonging to no one particular.[42] Thus the transcendental ego offers an "infinite field of pure investigation" inasmuch as experience of what is immediately given cannot be cancelled, suspended, or denied.[43] After the phenomenological reduction, what remains is *essentially* functioning consciousness *given as such*. Achieving the transcendental attitude means that phenomena in the fully phenomenological sense become the objects of consciousness.

After achieving the phenomenological reduction, the phenomenologist pursues two related purposes. First, he or she systematically explores the structure of functioning consciousness in order to reconstruct the depth, variety, and immediacy of human experience. Such efforts reveal the "*a priori* structural origins and foundational meaning"[44] of *our* world. Second, the transcendental investigator focuses on "the intersubjective impulse hidden in the apparent privacy of perception."[45] Within the transcendental sphere,

with all its truths, the "natural attitude" shows itself to the phenomenologist as a *constituted* situation, as the situation of the transcendental subjectivity which has objectified itself into man and which has gone outside itself, as the situation of the spirit's self-estrangement.[46]

Transcendentally, it also becomes clear that "phenomenology is centered in intentionality, that intentionality is opened up by reduction, that reduction involves origin, and that origin is the transcendental clue to existence."[47]

The phenomenological reduction gives way to *intentional analyses* that disclose and clarify the relationship between phenomena and acts of consciousness. Only the transcendental sphere provides absolute grounds for analyzing intentionality as the essential functioning of consciousness. The results of such analyses provide the substance of Chapters 2 and 3. The transcendental sphere permits constitutional analyses inasmuch as it opens for inspection the original "constitutive layer," the self-constituting intentionality of consciousness. The phenomenological reduction is, in fact, necessary for disclosing the double intentionality of consciousness. Without it, longitudinal intentionality remains hidden, for the nontranscendental, empirical "I" blocks its full discovery. The phenomenological reduction and intentional analyses thus give way to constitutional analyses.

Before turning to evidence and empiricism, I should make several points about the relationship between the results and the method of phenomenology.[48] Phenomenologists are single-minded in the belief that *any* epistemology must originate in phenomena and develop through their rigorous examination. As the sole line of access to phenomena, radically reflective consciousness is necessary for developing any adequate epistemology. Phenomenological method proceeds entirely through acts of radical reflection.[49] It involves rigorous reflection directed at the "ultimate thinkable suppositions" of knowledge. The fulfillment of its radicality discloses transcendental subjectivity as the absolute origin of all meaning.[50]

A full-fledged, essential integrity thus obtains between phenomenological method and phenomenological results. What phenomenologists describe depends completely on phenomenological method. Without reduction there are *no* results, only reports about "results."[51] Arrived at apart from the reflexive method of phenomenology, descriptions concerning consciousness and experience are mere reports resting on the naivetés that necessitate phenomenological method in the first place. The root meaning of the reflexivity of phenomenological method finally emerges: "Phenomenological method is itself phenomenologically derived."[52] Phenomenological inquiry reveals the natural attitude *at the very moment* that it reveals the need for the epoché of the general thesis; reveals essences at the moment it reveals the necessity of the eidetic reduction; reveals the transcendental ego at the moment it reveals the necessity of the phenomenological reduction. Method and finding arise together and are essentially bound together in phenomenological investigations. Therein lies the necessity of presuppositionlessness as a phenomenological ideal.

Evidence and empiricism

Phenomenological method reflects Husserl's concern with releasing consciousness from factual, contingent elements by progressing away from preconceptions and toward transcendental subjectivity. That progression from the contingent to the absolute concerns evidence in both the mundane and technical senses. First, phenomenological method establishes the conditions for disclosing what is nonevident in the life-world. In this sense, evidence concerns "seeing"; it requires suspending the preconceptions inherent in any life-world. It is the incorrigible, immediate givenness of an object of consciousness as *it itself*. In the first sense, then, evidence

consists in the *self-appearance*, the *self-exhibiting*, the *self-giving*, of an affair, an affair-complex (or state of affairs), a universality, a value, or other object, in the final mode: "itself there", "immediately intuited", "given originaliter."[53]

Phenomenological method also aims at eidetic assertions about "the things themselves." As we have seen, eidetic assertions specify the necessary boundaries of empirical particularizations as instances of a specific type of thing. Here phenomenology concerns evidence in the sense of verification. Thus phenomenologists seek evidence in the technical as well as the mundane sense. "Making evident" in both senses expresses a single orientation that we might call, in Husserl's programmatic words, a commitment to "philosophy as rigorous science."[54]

Both science and philosophy have in common

an *order of cognition, proceeding from intrinsically earlier to intrinsically later cognitions*; ultimately, then, *a beginning and a line of advance* that are not to be chosen arbitrarily but have their basis "in the nature of things themselves."[55]

The systematic pursuit of evidence begins *deliberately*, then. Although they start at different levels, both scientists and philosophers invoke a norm of "nonarbitrariness" in undertaking that pursuit. But every beginning short of transcendental subjectivity is ultimately arbitrary, since it presupposes some foundation. That foundation, which underlies predicative judging, involves prepredicative judging, which in turn involves intentionality and inner time-consciousness.

In the broadest sense, evidence denotes a universal primal phenomenon of intentional life, namely . . . the quite preeminent mode of consciousness that consists in the *self-appearance*, the *self-exhibiting*, the self-giving of an affair, an affair-complex (or state of affairs), a universality, a value, or other objectivity, in the "given originaliter." For the Ego that signifies: not aiming confusedly at something, with an empty expectant intention, but being with it itself, viewing, seeing, having insight into, it itself. Experience in the ordinary sense is a particular evidence. All evidence, we may say, is *experience in a maximally broad, and yet essentially unitary, sense.*[56]

Thus evidence concerns intention-fulfillment. So conceived, evidence is broadly the terminus intentional experience seeks; it is narrowly the deliberate pursuit of intention-fulfillment. In both senses, evidence is essentially experiential and, therefore, horizonal, variably given, and temporally constituted. Just as there can be no absolute beginning point (except transcendental subjectivity) in the pursuit of evidence, there can be no absolute stopping point (except transcendental subjectivity). Apart from the absolute ground of transcendental subjectivity, the diverse processes of verification belong essentially in the domain of the "I can,"[57] an idealization inherent in all lived experience.

Verification can proceed through various noetic modes, such as intending-as-possible, as-doubtful, as-likely, or as-real. Underlying all those modes is the bifurcation between intending-as-actual and intending-as-possible. Husserl labeled the former a "positional" and the latter a "quasi-positional" mode of consciousness. "To each . . . mode there correspond both a particular mode of evidence of its meant objects . . . and potentialities of making objects evident."[58] Husserl thus specified the major boundaries wherein individuals pursue different levels of evidence, using different modes of intention-fulfillment at each judicative level. His theory of evidence addresses both the noematic and noetic features of the experience of evidence. In that sense, the phenomenological theory of evidence is a theory of self-evidence.[59]

Husserl's use of "self-evidence" in no manner implies the infallibility of human perception and judgment. The concept does, though, emphasize that further experiences can correct any judicative experience. Husserl's approach implies, moreover, that either self-evidence is the final court of appeal or human knowledge is inescapably illusory.[60] Self-evidence is the experience of "itself-there" whose opposite is a "mere presentification" or indication.[61] The givenness of "itself-there" or "it itself" is an intentional experience with a horizon of endless possibilities for reidentification. In order to *verify* such givenness, one cannot fulfill all the empty intentions constituting its horizon. Of necessity, then, attempts at verification return the investigator to the self-giving experience of the more basic judgments underlying self-evidence.[62] "To the phenomenologist, evidence is not a hidden quality inherent in a specific kind of experience, but the possibility of referring derived experiences to an originary one."[63] In the strictest sense, then, self-givenness (evidence) does not point to anything beyond what is directly given. Such evidence is available only in the phenomenologically reduced sphere[64] that offers the indubitability of the simplest, original *immediate* judgments involving no inferences. Such judgments constitute the grounds of all other judicative activity. In the narrowest sense, then, self-evidence is the immediate self-givenness of intentional objects constituted through acts of transcendental subjectivity.[65] In a less strict, broader sense evidence of transcendental objects is always *more or less adequate*.[66]

Thus phenomenological claims, presumably resting on absolute grounds, are meant as incontrovertible. Seemingly, no clearcut grounds are available for proving them inadequate. That conclusion is false, however. Phenomenological assertions are eidetic claims about essential possibilities and impossibilities. As such, they are subject to two types of disconfirmation. One can either demonstrate that the asserted possibility or impossibility is logically inconceivable or one can find a *single* case that contradicts the assertion.[67] Given their nonprobabilistic form, phenomenological claims are, in fact, more readily subject to disconfirmation than are most empirically derived claims.

Thus the matter of the relationship between phenomenology and empirical sciences surfaces again. At the most general level, phenomenology and empirical sciences actualize the capacity to clarify the world; both emphasize the systematic pursuit of knowledge, evidence, and understanding; both admit, though reluctantly at times, a need for the other. Most importantly, phenomenology and the empirical sciences share a primordial belief in the intelligibility of "the" world. Their symbiosis rests on the empiricist drive to exploit that intelligibility by developing objective, factually based knowledge and the phenomenological drive to exploit it by developing objective, eidetically based knowledge.

6. Ethnomethodology:
an alternative sociology?

"Where there is smoke there must be fire" is the logic of stake-burning,
not of free inquiry.

Maurice Natanson, *Phenomenology, Role, and Reason*

To address itself, sociology must free itself from its practice; sociology
must desociologize itself.

Alan F. Blum, "Sociology, Wrongdoing, and Akrasia"

From the nineteenth century, phenomenological tendencies have informed
sociology. In a sense, Max Weber's sociology was strongly prephenome-
nological and Georg Simmel's sociology tended toward the phenomenological
method and spirit. Later social scientists such as James, Cooley, Mead,
and Thomas adopted phenomenologically relevant methodologies. Schutz
and, to a lesser extent, Scheler remain, though, the pacesetters among
phenomenological social scientists.[1] Current attempts to develop a phenomenological sociology are fairly widespread; the most influential individuals who appear aimed in that direction are ethnomethodologists. That
they often express indebtedness to phenomenologists, that their critiques
of sociology have a phenomenological tone, and that they draw some of
their major presuppositions and constructs from the phenomenological frame
suggest that ethnomethodologists lean toward phenomenological sociology.
Its historical and intellectual grounds also link ethnomethodology with phenomenology.

Throughout his works Harold Garfinkel, the originator and guiding figure
of ethnomethodology, cites phenomenologists. In his doctoral dissertation,
completed in 1952 under Talcott Parsons, Garfinkel frequently cited Husserl,
Schutz, and Gurwitsch. He acknowledged "many friendly meetings" with
Schutz and Gurwitsch that helped him clarify the relationship between phenomenology and sociology, and he cited Husserl's solution to the problem

of relativity in sociology.[2] In discussing the Hobbesian problem of order, Garfinkel used four of Schutz's postulates as "unquestioned givens."[3] In addition, he drew "inspiration and actual materials" from Schutz in his "structural comparison" of the natural and scientific attitudes.[4] In Garfinkel's first major work, the influence of Schutz's and Husserl's ideas is clear-cut.

A decade later Garfinkel wrote that

in a series of classical writings in sociological theory directed to the constitutive phenomenology of situations of daily life, . . . Schutz described those presuppositions whereby scenic occurrences were assigned by an actor the constituent meanings for him of the scene's feature, "known in common with others." In accordance with the program, attitude, and method of Husserlian phenomenology Schutz looked for the presuppositions and the corresponding environmental features intended by them that were invariant to the specific contents of actions and their objects.[5]

Garfinkel culled eight presuppositions from Schutz's works, including what Garfinkel calls the "et cetera assumption" ("that as events have occurred in the past, they will occur again in the future") and Schutz's general thesis of the reciprocity of perspectives.[6] Using those presuppositions, Garfinkel described eleven "determinations" that make an event an occurrence in the common-sense environment. Those features are "seen without being noticed"; actors invariantly presuppose them. Thus they are "constitutive of a situation of events as a world known in common and taken for granted."[7] As such, those features receive a "constitutive accent" and function as "constitutive expectancies" in daily life.[8] To illustrate such invariants, Garfinkel argued, one must "breach" constitutive expectancies in radical ways, since the natural attitude guarantees that people assimilate the "strange" into the "familiar" without dismantling the presuppositions undergirding a shared world. In his logic of inquiry, Garfinkel "borrowed" from Schutz "by accepting his findings that the situations of game, of play, of scientific theorizing, of dreaming, of staging in the theatre, of theatre going, are produced by modifying the presuppositions of the attitude of daily life."[9] Garfinkel also noted that "part of Schutz's great stature as a sociologist consists in having performed the fundamental work that makes it possible for sociologists to" study the natural attitude and the common-sense world as problematic phenomena.[10]

In his programmatic *Studies in Ethnomethodology*, Garfinkel cited Schutz, Husserl, and Gurwitsch (as well as Parsons) as major influences.[11] He pointed to Schutz as a "magnificent exception" among sociologists, who rarely see the sociological problem of how any common-sense world is possible.[12]

Almost alone among sociological theorists, the late Alfred Schutz, in a series of classical studies of the constitutive phenomenology of the world of everyday life, described many of these seen but unnoticed background expectancies. He called them the attitude of daily life. He referred to their scenic attributions as the "world known in common and taken for granted." Schutz's fundamental work makes it possible to pursue further the tasks of clarifying their nature and operation, of relating them to the processes of concerted actions, and assigning them their place in an empirically imaginable society.[13]

In addition, Garfinkel reiterated the eleven features of events that he had formulated using Schutz's ideas.[14] Somewhat later, Garfinkel and Sacks commented on the "endless directives" Schutz's ideas had provided.[15] They also cited Husserl's contributions concerning "indexical expressions," a term common among ethnomethodologists.[16] Aaron V. Cicourel, another influential ethnomethodologist, insists that Schutz's studies extend knowledge of social interaction beyond the insights of James and Mead. Moreover, according to Cicourel, Schutz's ideas are "quite compatible with the linguistic theory known as generative-transformational grammar," which Cicourel has adapted to his studies of interaction.[17]

Schutz's ideas were probably necessary but not sufficient for the emergence of ethnomethodology.[18] Even a cursory reading of ethnomethodological studies points to other influences, particularly sociological and linguistic ones. In his early works, Garfinkel often cited Parsons. Garfinkel's initial interests were the problems of social order and social action that Parsons treated throughout his career. Yet Garfinkel, initially approaching those problems by comparing Parsons's and Schutz's reactions to Weber's theories,[19] not only failed to synthesize their ideas but also obscured their differences. Mullins states that ethnomethodology derived from Garfinkel's studying both Parsons and Schutz.[20] An understanding of ethnomethodology necessitates, then, appreciating the incompatibility of the Parsonian and Schutzian frameworks. Specifically, "in the context of Garfinkel's work, Parsons and Schutz make the strangest of bedfellows."[21] In other terms, a "Schutz-Parsons Divide"[22] may elucidate tensions inherent in ethnomethodology. For example, Parsons himself identified Garfinkel as a "follower of Schutz" and *at the same time* disavowed Schutz's thinking.[23] Parsons's ideas did influence Garfinkel, and their incompatibility with Schutz's implies serious anomalies in Garfinkel's ethnomethodology.

Another influence on ethnomethodology is symbolic interactionism, although their relationship is far from clear-cut. Dreitzel contends that Natanson's exposure of a phenomenological dimension in Mead's thought[24] casts symbolic interactionism in a new light; he regards ethnomethodology as a joint derivative of symbolic interactionism and phenomenological philosophy.[25] Symbolic interactionism and ethnomethodology both focus on the subjective bases of social life.[26] Moreover, their common dissatisfactions with positivistic science establish a symbiosis between them.[27] In the labeling perspective on deviance, the two approaches seem to converge.[28] Yet the differences between symbolic interactionism and ethnomethodology are considerable. Douglas, who also cites Natanson's pioneering analysis of Mead, argues that no synthesis between the two approaches is possible.[29] Ethnomethodologists and symbolic interactionists pose different sorts of questions; the former study the underlying structures of common-sense situations, while the latter focus on meaning as a (self-evident) feature of social life.[30] Significantly, for symbolic interactionists language proffers signs of the self that represents the center of social life; for ethnomethodologists, the self points to language as the principal reality in need of explanation.[31] Phillipson, who delineates correspondences between symbolic interactionism and phenomenology, argues that the latter will subsume the former because of its greater refinement.[32] Perhaps some coalescence will occur through ethnomethodological theorizing. Yet the likely incompatibility of the two approaches[33] holds another clue to anomalous features of ethnomethodology and the difficulties sociologists face in situating it within the sociological domain. Although symbolic interactionism presents itself as the most appropriate base for grasping ethnomethodology, ethnomethodologists themselves reject comparisons with symbolic interactionism that aim to specify a common ground between conventional sociology and ethnomethodology.[34]

Similar points apply to the nexus between labeling theory and ethnomethodology. Although some ethnomethodologists have contributed to labeling theory,[35] others have criticized that perspective.[36] Pollner, for example, acknowledges an affinity between those two perspectives but stresses that no intellectual rapprochement has brought them into line with one another. He has shown that among scholars two versions of labeling theory, mundane and constitutive, compete. Some of the major formulations of labeling theory, including Becker's, confound those two versions. Ethnomethodologists endorse only the constitutive version and hence take issue with most labeling theorists.[37] Similarly, the naturalistic sociology of Matza and Goffman shares some concerns with ethnomethodology, but its goals and methods differentiate it from ethnomethodology.[38] Ironically, Douglas characterizes naturalistic sociology by its belief in the possibility of a presuppositionless understanding of everyday life; he correctly associates that belief with Husserl and Schutz but thinks that Farber, a contemporary phenomenologist, has discredited it.[39] The complexity thickens! Denser confusion develops when one considers Attewell's argument that Goffman himself is a major forerunner of Garfinkel's ethnomethodology.[40]

Finally, linguistic and hermeneutical scholars have influenced ethnomethodologists. The language philosophies of John Austin and Ludwig Wittgenstein stand out here.[41] Chomsky's linguistics has also shaped ethnomethodology, but the "ethnography of communication" associated with Basil Bernstein and William Labov has probably exerted more influence.[42] The "hermeneutical dialecticalism" that underlies some of the works of Sartre, Merleau-Ponty, Heidegger, and the later Wittgenstein has also shaped ethnomethodology. Arguing that "scientism" and the "logico-empiricism" of Ernest Nagel, May Brodbeck, and Carl Hempel undergird ethnomethodology, Mehan and Wood depict it as a synthesis of that scientism and the hermeneutical-dialectical tradition.[43]

The preceding overview implies the likely difficulty of understanding ethnomethodology as well as some tensions ethnomethodology itself incorporates. A sound grasp of ethnomethodology derives from attention to two questions implicit in the preceding discussion. First, in what ways does ethnomethodology reject conventional sociological methods and results? Second, in what ways does ethnomethodology incorporate phenomenological methods and results? Careful responses to those questions provide grounds for characterizing ethnomethodology. Here and in the following chapter, I undertake those responses. In Chapter 8, I integrate responses to those two questions by considering the broader relationship between phenomenology and sociology. In any event, the two questions belong together if one wants to understand ethnomethodology and eventually assess its merits and shortcomings.

The aims of ethnomethodology

In his major work, Garfinkel[44] indicated that ethnomethodology concerns "practical activities, practical circumstances, and practical sociological reasoning as topics of empirical study. . . ."[45] Practical activity is Garfinkel's paramount concern, particularly practical reasoning, whether lay or professional.[46] Ethnomethodologists aim to illuminate the world as an object of common-sense perceptions and actions.[47] More precisely, ethnomethodology is the empirical investigation ("-ology") of the methods ("method-") people ("ethno-") use to make sense of and at the same time accomplish communication, decision making, reasonableness, and action in everyday life. Ethnomethodologists emphasize not only the methodical but also the artful character of the processes they study. Furthermore, their work stresses that "members can be faced with the task of managing the observability of their own observational work."[48] Filmer, who abstracts four definitions of ethnomethodology from Garfinkel's introduction to that perspective, emphasizes two points common to the definitions. For ethnomethodologists, (1) sociology is the study of everyday life, including both its presumably trivial and profound aspects; (2) sociology itself is an everyday activity.[49] Ethnomethodology presents itself as a "reflexive social practice which seeks to explicate the methods of all social practices, including its own."[50]

Concern with practical actions and accomplishments logically entails concern with common-sense knowledge, sometimes conceived as "describably elegant knowledge." Sudnow, in fact, believes that ethnomethodology stands or falls on its capacity to show how practical actors methodically apply their elegant knowledge of the "workings of social structure."[51] Garfinkel apparently agrees, since he regards ethnomethodology as "an organizational study of a member's knowledge of his ordinary affairs, of his own organized enterprises, where that knowledge is treated by us [ethnomethodologists] as part of the same setting that it also makes orderable."[52] Thus ethnomethodologists reject the ironic attitude toward common-sense knowledge; they take issue with the sociological inclination to debunk that knowledge. Instead, they examine common-sense beliefs as necessary ingredients of "organized social conduct."[53] To that extent, they overcome sociologists' habit of treating common-sense knowledge as a residual category. At the same time, they undercut the distinction between manifest and latent functions that denigrates common-sense perceptions of social reality.[54] Yet ethnomethodology

is not the sociology of knowledge or the sociology of science, or the sociology *of* any other matter. It is the attitude by which any and all practices for constituting knowledge in and of the world of everyday life are revealed as members' practices.[55]

Ethnomethodology broadly concerns, then, the *how* of social structure – how social groupings emerge, how a sense of social structure builds up, how members make available to one another the organized character of their activities.[56] Thus ethnomethodology emphasizes process. Two general processes consistently receive attention, decision making in common-sense situations and reality maintenance.[57] Interest in those processes leads ethnomethodologists to examine not only mundane knowledge but also language, interpretive activities, and the structure of common-sense experience, all focal concerns of phenomenology.

Ethnomethodologists regard social reality as "the set of activities and interpretive processes of experiencing and depicting the social as factual";

they concern themselves with how common-sense actors create the inter-subjective character of social reality.[58] Ethnomethodologists investigate the *formal* properties of those practical activities that accomplish social structure.[59] And their concern with formal properties gives way to concern with actors' resources, including invariant ones (i.e., universal cognitive capacities) and culturally acquired ones (e.g., a specific language). Ethnomethodologists are not, however, concerned with resources like money, social status, and formal authority. Their interest lies in the "tacit resources" or "background understandings" that underlie the regularities of social life.[60] Members' presuppositions and formulations as well as setting features themselves represent such tacit resources.[61] "Ethnomethodologists . . . take as their aim (in their various ways) the description and analysis of the members' resources for finding what they find and doing what others will find them to have done."[62] Apparently, the finding, the "doing," and the communication that make practical activities observable constitute *social action* from the ethnomethodological perspective. In fact, as a "naturalistic observational discipline," ethnomethodology aims to specify the nature of social action in an empirical, formal manner.[63]

In sum, ethnomethodology might be conceived as the empirical study of social action, undertakings in the common-sense world accomplished by applying invariant and relative resources so as to continuously structure that world. Although this formulation resonates with phenomenological concerns about the life-world, it points to divergences from conventional sociology. Detailing those divergences provides further grounds for understanding ethnomethodology.

The ethnomethodological critique of professional sociology

John O'Neill contrasts ethnomethodology with conventional sociology:

What Garfinkel calls "ethnomethodology" invokes a version of sociological knowledge that is neither narcissistic nor alien with regard to the intrinsic generosity of the platitudes of commonsense values and knowledge of the social world.[64]

Ethnomethodologists claim to be more in touch with mundane realities than (other) sociologists. They stress that sociologists need to examine experience itself if they are to understand it.[65] Ethnomethodologically, a "return to experience" necessitates modifying techniques of theory construction[66] and data collection. Ethnomethodologists assume that everyday "phenomena" warp when viewed through the "grid of scientific description."[67] Thus sociologists need alternative approaches to description that enable them to treat "lived social realities." Because everyday discourse consists of concepts and speech that depart from formal logic, sociological accounts that ignore lived experience can portray practical actors as irrational when their behavior is merely incompatible with the requirements of literal description.[68] To that extent, sociological theories concern the possibilities of the scientific idiom and scientific discoveries more than they concern the social realities they appear to treat.[69]

Methodologically, ethnomethodologists reject the use of indicators, because they represent a commitment to causal explanation rather than means for tapping "experiential substance." As Mehan and Wood go on to put it, "Smoke is not the phenomenon of interest; fire is."[70] Similarly, ethno-methodologists regard interviewing techniques with some suspicion, since interviews are novel experiences only remotely related to the experiences they are meant to elucidate.[71] By and large, ethnomethodologists subscribe to some combination of "hard" empirical data – e.g., films, tape recordings, written descriptions – and firsthand observation and participation. In general, they criticize the unrealistic presuppositions of sociological theory and methods. In addition, they insist that sociology itself is a practical activity in need of reflexive examination.

Conventional sociological presuppositions. Ethnomethodologists largely reject traditional sociological assumptions about social reality. They emphasize that sociologists assume that a stable system of shared meanings and norms governs any social system. Moreover, sociological frameworks also assume a meaningful world external to and independent of social interaction; that assumption is an implicit resource underlying sociological concepts like "norms," "rule," and "structure."[72] According to most sociologists, interaction depends on normative patterns that, from an ethno-methodological viewpoint, are actually continuous accomplishments of interacting, practical actors. As positivistic scientists, sociologists unthinkingly apply the "object-constancy assumption." Instead of rejecting their assumption of stable norms and meanings when their data challenge it, they turn to explanatory factors compatible with the object-constancy assumption. Sociologists might, for example, account for deviant behavior by emphasizing "faulty socialization" or normative ambiguity rather than by questioning their assumption of a stable normative system. Although the data used for inferring inadequate socialization could be used to infer the relative absence of shared norms, the object-constancy assumption demands that the latter interpretation, though empirically tenable, be dismissed in favor of some variant of the former interpretation. Thus the object-constancy assumption is self-validating; sociologists use it to "reflexively support the reality that has produced the unexpected failure in the first place."[73] This "self-preservative reflexive process" characterizes both common-sense and scientific reasoning.[74]

For the object-constancy assumption, ethnomethodologists substitute the assumption of process.

Where others might see "things," "givens," or "facts of life," the ethnomethodologist sees (or attempts to see) *process*: the process through which the perceivedly stable features of socially organized environments are continually created and sustained.[75]

Thus "social facts" are members' achievements.[76] Ethnomethodologists aim to make social facts intelligible[77] by showing how sociologists and others create and sustain the presumption of a real, shared social world. As a constructed reality, the social world makes "progressive social interactions" possible by making them understandable and they become understandable by "being presented as being ordered systematically and rationally in commonsense terms."[78]

Ethnomethodologists take issue with the "normative paradigm," which insists that interaction is rule-governed and that sociological explanation should be deductive.[79] Thus much ethnomethodological work concerns norms and rules. Supposing that sociologists slight all that rule application concretely involves, ethnomethodologists focus on members' decision making.[80] Rather than assuming that actors know and follow rules in situations,[81] ethnomethodologists examine the methods actors exploit to make rules available and observable, thereby making their activities rationally "account-able." They assume that members' practical activities in concrete settings continuously establish the intent and meaning of rules and procedures.[82] More basically, ethnomethodologists work toward models of how actors store and process information[83] and how common-sense and sociological actors use speech as a resource.[84] They assume that " 'practical' actors make and find a reasonable world: their doing so is topically available for the social scientist."[85]

Unsurprisingly, ethnomethodologists reject sociological models of the practical actor. They refuse to assume that individuals' activities derive primarily from their social positions and that their actions fail to alter the world.[86] Ethnomethodologists stress that although sociologists assume that people assign meanings, they first assume that internalized norms provide "automatic guides" for assigning those meanings.[87] The sociological model of "actor competence and performance" fails to say how actors perceive and interpret, how they recognize the familiar and the acceptable, and how rules govern interaction.[88] Such failures overlook the "experiential essence" of daily life.[89]

From the start, Garfinkel insisted that "the empirical world of the sociologist is inhabited *only* by types."[90] Relying on Schutz's thinking, he stressed that the sociologist's actor is a "dummy," an interpretive product whose rationality resides in the procedures for constructing and using the model. Schutz's thinking illustrates the basis of Garfinkel's criticisms.

Yet these models of actors are not human beings living within their biographical situation in the social world of everyday life. Strictly speaking, they do not have any biography or any history, and the situation into which they are placed is not a situation defined by them but defined by their creator, the social scientist. He has created these puppets or homunculi to manipulate them for his purpose. A merely specious consciousness is imputed to them by the scientist. . . . The puppet and his artificial consciousness is not subjected to the ontological conditions of human beings. The homunculus was not born, he does not grow up, and he will not die. He has no hopes and fears; he does not know anxiety as the chief motive of all his deeds. He is not free in the sense that his acting could transgress the limits his creator, the social scientist, has predetermined. He cannot, therefore, have other conflicts of interests and motives than those the social scientist has imputed to him. He cannot err, if to err is not his typical destiny. He cannot choose, except among the alternatives the social scientist has put before him as standing to his choice.[91]

In effect, action is possible only by sabotaging the scientific conception of rationality. Were practical rationality what sociologists assume it to be, inactivity would rule the world.[92]

Sociological models also portray the practical actor as an unfeeling dope. They imply that the passions are antisocial.[93] Moreover, they imply that practical actors are "judgmental dopes," whose compliance produces the stable features of any society.[94] Sociological models treat practical actors as "inept scientists," "*as though they had intended to produce a science of their lives in the course of living them.*"[95] Whatever sociologists accomplish rests largely on such models as both resources and standards in their work.[96]

The naiveté of sociological models implies a blurring of the sociological and the common-sensical. Garfinkel suggests that professional sociologists and common-sense actors construct their worlds in similar ways. He argues that

a concern with the nature, production, and recognition of reasonable, realistic, and analyzable actions is not the monopoly of philosophers and professional sociologists. Members of a society are concerned as a matter of course and necessarily with these matters both as features and for the socially managed production of their everyday affairs. The study of common sense activities consists of treating as problematic phenomena the actual methods whereby members of a society, doing *sociology, lay or professional*, make the social structures of everyday activities observable.[97]

Garfinkel thus bifurcates sociology into lay and professional varieties. At the same time, he relegates professional sociology to the practical sphere.

Professional sociology as a practical activity. Ethnomethodologists emphasize the common-sense grounds of sociology. As a folk discipline, professional sociology is an integral part of the reality it studies.[98] Sociological inquiry rests on tacit, common-sense understandings.[99] For example, sociologists depend on their common-sense knowledge to recognize what interactants are doing.[100] Similarly, they treat the relationship among shared knowledge, a collectivity, and collective activities in common-sense terms.[101] With their "subjects," moreover, sociologists share assumptions about their own and others' knowledge in order to maintain a "sense of social structure."[102] Even social rates derive from subjective, common-sense activities. For example, suicide statistics involve coroners' judgments as to actors' intentions.[103] Inescapably, sociologists use common-sense understandings in attempting to expose social meanings.[104] But sociologists are unmindful of their reliance on mundane knowledge. Ethnomethodologists claim that sociologists naively confound resource (common-sense understandings) and topic (common-sense reality) by assuming that everyday social reality somehow exists independently of lay and professional inquiries. Thus, the "attitude of daily life" supplies both the context and concepts of sociological investigations.[105] Sociological findings are, then, preeminently "reasonable." In presenting their findings, sociologists invoke "reasonableness" to acknowledge their "practical circumstances" or "common sense situations of choice." "Reasonable findings," the outcome of "documentary work," are the principal product of sociological studies.[106]

Ethnomethodologists imply that "it is only when one knows the meaning and purpose of the science and how he comes to do as he does that he speaks responsibly under the influence of the unity of Logos."[107] Stressing that sociological theories and methods are socially organized and acomplished, they reject the privileged access to social reality that sociologists claim.[108] Ethnomethodologists advise sociologists to attend to the presuppositions and methods they use to accomplish their own status as well as their products. In the spirit of Schutz, who indicated that social scientists use constructs of the constructs everyday actors employ,[109] ethnomethodologists emphasize that sociology rests on "second-order objectifications" of everyday social experience.[110] Ethnomethodological investigations of sociological practice support the conception of social science as a practical undertaking naively implicated with all other practical activities. If ethnomethodology is in part a sociology of sociology, as I think it is, the ethnomethodological approach is distinctive because of its focus on the naive practicality of sociology.

Ethnomethodologists regard their own endeavors as uncovering the invariant features of social reality that professional sociologists commonsensically presuppose. They believe that those features are not available research topics among professional sociologists.[111] Although they do not deny sociologists' concern with the "formal structure" of everyday activities, they stress that "formal structure" means something different from their perspective than it does among professional sociologists. Garfinkel and Sacks articulate that difference in describing "ethnomethodological indifference."

Ethnomethodological studies of formal structures are directed to the study of such phenomena, seeking to describe members' accounts of formal structures wherever and by whomever they are done, while abstaining from all judgments of their adequacy, value, importance, necessity, practicality, success, or consequentiality. We refer to this procedural policy as "ethnomethodological indifference."

Our work does not stand . . . in any modifying, elaborating, contributing, detailing, subdividing, explicating, foundation-building relationship to professional sociological reasoning, nor is our "indifference" to those orders of tasks. Rather, our "indifference" is to the whole of practical sociological reasoning, and *that* reasoning involves for us, in whatever forms, inseparably and unavoidably, the mastery of natural language. Professional sociological reasoning is in no way singled out as a phenomenon for our research attention. Persons doing ethnomethodological studies can "care" no more or less about professional sociological reasoning than they can "care" about the practices of legal reasoning, conversational reasoning, divinational reasoning, psychiatric reasoning, and the rest.

Given ethnomethodology's procedure of "indifference," by *formal structures* we understand everyday activities (a) in that they exhibit upon analysis the properties of uniformity, reproducibility, repetitiveness, standardization, typicality, and so on; (b) in that these properties are independent of particular production cohorts; (c) in that particular-cohort independence is a phenomenon for members' recognition; and (d) in that the phenomena (a), (b), and (c) are every particular cohort's practical, situated accomplishment.

The above development of formal structures contrasts with that which prevails in sociology and the social sciences in that the ethnomethodological procedure of "indifference" provides for the specifications (c) and (d) by studying everyday activities as practical ongoing achievements.[112]

Thus "formal structures" concerns what is invariant in everyday activities. The insistence that such structures be studied derives from believing that sociological theory must relate institutional life to its latent structures.[113] Ethnomethodologists presuppose that institutions cannot be studied prior to understanding action. Specifically, findings about large-scale matters depend on valid findings about social interaction itself.[114] Thus ethnomethodology reacts against the "fallacy of abstraction," the belief that one can know in more abstract form what is not known in concrete or particular form.[115] It rejects the naiveté of sociologists "who argue against the basic proposition that all of the science of sociology necessarily begins with the understanding of everyday life. . . ."[116] Ethnomethodologically, such sociologists – and they are assumed to be the overwhelming majority – fail to see their evidence back to its original sources.[117]

Several implications of the ethnomethodological critique of sociology clarify ethnomethodology and its relationship to sociology. First, the critique implies that efforts to comprehend ethnomethodology from the epistemological standpoint of conventional sociology must fail because ethnomethodology mostly rejects that standpoint. Ethnomethodology, in fact, challenges three features of traditional sociology – its natural-scientific rationality, its objectivity, and the validity of its generalizations. To that extent, ethnomethodology demands an examination of the philosophical bases of sociology.[118] Thus without stepping outside their taken-for-granted framework sociologists are unlikely to make much sense of ethnomethodology. Second, the critique implies that sociology and ethnomethodology are methodologically distinct. Mehan and Wood maintain so, and Garfinkel has intimated that he is unconcerned with whether or not conventional sociologists can assess the compatibility between ethnomethodological findings and their own findings.[119] Moreover, at least one ethnomethodologist argues that ethnomethodologists somehow supersede instances of practical reasoning.[120] Given the ethnomethodological critique of sociology and claims to epistemological superiority, the likelihood of beneficial exhanges between ethnomethodologists and (other) sociologists seems seriously limited.

Ethnomethodological presuppositions and major constructs[121]

Presuppositions. Several presuppositions undergird most ethnomethodological work. By "presuppositions" I mean guiding principles that cannot be thoroughly validated but are accepted because they appear to increase one's understanding. Among ethnomethodologists the key presuppositions rest on the notions of rationality and situational integrity. Blum's definition of "rational practice" virtually prefaces one of the presuppositions: "The Rational practice is the practice that elects to provide for itself as an occasion of the self-same practice; it is the practice that analyzes itself as an instance of itself."[122] Garfinkel's ethnomethodology attempts to describe how people "produce rationality" and thereby the settings they take for granted.[123] Associated with "practical rationality" and the "accomplishment" of shared settings is the presupposition of *reflexivity*. Ethnomethodologists also concern themselves with the integrity of social situations: "Concrete human events are always to some degree dependent on the situational context in which they occur and can adequately be explained only by taking that context into account."[124] Associated with that conception of situational integrity is the presupposition of *indexicality*. These presuppositions underlie the major ethnomethodological constructs.

The presupposition of reflexivity is probably the most elusive idea in the ethnomethodological framework. Reflexivity concerns those practices that simultaneously describe and constitute a social setting. In other terms, reflexivity is a property of activities that both presuppose and make observable the same thing.[125] For example, "all talk is essentially reflexive or self-descriptive in that the resources being mobilized in establishing the sense of the conversation are also being invoked or consulted as part of the as-sembling of sense."[126] Members' formulations, therefore, continuously create a conversation (the setting) *and* describe that setting by demonstrating its comprehensibility. At one and the same time and through the same procedures, then, members construct and describe a setting as an observable reality. Ethnomethodologists study the "reflexive relationship between general patterns and their exemplars" by demonstrating that patterns are a resource members gloss in creating specific situations; the specifics point to the pattern and yet gain their identity from it.[127]

"Reflexivity" is a radical version of "definition of the situation."[128] Garfinkel refuses to separate definition and situation. He denies that actors enter some *type* of situation and then define *that* particular instance of the type. From his perspective, the defining is the situation. The situation is, in other terms, simultaneously resource and topic for its participants; they presuppose it yet at the same time make it available to one another. Actors treat accounts, the verbal processes and products of interaction, as if they "folded back" on their settings, making features of settings reportable and observable.[129] They treat accounts as belonging somehow to the same order of properties they report.[130] Interactants use accounts reflexively, then, to organize ordinary situations.[131] They take interactional continuity for granted at the same time they are accomplishing it.[132]

One of Garfinkel's studies illustrates the meaning of reflexivity. The study focused on "practical sociological reasoning" or "doing accounts" in "common sense situations of choice." Its setting was the Los Angeles

Suicide Prevention Center (SPC) where the medical examiner-coroner sent requests for "psychological autopsies." In discussing his findings, Garfinkel indicated that

the work by SPC members of conducting their inquiries was part and parcel of the day's work. Recognized by staff members as constituent features of the day's work, their inquiries were thereby intimately connected to the terms of employment, to various internal and external chains of reportage, supervision, and review, and to similar organizationally supplied "priorities of relevances" for assessments of what "realistically," "practically," or "reasonably" needed to be done and could be done, how quickly, with what resources, seeing whom, talking about what, for how long, and so on. Such considerations furnished "We did what we could and for all reasonable interests here is what we came out with" its features of organizationally appropriate sense, fact, impersonality, anonymity of authorship, purpose, reproducibility – i.e., of a *properly* and *visibly* rational account of the inquiry [*sic*].[133]

In other terms, how the SPC staff makes and accounts for its decisions not only describes their practical circumstances (their situation) but also constitutes those circumstances; to describe the setting is to constitute it.[134] "Reflexivity" refers to that equivalence between describing and producing interaction, between understanding and articulating the understanding. "Account" is the vehicle of that equivalence; it refers to simultaneously making something understandable and to expressing that understanding. "To 'do' interaction is to 'tell' about an interaction" represents, in effect, a triple equivalence in Garfinkel's work; namely, to interact is to do is to tell.[135] In sum, "reflexivity" presupposes "that the activities whereby members produce and manage settings of organized everyday affairs are *identical with* members' procedures for making those settings 'accountable.' "[136]

Closely connected to the presupposition of reflexivity is that of indexicality. Reflexivity concerns the simultaneity of doing and interacting and telling; indexicality concerns the contextual meaning of that simultaneity. The principle of the integrity of the situation, which undergirds situational ethnomethodology, is that concrete human events depend on contexts for their lived meaning; it is a principle of the "contextual determination of meaning."[137] Actors continuously negotiate and achieve meaning in specific social settings. All accounts – all manners of describing, schematizing, analyzing, idealizing, arguing, believing, judging, etc. – are contingent on settings that situate or occasion them (and which they simultaneously constitute); their meaning is contextual.[138] Ethnomethodologically, interaction is an *interpretive* process involving *documentary work* and *indexicality*.[139] "Routine everyday exchanges are cross-modal, self-embedding, self-modifying, and emergent in the act of their production."[140]

"Indexicality" is a technical term adapted from linguistics. It means that although a word has a trans-situational meaning, it also has a distinctive meaning in any particular situation where it is used.

For example, "he was there" has different meanings for both "he" and "there" depending on the particular occasion or situation in which the sentence was said. More generally, any sentence is understood in terms not only of the literal meaning of its words, but in terms of the surrounding conversation and knowledge of the people talking.[141]

Thus telling not only describes and constitutes a setting but also "indexes" its meaningful features. Talk, in other terms, stands for or indexes more than it offers literally.[142] Where and who the interactants are, their purposes, and their knowledge are all features of a setting that make exchanges understandable. Out of context sentences are neither meaningless nor replete with meaning.

Ethnomethodologists elaborate the linguistic reference of "indexicality." The notion presupposes that all symbolic forms – utterances, gestures, rules, actions – bear a "fringe of incompleteness" that is uniquely filled in when they occur, even though the completions themselves carry a "horizon of incompleteness."[143] Deriving their sense from specific settings, accounts and the "factual realities" of social situations rest on the "ways-in-which-they-are-known."[144]

Ethnomethodology's concern, in general, is the elucidation of how accounts or descriptions of an event, a relationship, or a thing are produced in interaction in such a way that they achieve some situated methodological status, e.g., as factual or fanciful, objective or subjective, etc.[145]

Ethnomethodologically, all the symbols and meanings the notion of social order presupposes among traditional sociologists have no existence apart from members' practices of accounting and describing.[146] Moreover, practical actors use "rule-of-thumb" procedures to make intention and other internal states observable. Through such procedures they effectively agree to act as if they had objective knowledge of such states and hence of meaning.[147]

Together, the presuppositions of reflexivity and indexicality imply an emphasis on language. For ethnomethodologists,

language is the principal mechanism by which members make their everyday activities "visibly-rational-and-reportable-for-all-practical-purposes", i.e., "accountable", as organizations of commonplace everyday activities. It is through the common terms of language that unique or personal experiences are given what ostensibly is taken to be objective expressions in members' accounts of them. These accounts, however, are rational versions of members' experiences partly because of the requirements of linguistic sense, so that shared language is the source of the reflexivity between members' accounts of their experiences and the experiences themselves. And finally, it is in the shared language in which accounts are framed that the context, in terms of which the experiences are to be understood and analyzed, is implied or explicitly stated. Language is used by Garfinkel, it should be stated here, in a much wider sense than the purely verbal, as comprised of common vocabulary, grammar and syntax, not only of words but of symbols, gestures, expressions, deportments and so on of all kinds. . . . [148]

Both presuppositions also imply a serious limitation of conventional sociology. All use of "natural language," whether lay or professional, involves indexicality; "indexicals" are unavoidable.[149] Thus nonindexical or "objective" expressions are matter of *reasonableness* that occur "within a swarm of never-specified caveats, et cetera clauses, and 'ceteris paribus' assumptions."[150] Ethnomethodologists regard the empirical clarification of objective and indexical expressions as programmatically relevant.[151] That general concern unites situational and linguistic ethnomethodologists, as does concern with determining the invariant features of interaction.

Finally, the two presuppositions imply a perspective on common-sense knowledge. Mundane knowledge is not only taken for granted but also contextual. Blum indicates that the social organization of knowledge concerns actors methodically assembling and organizing knowledge with some conception of an "adequate corpus of knowledge" regarding their conduct.[152] Both adequacy and conduct are, however, relative to situations. And expression, which both presupposes and creates knowledge, is indexical. In these respects, the ethnomethodological framework leaves open the issue of how knowledge comes to have coherence and continuity. Moreover, although ethnomethodologists on occasion mention relevances or "purposes at hand,"[153] by and large they fail to comment on the motives that account for the uniqueness of any actor's knowledge and his or her predispositions to elaborate that knowledge.

Major constructs. The constructs common among ethnomethodologists derive from the notions of reflexivity and indexicality. Only one other term is as fundamental to understanding ethnomethodological terminology. Garfinkel implies the central place of "rationality" in specifying the boundaries of ethnomethodology.

Members' accounts are reflexively and essentially tied for their rational features to the socially organized occasions for their use for they are *features* of the socially organized occasions of their use.

   That tie establishes the central topic of our studies: the rational accountability of practical actions as an ongoing, practical accomplishment.[154]

What distinguishes Garfinkel's conception of rationality is his insistence on its contingency; it depends on the taken-for-granted, reflexively generated "reasonableness" of everyday social settings. Specifically,

> sociological inquiry accepts almost as a truism that the ability of a person to act "rationally" – that is, the ability of a person in *conducting his everyday affairs* to calculate; to act deliberately; to project alternative plans of action; to select before the actual fall of events the conditions under which he will follow one plan or another; to give priority in the selection of means to their technical efficacy; to be much concerned with predictability and desirous of "surprise in small amounts"; to prefer the analysis of alternatives and consequences prior to action in preference to improvisation; to be much concerned with questions of what is to be done and how it is to be done; to be aware of, to wish to, and to exercise choice; to be insistent upon "fine" as contrasted with "gross" structure in characterizations in the knowledge of situations that one considers valuable and realistic knowledge; and the rest – that this ability depends upon the person being able to take for granted, to take under trust, a vast array of features of the social order. In the conduct of his everyday affairs in order for the person to treat rationally the one-tenth of this situation that, like an iceberg appears above the water, he must be able to treat the nine-tenths that lies below as an unquestioned and, perhaps even more interestingly, as an unquestionable background of matters that are demonstrably relevant to his calculation, but which appear without even being noticed.[155]

In other terms, "the kind of rationality necessary to sustain social interaction . . . is not the same kind of rationality . . . necessary for the solution of scientific problems."[156] These general remarks provide the context for the (indexical) meaning of most ethnomethodological constructs.

A recurrent term among ethnomethodologists is "member." The term refers not to persons but to perspectives; it presupposes reflexivity, indexicality, and practical rationality.

> The notion of *member* is the heart of the matter. We do not use the term to refer to a person. It refers instead to mastery of natural language, which we understand in the following way. We offer the observation that persons, because of the fact that they are heard to be speaking a natural language, *somehow* are heard to be engaged in the objective production and objective display of commonsense knowledge of everyday activities as observable and reportable phenomena. . . . What is it about natural language that makes these phenomena observable-reportable, that is *accountable* phenomena? For speakers and auditors the practices of natural language somehow exhibit these phenomena in the particulars of speaking, and *that* these phenomena are exhibited is thereby itself made exhibitable in further description, remark, questions, and in other ways for the telling. . . .
> We take the critical phenomenon to consist in this: With ubiquitous prevalence and insistence members do formulations as remedies for problematic features . . . of

indexical expressions, and, in actual occasions, provide objective expressions as substitutes for indexicals.[157]

"Member" refers to a "course of activity" whose direction and motives become recognizable through procedures that show "what is going on."[158] The concept concerns ways of looking, thinking, demonstrating, and recognizing, not affiliations or loyalties.[159]

In spite of ethnomethodologists' tendency to eschew conventional sociological terminology, it nonetheless enters their framework, albeit through the back door. "Member" is "social role" conceived in terms of its elementary features, preliminary to formalized considerations. Cicourel's treatment of status and role supports this contention.[160] Space does not permit me to demonstrate that "member" is ethnomethodologists' means of referring – with some innovative distinctiveness, I think – to what sociologists traditionally call "role." My main point is that, as a complement of "role," "member" may involve principles capable of linking ethnomethodology and traditional sociology and simultaneously refining role theory.

Zimmerman and Pollner introduced "occasioned corpus" to refer to those "features of socially organized activities which are particular, contingent accomplishments of the production and recognition work of the parties to the activity." The occasioned corpus is the "temporally situated achievement" of actors in a specific setting. According to Zimmerman and Pollner, it contrasts with any member's corpus of knowledge prior to activity in that setting.[161] Give the presupposition of reflexivity, the occasioned corpus represents members' methods for exhibiting the reality, orderliness, and relevance of a setting that connects with "society" through each member's corpus of knowledge. The occasioned corpus displays society "in back of" situated appearances.[162] Zimmerman and Pollner's purpose in introducing the concept was to "reduce" the features of everyday social settings to a set of practices and their properties in order to clarify the relationship between topic and resource.[163] Thereby researchers' reliance on common-sense understandings as an unanalyzed resource might be circumscribed. Specifically, by equating setting features and members' methods, the analyst short-circuits the common-sense tendency to regard those features as independent of participants' activities. To that extent the notion reveals the "strangeness of an obstinately familiar world";[164] it radically modifies the sociological view of the social world, including social-scientific investigation itself.[165] Although I think Attewell's description of occasioned corpus distorts its meaning, he does illuminate its theoretical purposes by indicating that the notion provides for getting at the specificity of any situation.[166] It does so by implying how reflexivity occasions the meaning of *this* setting as opposed to that of any other setting.

Ethnomethodologists also use "constitutive" with some frequency. Garfinkel uses "constitutive expectancies" to refer to those rules operative in all social situations and games.[167] They include (1) the framing of a set of alternatives the actor expects to choose from regardless of desires, circumstances, plans, interests, or the consequences of his or her choice for self or others; (2) the expectation that the same set of required alternatives is binding on others in the situation; and (3) the expectation that others expect that he or she will be bound by the same set of required alternatives as they are. These constitutive expectancies are a condition of stable concerted actions.[168] In part, they constitute the possibility of mutually coordinated action.

Somewhat less technically, Pollner uses "constitutive" in describing a model of deviance that makes the labeling process "constitutive . . . of the very possibility of any determination of deviance or rule violation. . . ."[169] That model considers the labeling process "constitutive of deviance." Given Pollner's references to Gurwitsch, Merleau-Ponty, and Schutz, one infers that he means "constitutive" phenomenologically. Such is also the case with Garfinkel's "constitutive expectancies." Yet such inferences remain hazardous at this point.

What distinguishes the ethnomethodological vocabulary is its emphasis on process. "Negotiated creativeness," for example, concerns finding and justifying the meaning of events by applying normative or syntactic rules.[170] "Contexted phenomena" refers to specific practices with the following features:

(1) They make up what a member is doing when he does and recognizes (the fact of relevant time, place or personnel); (2) they are done with or without formulating *which* now, or where, or with whom, or since when, or how much longer, and the like; (3) they make up members' work for which (practices of objective, clear, consistent, cogent – rational – language) is a proper gloss; and (4) they meet the first three criteria by satisfying the following constraints (to which we refer with the adjective *essential*).[171]

Garfinkel and Sacks go on to list the constraints of "speaking practices" that account for their invariant features. Process, whether conceptualized as activities, practices, accomplishing, or achieving, rests on invariants that account for its observable, though general, features. Ethnomethodologically, social reality is itself a continuous process structured within invariant limits. Several additional concepts illustrate this point.

"Shared agreement" is a common enough phrase in sociological discourse. Garfinkel defines it as

the various methods for accomplishing the member's recognition that something was said-according-to-a-rule and not the demonstrable matching of substantive matters. The appropriate image of a common understanding is therefore an operation rather than a common intersection of overlapping sets.[172]

Thus a "common understanding" necessarily has an *operational structure* that must be understood so that analysts avoid slipping their common-sense knowledge into their work in the same way lay members use that knowledge.[173] Closely related to shared agreement is "formulating," "conversationalists' practices of saying-in-so-many-words-what-we-are-doing."[174] Both shared agreement and formulating presuppose socialization, the acquisition of interactional competencies.[175]

Thus ethnomethodological conceptualizations do stress process. Moreover, they are nested with one another in fairly straightforward ways. The most logically fundamental conceptualizations presuppose invariants and the less basic terms presuppose the conceptualizations of the more basic ones. That is more or less expected. However, we also more or less expect that such interconnections be delineated by those masterminding the development of a distinctive framework. To my knowledge, no ethnomethodologist has pursued that task; novices must make those connections for themselves.

Methodology and methods

Methodology. Ethnomethodological concepts concerning everyday social reality and the ethnomethodological critique of traditional sociology imply a distinctive logic of inquiry. In some respects, the methods based on that logic differ from ordinary sociological methods. Thus understanding ethnomethodology necessitates grasping its methodology and methods.

Several general points underlie ethnomethodological methodology. First, ethnomethodologists claim a research style in line with their subject matter.[176] Their basic commitment is to investigate the "phenomena of everyday life" on their own terms, that is, to respect the integrity of phenomena.[177] Ethnomethodologists aim, then, to make the "phenomenon" and the method of investigating it "mutually constitutive."[178] Second, ethnomethodological conceptualizing, investigating, and describing focus on what is most fundamentally taken for granted in daily life.[179] Third, ethnomethodology inquires into the "we agree" implied in all social action and social settings. "We agree" represents an achievement of provisional unity that ethnomethodologists adopt as a topic.[180] It leads a group of people to limit their questioning to what can be "topicalized," thereby making answers appear as responses to questions that are somehow external to them.[181] Ethnomethodologists try to disclose the "we agree" that underlies the processes of daily life. That goal necessitates treating those processes as "anthropologically strange" and considering common-sense reasoning as a resource in one's own accounts of the everyday world.[182] Finally, as Garfinkel has noted, Husserl's studies and the phenomenological attitude itself offer grounds for a dogma-free methodology.[183] Ethnomethodology seeks such a methodology. As a set of "destratifying practices,"[184] it aims at empirically demonstrating the formal properties of practical activities.[185] Although that aim necessitates innovative methods,[186] thus far ethnomethodologists have offered only "limited program statements" that specify goals largely through example.[187]

The ethnomethodological logic of inquiry rests on Garfinkel's contention that traditional social scientists inescapably use terms like "objective world" and "real object," even though they draw on lay as well as professional frameworks.[188] Moreover, their decisions become reasonable to the extent that they overcome the problem of the relativity of perspectives.[189]

Sociologists appear to overcome that relativity by their assumptions about what actors understand. In effect, individuals become actors for sociologists when their conduct can be treated as displays of those assumptions.[190] "To formulate an actor is to construct an other who is ruled by his commonness; the reflexive actor is rendered the common-sense member both impersonating and impersonated by the ideal rational scientist."[191] In these ways traditional sociology uses unexamined, unproblematic features of practical activities as means of accomplishing its own "demonstrably rational" character.[192] In short, professional sociological inquiry shares with lay sociological investigations the "documentary method of interpretation,"

treating an actual appearance as "the document of," as "pointing to," as "standing on behalf of" a presupposed underlying pattern. Not only is the underlying pattern derived from its individual documentary evidences, but the individual documentary evidences, in their turn, are interpreted on the basis of "what is known" about the underlying pattern. Each is used to elaborate the other.[193]

Given the critical context of these observations, ethnomethodological methodology appears to demand that researchers be aware of the part common-sense understandings play in all inquiry. Specifically, ethnomethodological emphasis on the documentary method of interpretation focuses attention on the interpretive procedures inherent in all inquiry, lay and professional. "Documentary methods of interpretation" points, then, to the irretrievable quality of social life. The concept emphasizes that individuals make social reality available to one another through "pattern- and document-building work."[194]

The presuppositions of reflexivity and indexicality also shape the methodology implied in ethnomethodological studies. As Filmer has put it:

It is their reflexive, incarnate character, above all, that makes the formal properties of everyday social interactions such recondite phenomena from the point of view of traditional sociological analysis. And that they are to an important degree inseparable from their specific context, makes them effectively inaccessible to positivistic professional sociologists.[195]

Features of reality that emerge "upon analysis" represent particular instances of reflexivity.[196] Ethnomethodology takes reflexivity as a topic, assuming an ineluctable relation between the knowing subject and the subject known.[197] Ethnomethodologists reflectively incorporate the common-sense understandings that inform social-scientific inquiry. For example, they recognize that valid, reliable communication with members "presupposes an understanding of their language, their uses of that language, their own understandings of what the people doing the observations are up to, and so on almost endlessly."[198] The commitment to be aware of that reflexivity is, it seems, a methodological requirement of ethnomethodology.

It appears, too, that "naturally occurring situations" are the only strictly valid research sites from the ethnomethodological perspective.[199] Since "rigorous demonstration" is unattainable anyway, evidence derived from "artificially created" settings is inferior to that derived from naturally occurring situations.[200] Yet "naturally occurring situation" remains unclarified. For example, Garfinkel seems inclined to say that when an interviewer knocks on someone's door, that situation could be treated as naturally occurring.[201] He recognizes, though, that some of his colleagues disagree.

Speech occupies a prominent position in the ethnomethodological logic of inquiry. Concern with practical reasoning and practical accomplishments leads ethnomethodologists, both situational and linguistic, to emphasize the verbal communication whereby members achieve accountability in social settings. Some ethnomethodologists argue that the basic features of conversation hold the clue to social organization.[202] More commonly, they agree that the generative features of speech merit analyses sociologists generally sidestep.[203] In addition, inasmuch as "human experiences continually outstrip our ability to express them in speech acts," some ethnomethodologists stress the need to examine the organization of memory and the interpretive procedures strained by the indexicality of language.[204]

Unsurprisingly, given these methodological specifications, ethnomethodologists often assume that "the operations that one would have to perform in order to produce and sustain anomic features of perceived environments and disorganized interaction should tell us something about how social structures are ordinarily and routinely being maintained."[205] In the absence of incongruities, people do not expose the unarticulated knowledge and presuppositions underlying their routine accomplishments. Originally, Garfinkel proposed the use of epochē to determine the conditions where people experience incongruities,[206] but apparently he has since dismissed it. Yet Douglas advocates "reductions" for arriving at "the fundamental truths" of daily life;[207] Wieder claims that a form of phenomenological reduction generated some of his findings.[208] Commitment to phenomenological methods is widely lacking among ethnomethodologists, however. Rather, their methodology leads to methods for creating and observing incongruity, among other things.

Implicit in ethnomethodologists' methodology is the assumption that analyses of social reality are properly descriptive rather than explanatory. Ethnomethodologically, trying to explain social reality involves using as resources the very realities for which analysts attempt to account. Thus social-scientific explanation merely appears to elucidate what common sense cannot disclose. Given their presuppositions about everyday life and their critiques of traditional sociology,

it should be apparent that an important objective of ethnomethodology lies in the area of sociological description. At first glance it would seem that this should not be classified as an objective but rather as a strategy or even a procedure. However, owing to its phenomenological roots, ethnomethodological description clearly becomes more of a process to be achieved than an instrument of research. Description, in other words, becomes a problem intricately involved with the nature of social reality.[209]

Their descriptive orientation suggests why ethnomethodologists favor direct observation. Since descriptions presuppose meanings tied to members' practical circumstances,[210] adequate description demands the researcher's firsthand involvement in those circumstances.

Finally, the issue of evidence merits attention. To my knowledge, the sole published source of ethnomethodologists' comments on evidence is the edited transcript of a symposium on ethnomethodology that attracted several leading ethnomethodologists and a small number of non-ethnomethodologists, including both sympathizers and critics.[211] Since their explicit remarks on evidence seem to have occurred only in exchanges with others who forced that issue, one might infer that ethnomethodologists largely avoid or dismiss the question of evidence. Apparently, Garfinkel has adopted a pragmatic, I-take-what-I-can-get posture toward evidence. And when he pleads ignorance as to whether sociologists and witchdoctors use different "logics of justification," he simply dodges the issue.[212] Yet Sudnow and Sacks espouse a general criterion of evidence that may underlie much ethnomethodological work. Sudnow claims that the test of ethnomethodological analyses is whether they "reproduce reality."[213] Similarly, Sacks claims that his work generates rules that virtually give him back his data.[214] His position implies that evidence derives from descriptions so faithful to lived reality that they effectively regenerate their data "in the telling." Similarly, Scott argues that field workers have enough data when they can imagine writing instructions that would enable a stranger to reproduce the realities described.[215] A second criterion of evidence, apparently less strict, concerns temporal ordering. Sudnow claims that researchers can assess the plausibility of their descriptions by considering the temporal structure of the larger "course of action" that subsumes the described activity or event.[216] And Garfinkel emphasizes "action through time" or the "temporal ordering" of everyday reality,[217] implying support for Sudnow's criterion of evidence. Clearly, though, the ethnomethodological meaning of evidence remains unclarified. Perhaps the presuppositions of reflexivity and indexicality undermine the need to confront that issue. In short, the matter of evidence seems to concern non-ethnomethodologists considerably more than ethnomethodologists.

Methods. Hill and Crittenden indicate that ethnomethodologists and (other) sociologists disagree about meaning, consistency, inference, and the rules of evidence.[218] The two groups also lack a common ground regarding methods. In fact, what makes understanding ethnomethodological methods difficult is the admitted inability – or at least reluctance – of ethnomethodologists to adequately describe their methods.[219] Sudnow, for example, claims he cannot provide rules about what to focus on and what is of likely significance in ethnomethodological inquiries. He does stress, though, that what he recognizes as a specific phenomenon and what he chooses to say about it initially derive from sharing the culture of the members whose activities he studies.[220] Garfinkel, too, has indicated that because researchers are "members," they can locate and categorize objects of study. That capacity, however, represents both a problem and a phenomenon for investigation.[221] Garfinkel has also noted that ethnomethodological methods are only partially "tellable"; would-be ethnomethodologists must learn a great deal on their own.[222] In short, ethnomethodologists offer no handbook and few recipes for doing ethnomethodology. Unraveling ethnomethodological methods necessitates understanding that "the interests of ethnomethodological research are directed to provide, through detailed analyses, that accountable phenomena are through and through practical accomplishments."[223]

Ethnomethodological studies analyze everyday activities as members' methods for making those same activities visible-rational-and-reportable-for-all-practical-purposes, i.e., "accountable," as organizations of commonplace everyday activities. The reflexivity of that phenomenon is a singular feature of practical actions, or practical circumstances, of common sense knowledge of social structures, and of practical sociological reasoning. By permitting us to locate and examine their occurrence the reflexivity of that phenomenon establishes their study.[224]

Moreover, the novice should understand that ethnomethodological studies are often exploratory.[225]

One way to understand ethnomethodological methods is to juxtapose them with other methods. Ethnomethodological methodology suggests, for example, an affinity with analytic induction; Sudnow concedes that that procedure largely corresponds with his own approach.[226] Although ethnomethodology also suggests a taste for participant-observation, participant-observation and the methods of situational ethnomethodologists differ. In that connection Psathas says that

"performing as a member" and being able to describe and analyze the methods used by members are not the same thing. "Knowing how" to do something and "knowing" the hows (methods) by which activities are produced are not the same. . . . The claim by participant-observer sociologists that they "understand" how activities are accomplished is usually no different from the claim of ordinary members, namely, common sense understandings and "explanations" are drawn upon as resources for the description and explication of activities. When the social scientist is concerned with analyzing these common sense understandings (i.e., making them topics of study), they are not to be drawn upon as "explanations." The search for the formal or invariant properties of activities, the methods by which members produce an activity, requires an explication that is not identical to and bound by the same taken-for-granted understandings which members use since it is these taken-for-granted understandings which are topics of study.[227]

Thus the field researcher faces enormous interpretive difficulties. Zimmerman and Wieder advise regarding members' statements as "instructions" conveyed to the observer as an outsider or initiate. Members express themselves in natural language, however, "whose context is the same set of affairs the instructions seek to explain."[228] Interpretive problems are, therefore, inescapable.

Psathas considers ethnomethodological methods phenomenological insofar as they set aside all reports, interpretations, analyses, and theories of social reality.[229] He describes an "ethnomethodological reduction" whereby ethnomethodologists bracket belief in the social world except as constituted through the activities and accounts of members.[230] Although "ethnomethodological indifference" itself appears to involve no epochē, some ethnomethodologists advocate or claim the use of epochē.[231] In addition, one ethnomethodologist has used a method apparently similar to the method of free variation.[232]

Rejecting formal logic as a model of social action, ethnomethodologists commonly use ethnographic methods, perhaps most often to study "rule use." Since actors and rules and situations "inform" one another, ethnomethodologists assume that rule use is neither consistent nor automatic across situations.[233] Some ethnomethodologists have adopted ethnographic approaches to rules in highly formalized situations. They assume that finding "essential incompleteness" in such rules shows the likely incompleteness of all rules, including conversational ones.[234] Unsurprisingly, studies in such situations disclose "awesome indexicality" and thus undercut the need to consider social order.[235] Yet those studies do reveal the intricacies of members' work in completing the rules that formally define the boundaries of their activities. Ethnomethodologists have done such studies in legal, medical, educational, social-scientific, and other bureaucratic settings.[236]

Conversational analysis is another common method, even though many people fail to appreciate that such analysis represents an integral part of ethnomethodology.[237] Linguistic and situational ethnomethodologists do use different methods; conversational analysis is the major method of the former grouping. Its purposes are to enhance objectivity by investigating what is externally available and to disclose the meanings accomplished through language use.[238] Conversational analysts collect "talking-out-loud protocols" of telephone and other naturally occurring conversations; they also collect them after making everyday routines seem strange to subjects. Sometimes, too, linguistic ethnomethodologists collect protocols after asking subjects to describe activity or event and then providing an audio or visual tape of the same while asking for another account.[239]

Perhaps the best-known method of ethnomethodologists is the "demonstration experiment" or "incongruity procedures" or "breaching experiment." This method aims to uncover the processes of reality maintenance, reflexive accomplishments of situational order, the natural attitude, or the fragility of social reality. In developing ethnomethodology, Garfinkel used breaching or incongruity procedures in four instances that illustrate this method. First, in "Breaching the Congruence of Relevances" students collected data by insisting that others clarify their commonplace remarks.[240] Students refused to accept the taken-for-granted meanings of such phrases as "flat tire," "how are you?" "I'm tired," and the like; they insisted that subjects specify their meanings. In response, subjects made immediate, often frustrated, attempts to restore a "right state of (conversational) affairs." Second, in "Breaching the Interchangeability of Standpoints," students treated other customers in stores as clerks.[241] Third, students acted as boarders in their homes in "Breaching the Expectation That a Knowledge of a Relationship of Interaction Is a Commonly Entertained Scheme of Communication."[242] Finally, premedical students listened to what the researchers presented as a taped interview of a "premedical student" by a "medical school representative." The "student" was boorish and clearly lacked the qualities commonly thought necessary for medical school. Afterwards, the students received "official information" about the student that contradicted their impressions; they then listened to the tape again in order to reassess the applicant. This study, "Breaching What Anyone Like Us Necessarily Knows," showed that "students managed incongruities of performance data with vigorous attempts to make it factually compatible with their original and very derogatory assessments."[243]

Ethnomethodologists use a variety of methods, then, to validate their presuppositions and methodology. They have applied their methods to diverse social activities and situations. They have studied how the features of group therapy allow therapists to produce a special class of remarks; how people talk about and make sense of "behavioral episodes"; "glance-based interpretation"; and members' formulations of physical and social locations.[244] In addition, they have examined common-sense awareness of the temporal structure of activities, the methodic practices involved in walking, and the accomplishment of such things as ideology, newsworthiness, and gender.[245] Further, ethnomethodologists have studied how members sustain "proper" topics in conversation and how they reestablish a topic after interruptions; how members apply the category "nonsense"; how members of different cultures communicate with one another; how members negotiate meaning in traffic court; how news headlines and stories create "the news"; and how citizens describe automobiles when they call the police.[246] Finally, ethnomethodologists have investigated marijuana smoking, formal organizations, and women's subordinate roles in conversation as well as members' conceptions of "lifetime" and the practical differences between "teenager" and "hotrodder."[247] To date, two types of methods predominate among ethnomethodologists. On the one hand, they examine, more or less technically, how members use language to typify actions and people and to accomplish decision making and practical circumstances. On the other hand, they breach background expectancies to reveal the assumptions about normality and rationality that sustain the "objective" nature of social settings for members.[248]

Findings

Meaning. Garfinkel has indicated that ethnomethodologists are unlikely to talk about meaning, preferring to focus on setting features, accounting, and other members' practices.[249] Yet his own as well as others' work betrays that position. Douglas argues that *the* focal problem in sociology is the objective determination and analysis of social meanings.[250] Ethnomethodologists approach that problem by assuming that meaning is "self-organizing" and derives from a "reflexive interaction" among memory, practical reasoning, and talk.[251] Typically, ethnomethodologists stress that meaning is situated. Cicourel, for example, argues that

the interactional context, as reflexively experienced over an exchange, or as imagined or invented when the scene is displaced or is known through a text, remains the heart of a general theory of meaning.[252]

Yet situation or context provides only a partial basis for meaning. What worked previously is largely reconstituted in each new situation. Moreover, the discovery of regularities "reflects the normative organization of everyday experience by an inescapable reliance on memory and practical reasoning."[253] Meaning rests, then, on trans-situational as well as situational grounds; cognitive capacities underlie its genesis and continuity. In that connection, Douglas has distinguished between the "situated meanings" that immediately affect action and the "abstract meanings" that individuals use primarily for rhetorical purposes.[254] Though helpful, Douglas's distinction leaves intact a pressing problem still facing ethnomethodologists, the task of accounting for the trans-situational ordering of members' lives.[255]

Meaning has its roots in the situations where social action occurs and in the cognitive continuity members experience apart from as well as within such situations. Meaning presupposes *basic rules* that provide for the identification of settings and appropriate invocations of *surface rules* or norms. In their models of the common-sense actor, then, ethnomethodologists presuppose interpretive and inferential capacities as well as memory.[256] New settings necessitate normative reconstructions of speech, social identity, and culture.[257] The taken-for-granted assumption that events will be meaningful implies members' inherent past- and future-orientations. Members are past-oriented in assuming that what has already occurred forecasts the future and future-oriented in assuming that what will occur will make sense.[258]

Thus the definition of every situation contains both reconstructive and prophetic elements.[259] Finally, practical reasoning and decision making are retrospective; outcomes precede conscious decisions. For example, jurors seem not to understand what makes their decisions "correct" until they decide what they did to make them so.[260] Thus cognitive capacities and functions are central to analyses of social meanings.

Ethnomethodologically, meaning also requires attention to rules. McHugh's treatment of "definition of the situation" and Cicourel's conceptualizations of "negotiated creativeness" and "interpretive procedures" suggest Winch's observation that "all behavior which is meaningful is *ipso facto* rule-governed."[261] Maryl indicates that despite their differences Garfinkel's "rational properties," McHugh's "definition of the situation," and Cicourel's "basic rules" (interpretive procedures) all concern the production and communication of meaning. In spite of his disclaimers, Garfinkel has expressed concern with the process "whereby the basic meaning of a situation is produced by a participant along with a process whereby this meaning is communicated to 'cultural colleagues.' "[262] All three ethnomethodologists, together with most of their colleagues, appear to agree with McHugh that defining situations requires more than describing (incomplete) rules.[263] Meaning itself might be regarded as the rule whereby individuals formulate the content of their routine descriptions.[264] That position, though, is not commonplace among ethnomethodologists. Bittner, for example, holds that individuals clarify the meaning of actions retrospectively by invoking rules.[265] Insofar as ethnomethodologists assume a linkage between rules and meaning, they need to answer this question: "What does an action look like with regard to the *concrete observables* that would *describe* for us the activity proposed as rule-governed?"[266] To date, ethnomethodological approaches have concerned the construction, interpretation, and implementation of rules[267] more than the establishment of meaning as such. Nonetheless if "the social" involves sense-making,[268] ethnomethodological attention to common-sense accounts and interpretive activities expresses a consistent concern with meaning. And, of necessity, that concern meshes with an emphasis on process:

If social facts are to be treated as things, then socially organized meanings are to be treated as "ings." To attend to the -ing of things involves a radical modification of the attitude of everyday life, for it requires attending to the processes of constitution in lieu of the product thus constituted. In attending to the -ing of things one focuses on the course of activity – the form of life – which presupposes, preserves, and thereby produces the particular things.[269]

Much of the ethnomethodological concern with meaning reverberates with such phenomenological overtones.

Social reality. Concerned with the practices whereby members make settings available to one another as the kinds of settings they take them to be, ethnomethodologists view everyday exchanges as "invariably contingent productions embedded in emergent, context-sensitive informational environments."[270] Insofar as they also concern themselves with background expectancies, the negotiation of meaning, and the tacit knowledge that underlies social action,[271] they regard rationality as a reflexive, contingent accomplishment.[272] In short, ethnomethodologists emphasize five features of social reality, including reflexive activity, knowledge, interaction, fragility, and permeability.[273]

Mehan and Wood illustrate the meaning of reflexivity with a simple example. To greet with "hello" creates and sustains with some immediacy a world where people acknowledge that they sometimes see one another, that they signal to one another, that they expect to be signaled back to, and that they expect only certain others to signal back. When the response to that greeting is "hello," that utterance masks reflexivity for the participants. When the response is a scowl or silence, however, one experiences failure to create a "scene of greetings." Rather than question the "reality" of greetings and what they presuppose, the typical actor affirms that reality by accounting for the *apparent* inapplicability of the background and other expectancies that the failure might have called into question.[274] Ethnomethodologically, all social reality involves such reflexivity.

From the ethnomethodological perspective, social reality is also in some sense knowledge. Sacks says that culture does more than make us roughly similar; it "fills our brains" so that they are alike in fine detail.[275] Thus much "effective rationality" derives from culturally shaped subjective processes rather than adherence to rules per se.[276] As Garfinkel noted in studying jurors, "a person is 95 per cent juror before he comes near the court."[277] The competent use of rules rests, then, on members' practical grasp of what particular actions an occasion demands in order to produce a "normal" situation; that grasp involves common-sense knowledge.[278] Although members fail to recognize their methods of accomplishment, they are nonetheless part of members' knowledge.[279] In everyday life, the methods people use are resources, not topics: "To direct one's attention to the resources being used is to change one's activity to that of inquiring into the methods rather than using the methods."[280] Thus, ethnomethodologically, "knowledge" refers to a structure of activity, most fundamentally the know-how underlying recognizable sentences.[281] In short, social reality is knowledge that blurs, for all *practical* purposes, the distinction between the contents and processes of knowing.

Social reality is also interactional from an ethnomethodological viewpoint; namely, it is a shared coherence derived from interaction. Although it does not imply chaos, the ethnomethodological view of interaction does emphasize contingency. No matter how specific and explicit the terms of a common understanding, interaction always has a "wait and see" quality; an "et cetera" clause makes it open-ended. Although rules can be inferred by observing interaction, inferences are interpretive and embedded in settings of common-sense decision making.[282] Thus ethnomethodologists concern themselves with the *judgmental work* whereby members show that their behavior *essentially* satisfies the provisions of given rules.[283] Zimmerman's study of receptionists in a public assistance agency illustrates the interactional character of social reality. He examined the judgmental work of receptionists who assigned applicants to caseworkers by determining among themselves the relevance and meaning of organizational policies and procedures. The reasonableness of their decisions rests on a taken-for-granted understanding of their practical circumstances.[284] Thus rules and interaction dovetail with the interpretive work whereby members define their circumstances and make decisions accordingly. Members, too, sometimes create rules from scratch. Some of Garfinkel's breaching experiments provoked reactions from subjects that implied their construction of principles that reinstated the research situation as organized and rationally accountable.[285]

To understand social reality requires, then, investigating interaction, which in turn necessitates attention to the social rules members invoke and interpret. Reflexive interpretive procedures provide continuous instructions to members in every setting.[286] Those procedures are invariant properties of interaction and practical reasoning. They establish bases for assigning sense to surface rules (norms), which are open until members interpret them in specific situations.[287]

The two final features of social reality – its fragility and permeability – derive directly from the preceding characteristics. Social reality is fragile inasmuch as it is ineluctably contingent, though members do not experience it as such. Social reality is neither pregiven nor guaranteed as coherent and stable; members reflexively, interactionally accomplish it. Thus it is permeable, that is, inherently amenable to sharing by members of the same setting. Moreover, because of its reflexive character and the cognitive capacities underlying interpretive procedures, social reality can also be shared as a trans-situational reality. Ethnomethodologists, however, do not emphasize that point.

Social order. According to Psathas, the distinctive focus of ethnomethodology is "the methods used by members to create and sustain their sense of social order."[288] Ethnomethodologists investigate the linguistic and cognitive practices members use to create a sense of social structure and thereby sustain social structure itself.[289] Garfinkel has linked "meaning" and "sense of social structure." Because of his concern with common-sense knowledge of social structures, he focuses on the everyday "work whereby decisions of meaning and fact are managed and how a body of factual knowledge of social structures is assembled in common sense situations of choice."[290] He assumes that "the persistence, continuity, reproducibility, standardization, and uniformity of social structures are emergent products. . . ."[291] Garfinkel's work implies distinctions among *sense* of social structure, *knowledge* of social structure, and social structure itself. His ethnomethodology emphasizes the continuous emergence of those intertwined phenomena and their nexus with meaning in mundane experiences.

Surprisingly, the distinction among the sense of social structure, knowledge thereof, and social structure remains unconfronted. Despite ethnomethodological attention to knowledge and the presuppositions of reflexivity and indexicality, it remains unclear how to distinguish those three phrases in describing everyday life. Turner thinks ethnomethodological research focuses on the methods members use to construct, maintain, and change a *sense* of order in social settings.[292] Wilson views all the papers in Douglas's anthology as responses to the question of how members produce and sustain the *sense* that they act in an orderly world.[293] Others refer primarily to *knowledge* of social order. McHugh discusses the documentary method as a formula for generating a knowledge of order; Garfinkel discusses social structure in terms of "knowledge of" and "perceivedness."[294] Schegloff and Sacks seem also to focus on knowledge of social order:

Our analysis has sought to explicate the ways in which the materials are produced by members in orderly ways that exhibit their orderliness and have their orderliness appreciated and used, and have that appreciation displayed and treated as the basis for subsequent action.[295]

Yet ethnomethodologists also use "social order" and "social structure" without connotations of "sense" or "knowledge."[296] Perhaps the conceptual ambiguities concerning social structure derive from the tendency of ethnomethodologists to underplay structure as constraint and to emphasize structure as process.[297]

Two scholars provide bases for clarifying ethnomethodologists' use of "social order." Psathas formulates the problem, in effect, by specifying its major dimensions.

Social order is, when viewed ethnomethodologically, an accomplished order whose stability is both an interpretation and an accomplishment. As an accomplishment, it is necessary to study the methods by which and through which it is accomplished; as an interpretation, it is necessary to study how the interpretation of social order is itself accomplished. The ethnomethodologist may choose to focus on either or both of those activities, which themselves accomplish social order or the activities which are involved in the recognition and achievement of a sense of social order. There is a necessary relation between activities and their recognition since the manner in which order is accomplished contains within it possibilities for the recognition and description of that production. Moreover, as we shall note . . . , members' recognition, description, or account of order is essential before the ethnomethodologist can say that order does "exist" for members.

. . . For the ethnomethodologist, society is the perceived order which members accomplish by themselves and with others either in direct or indirect social relationships. Society is not a "thing" or "object" of study apart from its members' activities. And since society or social order is an accomplishment whose "permanence" and "stability" is an interpretation, i.e., an interpretation by members at each and every occasion when its recognition is required by them, it becomes important to continually examine what the interpretation or recognition is at whatever time it is accomplished. The content of "society" or the knowledge of what it "is" cannot be specified in advance of members' "doing" it. That is, what members "know" cannot be known in advance of their demonstrations or performances of the "possession" of such knowledge. (Contrast this with Schutz, whose analyses would imply that once we understand the content of members' knowledge, we can expect that each new situation will be seen by them as typically the same.)

This does not mean that the ethnomethodologist believes that society or social order are ephemeral, or "mere figments" of the imagination, or constantly changing, but rather that whatever it is for members, its character . . . is an interpretation, regardless. Since it is an interpretation, the ethnomethodologist focuses on the manner by which the interpretation-of-the-stability-of-society is accomplished or, the interpretation-of-the-instability, or whatever.[298]

Cicourel, on the other hand, addresses the problem by offering clues to its resolution. In his view, the problem of meaning concerns how members acquire the sense of social structure that enables them to negotiate their everyday activities.[299] He emphasizes that basic rules or interpretive procedures underlie members' trans-situational sense of social structure, while surface rules or norms provide institutional or historical validity for social action.[300]

The distinction between basic rules and norms is tied to the difference between consensus or shared agreement and a sense of social structure. Basic or interpretive rules provide the actor with a developmentally changing sense of social structure that enables him to assign meaning or relevance to an environment of objects. Normative or surface rules enable the actor to link his view of the world to that of others in concerted social action, and to presume that consensus or shared agreement governs interaction. . . .

The basic rules provide a sense of social order that is fundamental for normative order (consensus or shared agreement) to exist or be negotiated and constructed. The two orders are always in interaction, and it would be absurd to speak of the one without the other. . . . The distinction is necessary and presupposed in a reference to how the actor recognizes social scenes as normatively relevant, and in the differential perception and interpretation of norms and action scenes vis-à-vis role behavior. But unlike the rather static notion of internalized attitudes as dispositions to act in a certain way, the idea of basic or interpretive rules must specify how the actor negotiates and constructs *possible* action and evaluates the results of *completed* action. Our model of the actor must (1) specify how general rules or norms are invoked to justify or evaluate a course of action, and (2) how innovative constructions in context-bound scenes alter general rules or norms, and thus provide the basis for change. . . .

A more refined conceptual frame for understanding norms will have to specify basic rules as a set of invariant properties governing fundamental conditions of all interaction so as to indicate how the actor and observer decide what serves as definitions of "correct" or "normal" conduct or thought. The basic rules would suggest the nature of minimal conditions that all interaction presumably would have to satisfy for actor and observer to decide that the interaction is "normal" or "proper" and can be continued. The acquisition and use of interpretive rules or procedures over time amounts to a cognitive organization that provides a continual sense of social structure.[301]

In sum, ethnomethodology provides many clues but no definite answer to the question of how members create something that transcends themselves and at the same time continuously express themselves as practical reasoners. Perhaps the nexus between social action and social order provides ethnomethodology the site where it will, both theoretically and empirically, make or break itself as an *alternative* to the sociology it consistently criticizes.

7. Ethnomethodology:
a phenomenological sociology?

No brain has ever seen itself.

> Erwin W. Straus and Maurice Natanson, Preface to *Psychiatry and Philosophy*

That Garfinkel and other ethnomethodologists acknowledge a phenomenological influence on their work does not necessarily mean that they intend their endeavors as phenomenological. Yet Garfinkel has labeled his work phenomenological and existential.[1] Although not all ethnomethodologists accept that characterization,[2] Garfinkel's claims provide grounds for supposing that many ethnomethodologists regard their work as more or less phenomenological. Just as importantly for purposes at hand, non-ethnomethodological sociologists commonly consider ethnomethodology a variety of phenomenological sociology, sometimes even equating it with phenomenological sociology.

Commentators vary in their judgments about the relationship between ethnomethodology and phenomenology. Kando reports that ethnomethodology *claims* to carry on the phenomenological tradition; Craib suggests an *unsystematized* relationship between Garfinkel's ethnomethodology and phenomenology; Dallmayr and McCarthy regard ethnomethodology as an *offshoot* of phenomenological sociology; O'Neill considers the ethnomethodology of Garfinkel and Cicourel as a development *in* phenomenology; Morris maintains that phenomenology lies at the heart of ethnomethodology; Mayrl states that ethnomethodology and phenomenology have esssentially the same aims and procedures and that ethnomethodology is a phenomenology.[3] Heap and Roth maintain that ethnomethodology creates a unique domain by combining some phenomenological and sociological concerns without distorting either framework.[4] On the other hand, Zimmerman argues that errors are likely if scholars regard ethnomethodology as a phenomenological sociology; Spurling contends that ethnomethodology and phenomenology are partially incompatible and that phenomenologists would criticize some aspects of ethnomethodology, particularly its narrow approach to language.[5] Whatever the relationship between the two, ethnomethodologists frequently define themselves and are defined as phenomenologically disposed.[6] To that extent, the question of the actual relationship between ethnomethodology and phenomenology is important, for ethnomethodologists' judgments about sociology are often taken as phenomenologically based; for many scholars, phenomenology may be discredited as a result. At the same time, (other) sociologists' judgments about ethnomethodology are often meant to address phenomenological sociology in general, as if ethnomethodology obviously represents phenomenological sociology.

In the case of Schutz's thought, a similar situation obtains. Although many sociologists know his works through Natanson's expositions and Berger and Luckmann's work,[7] some sociologists' familiarity with Schutz's ideas probably derives from the ethnomethodological literature. Such sociologists may take ethnomethodological interpretations of Schutz's ideas as expository; their judgments of those interpretations are often intended as addressing Schutz's thought itself. Thus the question of the relationship between Schutz's and ethnomethodologists' views of action, daily life, and related matters is significant. Again commentators diverge about the closeness of that relationship. Dallmayr says that ethnomethodology carries on the *impulse* of Schutz's work; Craib, that Schutz's work *appears* to have influenced Garfinkel; Mehan and Wood, that many ethnomethodologists *adopt* Schutz's conception of reality; McNall and Johnson, that Schutz's general thesis of the reciprocity of perspectives *lies at the core* of much of Garfinkel's empirical work; Deutscher, that the *direct line of descent* to ethnomethodology is from Kant to Brentano to Husserl to Schutz to Garfinkel; Dreitzel, that ethnomethodology *relies heavily* on Schutz's work; McKinney, that there is a *clear and salient* relationship between ethnomethodology and Schutz's phenomenology; Bauman, Morris, and Poloma, that Schutzian phenomenology is the *foundation* of ethnomethodology.[8] Giddens indicates, though, that Garfinkel exhibits no interest in the kind of "motive-analysis" Schutz favored; Douglas contends that ethnomethodology differs from Schutzian phenomenology; Lemert argues that its stance toward language takes ethnomethodology beyond Schutz's phenomenology; Mennell concludes that its indebtedness to linguistic philosophy rather than Schutzian phenomenology distinguishes ethnomethodology from traditional sociology and from "other varieties" of phenomenological sociology.[9]

Given such heterogeneous perceptions, the question of whether or not ethnomethodology represents a phenomenological sociology presents itself as a difficult problem. At the same time, the question looms as an important one. The absence of a phenomenological examination of ethnomethodological methods, theory, and epistemology helps perpetuate assumptions that may be ill-based and that stand in need of careful examination in any case.

As a sociologist, I somewhat relish the emergence of ethnomethodology and view its shortcomings with as much patience as criticism. As a complement to extant sociologies, ethnomethodology extends concrete possibilities for a more reflexive, humanistically significant sociology. Ethnomethodologists challenge the rest of us to take a step back from our endeavors and examine their relation to our common-sense experiences and knowledge. Their challenge is that we consciously exploit reflexivity in our theorizing, data collecting, and data analyses so as to make explicit the grounds of our discipline. Ethnomethodology also demands respect for the routine accomplishments of common-sense actors by rejecting the bifurcation between "them," naive people carrying on their daily affairs, and "us," intellectually refined analysts presumably clarifying what naiveté cannot grasp, let alone elucidate. In that fundamental respect, ethnomethodology promises a fresh basis for pursuing a humanistic sociology. My immediate purpose, however, is neither to explore the actual and potential benefits ethnomethodology offers nor to delineate its shortcomings as an alternative to predominant sociological models and methods. Rather, I want to show that ethnomethodology is *not* significantly phenomenological in its conceptualizations and methods. Thus we should not regard it as an example or test case of the possibilities and limits inherent in applications of the phenomenological frame to sociology.

Superficially examined, ethnomethodology exhibits no consistent relationship to phenomenology. In general, its terminology is not phenomenological. "Life-world," "natural attitude," "consciousness," "ego," and "horizon," for example, appear rarely in the ethnomethodological literature, and ethnomethodologists use "phenomenon" with a looseness that betrays its phenomenological meaning. A second clue to the non-phenomenological status of ethnomethodology is its neglect of the work of post-Schutzian phenomenologists who have investigated will, role, situation, interaction, alienation, common sense, constitution, and everyday life. That ethnomethodologists have not made use of the findings of Maurice Natanson, Erwin Straus, Robert Sokolowski, Paul Ricoeur, and others strikes me as peculiar among individuals who purport a phenomenological orientation. Even the work of Berger and Luckmann receives little attention from ethnomethodologists. Third, and most significantly, ethnomethodologists make rare reference to and adopt no clear position on human consciousness. The hallmark of the phenomenological perspective is its insistence on the priority of consciousness and its concern with methodically demonstrating that priority. Some might argue that ethnomethodologists are thoroughly concerned with human consciousness, since they analyze practical reasoning, decision making, and judgmental work. The general and, I think, highly relevant issue that position raises is the possibility that ethnomethodology is *implicitly* phenomenological, that is, that its phenomenological character is implied in its general orientation and some of its specific emphases regarding social reality. Even more fundamental an issue is the question of precisely what it means to adopt a perspective or frame. In this case, what do those social scientists imply who claim to adopt a phenomenological viewpoint? Only a systematic juxtaposing of phenomenology and ethnomethodology provides bases for determining (1) what a phenomenological standpoint entails when adopted by nonphilosophers, (2) whether ethnomethodology is a phenomenological sociology, and (3) if ethnomethodology is not phenomenological, how did it come to be defined so, both from within and from without?

Consciousness and constitution

The ethnomethodological critique of sociology specifies some basic goals and major dissatisfactions. In general, that critique finds fault with sociology for naively using second-order constructs of social life derived from the first-order constructs of practical actors who, it implies, are naive or even rather mindless creatures. While using their models of mundane actors, sociologists overlook that they themselves draw on the understandings that undergird the naive world they implicitly denigrate. Ethnomethodologists reject the traditional sociological standpoint by stressing that practical actors accomplish practical reasoning, decision making, and accounting. In addition, they refer to "lay" and "professional" sociology so as to stress the similarity between those who do not and those who do identify themselves as sociologists when interpreting social reality. From a phenomenological viewpoint, the first position is defensible; the second is less clearly justifiable. Examining these two points is best accomplished by focusing on consciousness and constitution.

The ethnomethodological insistence that practical actors accomplish the realities they simultaneously assume as given seems to imply a model of the mundane actor that emphasizes consciousness and constitution. The ethnomethodological conceptualization of everyday social reality as an achievement appears to incorporate the idea of constitution, though the term itself occurs infrequently. Ethnomethodologists seem to insist that practical actors constitute a practical world. But the full meaning of constitution fails to inform their portrayal of mundane social reality.

Constitution *is* a process of accomplishing that establishes, most importantly, identity and objectivity. We commonly experience certain achievements of consciousness as objectively given, as if they somehow existed independently of consciousness. Ethnomethodologists largely ignore that experience of objectivity. Their emphasis on social facts as practical accomplishments is phenomenologically acceptable; their virtual denial that social facts are objective is, however, phenomenologically indefensible. By their inattention to the objective quality of social facts, ethnomethodologists imply that whatever members accomplish through practical reasoning and decision making is situationally contingent; namely, actors may or may not actualize the social facts associated with any given type of situation. Ethnomethodologists thus undercut the awesomeness of constitution by ignoring the achievement of "objectivity" out of "subjectivity." In fact, they disattend human subjectivity. Similarly, by ignoring the constitution of identity ethnomethodologists provide no adequate account of how people can knowingly return to *this same thing* as they pursue their practical affairs. By neglecting the constitution of identity and objectivity ethnomethodologists, in effect, maintain that in some sense practical actors are always starting from scratch or starting here and now rather than continuing on, renewing, or returning. Their inattention to human consciousness underlies the truncated, distorted attention ethnomethodologists give constitution.

Constitution cannot be treated apart from consciousness. Attempting such a treatment not only involves abandoning the phenomenological frame but also conceptualizing, at least implicitly, "process" as flux without form or activity without structure. Ethnomethodologists, though, consistently express interest in the invariant forms underlying the production of accountable situations. Yet they fail to acknowledge the invariant structure of the intentional acts that constitution presupposes. To date, ethnomethodological concern with the invariant features of conversation, speech, and interaction has neglected the foundation of those activities. Specifically, without careful attention to human consciousness descriptions of such invariants fall short of their full social-scientific and philosophical import. At the same time, constitution remains enigmatic inasmuch as its continuity and structure cannot be accounted for.

Ethnomethodologists neither acknowledge the essential intentionality of consciousness nor adopt any position regarding givenness and horizon. In fact, Garfinkel has said that nothing in actors' heads concerns ethnomethodologists; there are only brains.[10] Given that implicit rejection of the centrality of human consciousness to constitution and to all other human accomplishments, one can better understand why indexicality predominates among ethnomethodological presuppositions. Phenomenologists have no quibble with the propositions that every situation is unique and that context and meaning are essentially implicated with one another. Ethnomethodologists implicitly stretch "horizon," however, so as to equate radical incompleteness and open-endedness with uniqueness. Phenomenologically, analysts must guard against exaggerating the incompleteness of any situation lest they deny the now-retention-protention structure of consciousness and imply that sense is pathetically fragile. Without considering the essential structure and functioning of consciousness, the presupposition of indexicality seems worthy of support. Phenomenological findings about consciousness, though, render that presupposition an untenably radical version of an essentially valid proposition, that every situation is fundamentally unique. Consciousness never confronts the absolutely new. Ethnomethodologists often imply, though, that that possibility is always imminent. In that respect, they virtually siphon off the "now" from the now-retention-protention structure of consciousness and overlook the temporal horizon the present essentially bears. In other terms, inner time-consciousness does not enter into ethnomethodological reconstructions of practical reasoning, decision making, and other accomplishments of common-sense actors.[11]

Similar comments apply to the ethnomethodological use of "reflexivity." In effect, ethnomethodologists take a phenomenologically appropriate notion and, by neglecting consciousness, radicalize it to the point of phenomenological inaccuracy. To define the situation is *in a sense* to accomplish the *social* situation as such, but the defining necessarily cannot commence with the situation. (From a phenomenological perspective, "define" here is more accurately "intend" or "co-intend." Furthermore, "situation" here must refer to a narrowly social situation, since no participant's situation corresponds fully with the situation interaction establishes.) Individuals enter every situation with typifications that variously specify the kinds of defining and accounting that make the type of occasion they *pre*suppose it to be. This does not imply, as ethnomethodologists seem wont to conclude, that norms exist independently of those who situationally interpret and apply them. Rather, from the phenomenological standpoint *this* situation and *that* situation are not absolutely discrete and independent, just as no act of consciousness is absolutely separate from another act and no act of consciousness is entirely arbitrary. Social situations presuppose human consciousness which, by virtue of its essential structure, makes every situation part of a temporal succession of situations and thus fundamentally nonarbitrary.

The model of the practical actor that predominates among ethnomethodologists fails to respect the essential complexity of consciousness. Ethnomethodological attempts to account for the constitution of social situations without treating consciousness imply a model that frees mundane actors from the status of judgmental dopes only to cast them as situation-bound mechanics.[12] Ethnomethodologists do not intend such a portrayal any more than most sociologists intend a model of judgmental dope. Yet their inattention to intentionality, inner time-consciousness, givenness, the now-retention-protention structure of consciousness, and horizon leaves them with a model whose implications are as unpalatable as those of the more conventional model they criticize.

The ethnomethodological use of "sociology" to refer to both lay and professional interpretations of social reality not only implies that the latter rests on the former but also suggests that the two sets of practices are substantially the same. In espousing that viewpoint, ethnomethodologists equate active and passive constitution and, therefore, override a longstanding phenomenological finding. That active constitution presupposes passive constitution does not mean that the two processes are equivalent. Phenomenologists distinguish between the two levels of constitution by using a number of adjectives, including prepredicative and predicative, prereflective and reflective. Those adjectives are strikingly absent from ethnomethodological descriptions. That absence obfuscates the difference between the passive and the active genesis of interpretations of social reality. From Husserl onward, phenomenologists have shown that science presupposes the life-world, that it builds on common-sense understandings, and that it fails to recognize the necessary infiltration of those understandings into its models and other interpretive schemes. Those findings do not, though, make of science, nonscience; of the theoretical attitude, the common-sense attitude; of reflective grasping, prereflective grasping. As a human activity, scientific work "constitutes the archetype for rational interpretation and rational action."[13] Again it seems that ethnomethodologists exaggerate phenomenological findings to the point of sacrificing their validity. In no manner do phenomenologists deny the differences between scientific and nonscientific reasoning or idealize the latter at the expense of the former. In making sociologists of us all, ethnomethodologists perhaps impose a definition on common-sense people that many would just as soon forego. That definition may only add insult to the injuries already imposed by the "judgmental dope" model. In fact, in obfuscating the differences between active and passive constitution ethnomethodologists may indulge in a reverse elitism.

Their position hints at the superiority of sociologists by making it seem desirable for us all to participate in the activity ethnomethodologists overtly criticize. In any case, their insistence on using "sociology" to refer to professional and lay interpretations serves no clear purpose and, more importantly, betrays the phenomenological distinction between active and passive constitution.

Experience, meaning, and the self

The failure of ethnomethodologists to treat human consciousness seriously limits their possibilities for clarifying mundane experience. Although some ethnomethodologists advocate a "sociological" return to mundane experience, the programmatic meaning of their recommendations remains unclear. In fact, a survey of ethnomethodological studies reveals that experience as such is not an explicit concern. That receptionists, jurors, pedestrians, police officers, sociologists, and others demonstrably engage in the practices that accomplish the rational account-ability of their situations does not imply anything about their lived experiences. And analyses of the structure of conversations do not in themselves disclose the experience of conversing. Perhaps, though, ethnomethodological attention to situations (or settings) elucidates experience. Juxtaposing the ethnomethodological and phenomenological conceptions of a situation provides grounds for determining whether or not ethnomethodologists adopt a phenomenological conception of lived experience.

Phenomenologically, a situation is the fundamental unit of lived experience. Thus ethnomethodological emphasis on situations suggests a compatibility, at least terminologically, with phenomenological findings about the essential structure of experience. By "situation," though, ethnomethodologists usually mean a manifestly social setting, an occasion of social interaction. Schutz and Luckmann mean by "situation" – as did Husserl, I believe – the primal unit of experience, whether or not it involves social interaction. Situations are social in a broad and in a narrow sense. Broadly, an individual's situation is social inasmuch as he or she uses categories of determination that have social origins and are socially objectivated, especially in language; narrowly, situations are social inasmuch as partners in a situation reciprocally determine it.[14] Ethnomethodologists concern themselves with narrowly social situations, which is patently understandable and need not involve a departure from phenomenological findings about experience. Yet phenomenologists have found that individuals experience no clear-cut disjunction between situations that are social in the broad sense and those that are social in the narrow sense. To imply such experiential cleavage, if only by omission, runs counter to phenomenological results. Thus ethnomethodologists' inattention to broadly social situations separates them from phenomenologists and at the same time diminishes their possibilities for illuminating lived experience.

Each individual at any moment is

in a biographically determined situation, that is, in a physical and sociocultural environment as defined by him, within which he has the position, not merely his position in terms of physical space and outer time or his status and role within the social system but also his moral and ideological position. To say that this definition of the situation is biographically determined is to say that it has its history; it is the sedimentation of all man's previous experiences, organized in the habitual possessions of his stock of knowledge at hand, and as such his unique possession, given to him and to him alone.[15]

At any moment the individual's circumstances, whether broadly or narrowly social, are biographically determined. To those circumstances belongs "the experience that some elements of the world taken for granted are imposed upon me, while others are either within my control or capable of being brought within my control. . . ."[16] That experience raises a major philosophical and social-scientific problem: How do a unique biographically determined situation, a finite province of meaning, and interaction connect in individuals' lived experiences so as to permit a *shared* situation? Characteristically, ethnomethodologists ignore individuals' biographically determined situations as well as the finite provinces of meaning that underlie all situations. Instead, they focus on interaction as the doing that is the accounting of this situation as an observable, shared, and reasonable one. In and of itself, that focus sheds little light on lived experience.

From a phenomenological standpoint, ethnomethodologists also fail to give sufficient attention to the "epistemological domestication" that marks mundane experience.[17] Taken-for-granted reality is "epistemically precious" to common-sense actors.[18] Ethnomethodologists might seem to acknowledge that principle by attention to "glossing." Yet their conceptions of "situation" rule out that interpretation of "glossing." From their standpoint, every social situation seems inescapably problematic inasmuch as *this* accomplishing is treated as if it were independent of past similar practices, knowledge derived from past experiences, and the idealizations of continuity and repeatability.[19] We need, though, to distinguish routine situations from problematic ones where actors must acquire new knowledge or clarify their current knowledge.[20] To lump together comfortably familiar and sorely unfamiliar situations is to overlook a key principle about mundane experience. "Glossing" does not discriminate between familiar and unfamiliar situations.

It refers not to a practice for achieving taken-for-grantedness but to a practice imposed by the essential reflexivity of interaction. At best, then, ethnomethodologists relegate familiarity to an unimportant level in their portrayals of social situations.

Similar points emerge concerning the temporal and horizonal character of mundane experience. In describing social situations, ethnomethodologists also give these matters a peripheral status. The one point where the phenomenological and ethnomethodological views of experience seem to correspond concerns the interpretive quality of lived experience. Ethnomethodologists' emphasis on members' interpretive practices and judgmental work represents, at root, a phenomenological orientation toward interaction. But inattention to the structure of intentional acts and the stream of consciousness makes the application of that orientation only subtly phenomenological. Again, lack of attention to inner time-consciousness, typification, biographically determined situations, and the like makes the ethnomethodological stress on judgmental work phenomenologically deficient. Although ethnomethodologists insist that interaction is continuously interpretive, they neither stress the difference between prereflective and reflective interpretation nor explicitly treat the selective, self-correcting features of common-sense interpretation. More seriously, I think, their inattention to breakoff points and interests makes of judgmental work a continuous practice without pauses, respites, or subjectively meaningful stopping points. In other terms, the ethnomethodological view of mundane interpretive practices neglects the variable tensions of consciousness. Moreover, ethnomethodologists only vaguely treat common-sense knowledge as an interpretive scheme, in part because they virtually ignore the processes of typification and anonymization whereby individuals interpretively elaborate their knowledge. Ethnomethodologically, interaction is a continuous interpretive plane cordoned off from other lived experiences and from the objectivated constructions whose ground is human consciousness.

Ethnomethodologists cannot, then, account for the coherence of experience. Until they make room for subjectivity[21] itself in their schemes, coherence will remain an enigma. Meaning itself remains similarly problematic. Although some ethnomethodologists, most prominently Cicourel and McHugh, discuss the problem of meaning, their efforts remain preliminary, both ethnomethodologically and phenomenologically. Cicourel's attention to memory and other cognitive capacities appears to place him on grounds that are potentially phenomenological. Yet Coulter notes that Cicourel distinguishes three layers of reality – thought, language, and meaning – as "independent phenomena" that are loosely interrelated.[22] Phenomenologically, the three are closely interrelated. In a scheme like Cicourel's, the distinction between meaning-endowment and meaning-fulfillment might be useful in accounting for the continuity *and* adequacy *and* essential incompleteness of meaning. In addition, that distinction is necessary for understanding that only past experiences are fully meaningful. In analyses of meaning, the now-retention-protention structure of the stream of consciousness must also be given prominent attention, as must the principle that meaning concerns the "whatness," not the "thatness," of lived experience. Thus typification, too, is central to an adequate treatment of meaning.

Ethnomethodologists have not offered bases for understanding how meaning can be trans-situational as well as situational, a feature of both mediate and immediate experiences. They have not accounted for the complex achievements of consciousness manifest in the facts that

it is not only the currently comprehended action of my fellowmen (or of myself) that is subjectively experienced as motivated and purposeful behavior, that is as meaningful; it is also the institutionalizations of action in social settings. . . .

This holds analogously for objectifications of human intentions in sign systems and language, and also for the objectivated results of human acts, such as works of art. They all refer to original meaning-bestowing acts of reflective explications, subsequent acts of re-explication, and their habitualization in what my predecessors and colleagues in tradition and the relative-natural world view take as meaningful and self-evident. . . .

In the natural attitude, these diverse cultural strata of meaning always adhere to the object, even when I do not reflectively hold the meaning-bestowing acts in front of me.[23]

Ethnomethodologists need to come to grips with the profound significance of the symbolic in human experience and thereby with its transcendent dimension. Natanson comments that

the symbolic . . . is that which announces, presents (or "appresents") meaning whose elements are in the mundane world but whose qualitative unity and coherence are strange to common sense. The transcendent, in this approach, is not opposed to the mundane but penetrates it in such a way that the naive attitude of daily life is forced to the edge of its limits.[24]

At root, the symbolic is the line of access to and expression of the transcendent capacities every mundane ego bears.

Meaning necessitates the topic of ego or self, a notion foreign to ethnomethodological literature. "Member" is the closest facsimile of "ego," but its referential force lies almost exclusively with activity in narrowly social situations. "Member" is a course of activity that establishes occasion-appropriate (accountable and therefore reasonable) behavior that meshes with other participants' behavior. Although "member" presupposes "ego," it offers scant grounds for inferring the full set of capacities it presupposes. "Member" focuses attention on the uses of natural language and on judgmental work, leaving unaddressed the nature of the user-worker who originates every social situation. "If 'our' world is rooted in 'my' world, then the sociality of the intersubjective must be sedimented in the aloneness of the ego."[25] Without egos or selves, social situations seem engineered by automatons, however successful they may be. "Member," in short, needs conceptual amplification in the direction of its major presupposition, ego or self, and its major consequence, social role.[26] That ethnomethodologists rarely treat self and role is a shortcoming that is phenomenologically inexcusable and sociologically incomprehensible.

Phenomenologically viewed,

man and history seen in their *becoming*, as features of the development of the self and its social allies, are expressions of the ego's mobility, its capacity to confront and engage mundane existence through the constructions of consciousness. In this context, social role may be understood as a clue to what is both hidden and manifest in the world.[27]

Projected toward the world it helps to constitute, the self is the "directional activity" of consciousness whose intersubjective dimension is best treated through the concept of social role.[28] A phenomenology of social role and a phenomenology of social process are "root-related" procedures.[29] Ethnomethodological attempts to elucidate micro-level social processes apart from role taking are phenomenologically unjustifiable. Roles and role playing are the *forms* of typification that establish the spectrum of intersubjectivity stretching between the taken-for-granted situation and the anonymous constructs of the public world that subsume distance and absence.[30] Without attention to roles, the typified grasping and interpreting of others and of the socio-historical world cannot be accounted for.[31] From a phenomenological standpoint,

historicity, intersubjectivity, and identity are selected aspects of a larger complexus of the noematic possibility of social role. Taken together, perhaps they help to clarify somewhat the nature of the transcendental level of roles as pure features of societal process.[32]

The neglect of historicity, intersubjectivity, and identity as possibilities that common-sense actors actualize leaves ethnomethodologists without conceptual recourse to self and role. To that extent, they lack the means to account for how members transcend narrowly social situations. Nonetheless, it might seem that the point of a phenomenology of social role is not altogether dissimilar from Garfinkel's experimental antics: to dramatize the assumptions we all make about roles, to throw into fundamental relief a segment of the social world which we ordinarily presuppose, and, with a modicum of embarrassment and even pain along the way, to compel the onlooker to admit his complicity in the disguises of daily life. The position which I have presented is qualitatively different. Everything is not role. Bad Faith is not an eternal victor. The trick is not to make the details of the everyday crystallize but to thematize that believing in the reality of the mundane which gives to details their horizontal placement. In sum, the point of a phenomenology of social role is to illuminate the structure of any sociology or psychology of role by reconstructing the conditions which must be fulfilled if roles and role-taking are to be possible. Such reconstruction is a task for transcendental phenomenology. Within the life of the transcendental ego there may be found the distinctive promise of a social world built out of roles understood as pure possibilities. . . . The genesis of social role, including the internalization of gesture, is one side of the world we seek to understand. It is the side that is always *already there*, intentionally though naively grasped by all of us in the course of our daily lives, indeed, strictly speaking, *through* the course of mundane existence. That givenness of role is a bulwark of the natural attitude; it is taken as sure ground for the construction of sociological and psychological theory; but it is the subject matter of phenomenology which is determined to vindicate the typical. The recognition that typicality is inescapable for human reality is the acknowledgment of the other side of our world – the transcendental.[33]

Clearly, ethnomethodological inattention to the "other side" of what *our* world encompasses involves the failure to address the life-world.

The life-world

Ethnomethodologists' neglect of consciousness, experience, the self, meaning, and essentially related phenomena implies their neglect of the life-world and its structure. Since any life-world is necessarily historical, the ahistorical thrust of ethnomethodology also precludes its effective treatment. Yet some notions relevant to the life-world do inform the ethnomethodological perspective and merit careful attention, particularly inasmuch as ethnomethodologists do not appropriate them in a strictly phenomenological manner.

To some degree, Garfinkel's early breaching experiments illuminate the natural attitude. The results of those studies suggest, among other things, that people prereflectively expect the reciprocity of perspectives to govern their routine affairs and that they prereflectively fill in the linguistic gaps that attest to the familiarity they share. Breaching experiments cannot, however, disclose the most fundamental presuppositions of the natural attitude, including its general thesis. In undertaking his breaching experiments, Garfinkel raised the topic of the natural attitude, but then he interpreted the findings so as to deny its full breadth. One could interpret Garfinkel's findings using a scheme that taps the complexity of the phenomenon his data indirectly illustrate. A phenomenological sociology demands such interpretive elaboration; in its absence one has little, if any, reason for introducing the notion of natural attitude at all.

Similar but, I think, more serious problems underlie the ethnomethodological approach to members' knowledge. Ethnomethodologists have investigated the elegance of that knowledge as well as its relevance to social structure. But, as Psathas puts it, Garfinkel – and, more generally, other ethnomethodologists –

radically transforms knowledge within the natural attitude to only that which is "known" by members on the occasion of their "doing." Members' "knowing" consists of whatever it is they "do" and an analysis of what the activity consists of is sufficient for all practical purposes to reveal whatever it is they "have in their minds." And, in this respect, the concept of "contents of mind" becomes unnecessary.[34]

Psathas's characterization is apt. Ethnomethodologists do seem to equate knowing and doing. Although Husserl rejected the notion of contents of mind or consciousness in a narrow sense, his concepts of constitution and sedimentation indicate that the scope of knowledge necessarily exceeds that of action at any moment. Husserl would have taken issue with the idea that observable behavior discloses what actors know.

Schutz, too, would have disagreed with the ethnomethodological characterization of mundane knowledge. He emphasized the social distribution of knowledge, the socialization of common-sense knowledge, the distinctive features of role-specific knowledge, and the presuppositions undergirding a social stock of knowledge,[35] in addition to the dimensions of the stock of knowledge I already specified. For Schutz, and for phenomenologists generally, knowledge is prior to action and is denser and more complex than action itself can disclose. Contrary to the claims of ethnomethodologists, their approach to common-sense knowledge undercuts rather than reveals the elegance of its structure and the density of its elements. Brotz argues that ethnomethodologists view the world like the positivistic scientists they castigate. In his judgment, they fail to "take the *sense* in common sense seriously," mostly by refusing to distinguish it from nonsense. To that extent, ethnomethodologists provide no bases for a progression from common sense to a humane social science capable of complementing and correcting it.[36] Similarly, Mennell suggests that ethnomethodologists seem not to accept people's explanations of their meanings and intentions; if they did, they would emphasize indexicality considerably less.[37] More generally, ethnomethodological neglect of consciousness not only departs from the phenomenological perspective but also implies a kind of behavioristic outlook. In the equation of knowing and doing lurks the suggestion that consciousness is only peripherally important to social action and its major consequences. Phenomenology utterly opposes such a viewpoint. The phenomenological rejoinder to such a stance is that

the familiar everydayness of our experience in the world of daily life is the result, the creation of an immensely complex apparatus of consciousness and that consciousness, far from being divorced from the real, is the secret of its practicality and power.[38]

Lemert incisively pinpoints the grounds of ethnomethodological disregard for human consciousness. First, ethnomethodologists make language rather than consciousness "the sociological problematic." Second, that priority leads them to study methods rather than people; their conceptualization of member as a "competent language user" underscores their focus on methods. Third, "accountable rationality" derives from the "infinitely regressive discovery that talk is accountable and rational because it succeeds as talk"; such rationality, therefore, does not operate as a "substantive integrating norm." Fourth, ethnomethodology may rupture rather than radicalize sociology by shifting attention to members' practices for producing a sense of social structure. That shift instantiates the broader tendency to "deconstitute the center" or displace the human subject as the center of social life. Lemert's argument rests on the thesis of a homologous relationship between ethnomethodology and structuralism. Both frameworks, he argues, exploit language as their principal theoretical resource and take issue with the sociological conception of "core values." In other terms, ethnomethodology and structuralism "rearrange the priority between language and the social subject," and in the process they dismiss the idea of a social reality derived from and organized by a human center. Contemporary linguistic theory, particularly structuralism, treats language "as a phenomenon obedient to its own laws and independent of subjective human creativity."[39] Insofar as ethnomethodology is a homologue of structuralism, its inattention to human consciousness becomes comprehensible.

Philip Pettit's monograph on structuralism supports Lemert's points. At the same time it provides a clear, concise perspective on ethnomethodology. Pettit points out that structuralism offers systematic grounds for any semiological study, that is, "any study concerned with the production and perception of 'meaning.' " He delineates the linguistic model based on structuralism and surveys the diverse scholars "whose work, wittingly or not, illustrates the extension of the linguistic model to non-linguistic fields." Among those scholars, according to Pettit, is Garfinkel (as well as Goffman).

Pettit indicates that "much of the structuralist debate in France has been a debate . . . with phenomenology. . . ." Structuralist thinkers reject phenomenology and the standpoint of subjective consciousness. Their viewpoint is that "the conditions determine subjective consciousness to the extent that its self-understanding . . . is quite discontinuous with the understanding which a scientific study of those conditions yields. . . ." That viewpoint shows up in their posture toward language.[40] Together, Lemert's and Pettit's ideas offer grounds for understanding why ethnomethodological reports often leave their readers with little sense that social action, interaction, experience, the self, and consciousness lie at the heart of a taken-for-granted, shared world. The homology between ethnomethodology and structuralism accounts for the marginal position those matters occupy in most ethnomethodological studies.

Similarly, the ethnomethodological approach to knowledge implies an unduly narrow conception of social action. From that perspective, social action seems no more than the activity that expresses members' knowledge in a given setting. Absent from the ethnomethodological perspective is Schutz's emphasis on projecting as an essential feature of social action. Gone, too, is covert social action, including negative action. Phenomenologically, action is subject-bound.[41] As subjects, human beings act through and within situations, the primal units of experience. Social action has a "periodic cast"[42] resting on situations that effectively partition any actor's experiences. Action and meaning are inseparable in their epistemic functions,[43] and the mundane ego bears that undividedness. The ego's projection of acts underlies the meaningful structure of the social world.[44] Moreover, the intentionality of role taking may be a model for the sedimentation of meaning inherent in social action.[45] Intentionality constitutes roles and role taking (as well as alienation), establishing the possibility rather than the instantiation of social action.[46] Such phenomenological explorations need sociological elaboration that respects their philosophical basis. Ethnomethodology, however, departs from rather than elaborates extant phenomenological studies.

Finally, the micro-level focus among ethnomethodologists merits mention. Insofar as it excludes explicit attention to institutions, collectivities, the social stock of knowledge, and other macro-level social realities, the ethnomethodological perspective diverges from the Schutzian phenomenology of the life-world. Schutz emphasized the *social relations* mundane actors have with their contemporaries, considered at a number of levels of mediacy, and with their predecessors and successors. When people constitute the meaning of their experiences, they take into account their social relations with people they may never know as co-partners in a narrowly social situation. Social action bears the weight of those social relations in diverse ways and thus implies the transcendent dimension of the life-world that presupposes those same relations. Within the ethnomethodological perspective, though, the transcendent character of the life-world is not discernible. In other terms, whether or not ethnomethodologists adequately treat social structure remains equivocal. One's judgment rests, ultimately, on the analytic status given social structure in relation to social action.[47] Heap observes that "the master category of 'the social' is an unnoticed, unclarified resource for ethnomethodological analysts – a resource necessary for locating candidate phenomena."[48] Heap goes on to offer grounds for reconceptualizing the social. In the meantime, though, the social itself remains ambiguous within the ethnomethodological sphere. Like the individual, the social seems absent from most ethnomethodological considerations. "Social relations" becomes the immediate, face-to-face "doing" of a situation and refers to no more and no less than that. Scenarios do not a life-world make, however.

Methodology and methods

The ethnomethodological literature exhibits terminological affinities with phenomenological method. First, some ethnomethodologists refer to "epoché." Psathas, in fact, maintains that an ethnomethodological attitude called "epoché" or "bracketing" or "reduction," though distinct from phenomenological reduction, represents a phenomenological commitment. He says that the ethnomethodological attitude or epoché sets aside belief in society as an objective reality *except* as it is accomplished in and through the ordinary activities of members.[49] Thus "the specific epoché adopted by the ethnomethodologist requires that the emphasis or focus be placed on what for members is a meaningful, identifiable and recognizable activity. The epoché involves suspending belief in any other reality."[50] Stoddart used a type of "suspension" when he studied the methods of recognizing and locating argot. He maintains that effective access to such methods necessitates suspending the belief that the argot exists independently of the inquiry that makes it observable and making problematic the constitution of any collection of items.[51] Similarly, Zimmerman and Pollner used "occasioned corpus" to "reduce" the characteristics of everyday situations to a set of practices and their properties.[52] Significantly, however, they say that what their reduction reveals belongs to a different order than the phenomena phenomenological reduction discloses. Finally, Garfinkel and Sacks's "procedural policy" called "ethnomethodological indifference" involves conscious disregard for practical sociological reasoning in the interest of revealing members' recognitions and accomplishments.[53]

My reaction to "ethnomethodological indifference" and related procedures is skeptical. They exhibit little that is distinctively phenomenological. Rather, the so-called suspension undertaken is thoroughly sociological; it is also a "naive epochē." On the one hand, the ethnomethodological epochē suspends a particular set of beliefs, as does *all* sociological research aimed at valid, reliable findings. A long-standing sociological tradition advocates the suspension of sociopolitical and moral values; a natural-scientific tradition requires suspending beliefs about the characteristics of the matter under investigation. Although ethnomethodologists merit commendation for the wide range of beliefs they attempt to suspend, there seems little reason to attach a phenomenological term to their attempt. To do so obfuscates the relationship between ethnomethodology and phenomenology, perhaps falsely implying a methodological similarity between them and deemphasizing a methodological similarity between ethnomethodology and other varieties of sociology. On the other hand, a series of "naive epochēs" occur in the life-world, for example, in social roles. Lived experience involves numerous instances when actors suspend certain interests, convictions, or values in order to enact roles. What ethnomethodologists intend by their "indifference" seems qualitatively similar to that mundane experience. To that extent, it again seems misleading to label their indifference so as to suggest a phenomenological import. The term "epochē" loses its methodological force when applied to ethnomethodological techniques for getting at mundane realities.

Several other phenomenological terms sometimes appear in a methodological context in the ethnomethodological literature. Garfinkel and Sacks refer to the "invariance" of speaking practices; Zimmerman and Pollner refer to the "invariant properties" of members' practices across settings.[54] Although those researchers might intend a phenomenological connotation, it is largely absent. Phenomenologists typically refer to "invariant" characteristics or features in discussing the "eidos" of a phenomenon; ethnomethodologists do not say whether or not they intend the same focus when they use that term. In sum, phenomenology and ethnomethodology appear to involve dissimilar methodologies and methods. Yet by their use of some phenomenological terms ethnomethodologists obfuscate the dissimilarities between the two frameworks, if not imply similarities that do not relate the two.

A phenomenological sociology?

The weight of the preceding remarks is that ethnomethodology does not represent a phenomenological sociology. Nonetheless, in several respects ethnomethodology hints at a phenomenological sociology, most obviously in its insistence on "social facts" as members' accomplishments and its commitment to disclosing the practices that establish those accomplishments. Its processual emphasis also bends it broadly toward phenomenology, as does its concern with the "forgetfulness" of social science, specifically sociology. But these phenomenologically relevant elements of the ethnomethodological perspective represent, at best, a narrow extraction from the phenomenological frame. Ethnomethodology does not build on or even make use of the far-reaching relevance of phenomenology. Indeed, one could scarcely infer the nature of phenomenology from ethnomethodology. Yet ethnomethodologists as well as commentators on their work frequently maintain that the ethnomethodological and phenomenological perspectives are substantially linked. That fact raises the questions of how that belief originated and what maintains it.

Any attempt to answer those questions must begin with the ideas of Harold Garfinkel. By the time he wrote his doctoral dissertation, Garfinkel had steeped himself in the ideas of Husserl, Gurwitsch, Schutz, Farber, and other phenomenologists. His attraction to some of their ideas is discernible in his dissertation, as is his conviction that phenomenology advances the understanding of social action and social order. That Garfinkel masterminded a dissertation articulating such a position in 1952 attests to his ingenuity, for in the United States at that time phenomenology had not come of age as a widely recognized, let alone respected, philosophical frame.

Garfinkel's aim to link phenomenology to sociology made him a would-be pathfinder. Yet his tie to Talcott Parsons, his dissertation director, and his attraction to some of Parsons's ideas doomed his efforts. He laid a path away from traditional sociology but failed to specify where the path led. In effect, Garfinkel attempted to integrate some phenomenological ideas, most prominently Schutz's, and some ideas of Parsons. That attempt undergirded Garfinkel's (1952, 1963) early works and still informs the ethnomethodological perspective in some respects. But Schutz's and Parsons's ideas regarding sociology, social action, and social order are seriously incompatible. Garfinkel did not come to grips with that incompatibility and to that extent distorted or even rejected both the Parsonian and Schutzian frameworks. In large measure, the result was ethnomethodology. Its intellectual tensions and theoretical confusions derive, I think, from the double-edged rejection that marked Garfinkel's attempted integration.

Garfinkel's dissertation provides clear evidence of attempting to integrate Parsons's and Schutz's ideas concerning social action and social order. Having surveyed phenomenological ideas, foremostly Schutz's and Husserl's, Garfinkel characterized phenomenology in a peculiar way:

> The term phenomenology refers only to the rules that will be found operating in any perspective whereby certain areas of experience are made non-relevant to the problem at hand while with reference to others a "position is taken."[55]

How phenomenology can be reduced to rules, namely those partitioning experience into the nonrelevant and the immediately relevant, is incomprehensible, even within the context of Garfinkel's exposition. Garfinkel went on, however, to hint at the sources of his distorted definition; he described *two* "leading phenomenological attitudes." On the one hand is the neo-Kantian phenomenological attitude of Cassirer, Lewin, Freud, Weber, Mead, and Parsons; on the other hand is the Husserlian phenomenological attitude of Schutz.[56] Thus Garfinkel stretched "phenomenology" to cover an inappropriate mix of scholars. That conception provided for Garfinkel's definition of his own work as a phenomenological undertaking. Moreover, his conception of phenomenology accounts for his sense that Parsons's and Schutz's ideas are complementary. At one point Garfinkel sketched that complementarity explicitly; in his view, Parsons studied how we *can* believe our eyes and Schutz studied how we *do* believe our eyes.[57] In brief, Garfinkel undertook an intractable task and saw it through by distorting the philosophical frame he had envisioned as the basis for integrating the ideas of two highly influential scholars.

Among the expositors of ethnomethodology Filmer most clearly appreciates that

> in the context of Garfinkel's work, Parsons and Schutz make the strangest of bed-fellows. For Parsons's work would appear to be in many ways archetypical of precisely the neglect that Garfinkel bemoans in much sociology, of explaining how the commonsense world is possible; and to which neglect Schutz's work is dubbed such a "magnificent exception"![58]

Filmer argues that "Garfinkel would appear to be acknowledging an equally positive debt to both Schutz and Parsons, which adds up to an implied contradiction in his explanations of the ordered character of the everyday activities of collectivity members."[59] After delineating the major incompatibilities between Schutz's and Parsons's ideas, Filmer shows that they cannot be reasoned away. Parsons and Schutz hold different conceptions of "actor" or individual, and they assign vastly different weights to socialization and internalization. Moreover, Parsons's emphasis on the functional prerequisites of social systems has no counterpart in Schutz's thought.[60]

In a lengthy footnote, Filmer indicates that from conversations with Garfinkel in 1971 he understood Garfinkel to have drafted a manuscript in 1959 aimed at reconciling "the works of Parsons and Schutz on social action."[61] Filmer's understanding is that Parsons's subsequent work on socialization and systems theory made it practically impossible for Garfinkel to proceed. Although Garfinkel failed to integrate Parsons's and Schutz's ideas around the theme of social action, that goal did inform his dissertation and, I think, his formulation of ethnomethodology. As Filmer's exposition suggests, "member" symbolizes the Parsonian influence.[62] Thus "member" offers a conceptual key to the anomalous juxtaposition of Parsons's and Schutz's ideas in Garfinkel's work.

Garfinkel meant "member" in "strict accord" with Parsons's conceptualization of "collectivity member(ship)."[63] Unsurprisingly, then, "member" seems to connote role and refers to a "perspective" and a "course of activity" rather than an ego or self. Yet member as a practical actor with purposes at hand infuses Garfinkel's usages of the term. Significantly, those usages suggest an orientation compatible with Schutz's concerns. In short, "member" illustrates the attempt at a Parsons–Schutz synthesis that Garfinkel began during his doctoral studies. To that extent, its enigmatic status within the ethnomethodological framework is as understandable as it is inescapable.

Garfinkel wanted, then, to unite under the aegis of phenomenology Parsons's and Schutz's ideas on social action and social order. The recent publication of the Schutz–Parsons correspondence during 1940–1941 reveals their fundamental irreconcilability on those topics. Certainly both scholars

are deeply concerned with the theory of social action, with the status of the subjective interpretation of meaning, with the relationship between common-sense and scientific constructions of social reality, with the problem of rationality in human action, and despite everything which divides them, with the meaning of theory in social science.[64]

Yet their discussion reached an impasse. In Natanson's view, what divided Parsons and Schutz is the meaning of philosophy for the social sciences:

For Schutz, sociology cannot ground itself; epistemology is not a luxury but a necessity for the social scientist. . . . For Parsons, the demand is for demarcating science and philosophy, for allowing philosophy to enter the discussion only when it is needed.[65]

Garfinkel's ethnomethodology is an emblem of the very issue cementing the Schutz–Parsons Divide, for it fails to clarify the proper relation of philosophy to sociology. Although they advocate a philosophically, even phenomenologically, based sociology, ethnomethodologists have yet to produce such a sociology. Indeed, that possibility remains unlikely inasmuch as both Parsons's and Schutz's ideas do inform ethnomethodology, creating serious inconsistencies that hinder ethnomethodologists who seek an alternative to the philosophically deprived tradition they soundly oppose.

One question still remains: How do sociologists continue to regard ethnomethodology as a phenomenological sociology? Garfinkel invited as well as used the label "phenomenological" with reference to ethnomethodology. That the appropriateness of his designation goes largely unquestioned among sociologists suggests their relative unfamiliarity with phenomenology. Apparently, few sociologists have grounds for determining whether or not ethnomethodology is phenomenological. Tending to accept ethnomethodologists' own definitions, we sociologists evidence the decided influence of figures like Parsons, who relegated philosophy to a peripheral, unimportant position in the sociological domain. Thus it remains necessary to examine the features a phenomenological sociology would exhibit.

8. The idea of
phenomenological sociology

A science without philosophy would literally not know what it was talking about.

Maurice Merleau-Ponty, *Sense and Non-Sense*

If analogy is not a method of demonstration in the true sense of the word, it is nevertheless a method of illustration and of secondary verification which may be of some use. . . . In fact, analogy is a legitimate form of comparison, and comparison is the only practical means we have for the understanding of things.

Emile Durkheim, *Sociology and Philosophy*

Since human beings are born of mothers and not concocted in retorts, the experience of the existence of other human beings and of the meaning of their actions is certainly the first and most original empirical observation man makes.

Alfred Schutz, "Conception and Theory Formation in the Social Sciences"

Sociologists sometimes castigate themselves and their discipline for a past of false starts and inconsistent progress, as if sociology should somehow overcome the fate of all other human endeavors. Among such critics I stand uncomfortably. I have no doubt that sociologists must illuminate sociality, personhood, and community more intelligibly and incisively than they have to date. Yet I know the positive difference sociology has wrought in my own thoughts about, involvements in, and sensitivities toward *our* world. Moreover, I have observed time and again the open-ended wonder and open-minded queries sociology evokes in some students.

In spite of its shortcomings, sociology stimulates appreciation of the ambiguities and complexities of the modern world; it solicits distinctive, valuable attention to one's self, other selves, and the bonds connecting us; it discourages premature judgments about and simplistic solutions to the problems we have created or re-created, both through misapplied effort and inaction. Sociology, in short, addresses us and our times even though its proponents often speak with garbled voices, tell us what (we think) we already know, or seem only to remind us that our world is profoundly difficult to understand. Even the severest critics among us affirm something, if only the intellectual and cultural promise of "alternative" sociologies. And I sense that self-satisfied sociologists appreciate the necessity of sociological consciousness for heightened understanding of self and others. Despite their diverse pedagogical, theoretical, and methodological commitments, at root sociologists share the convictions that human beings need to understand social reality and that sociology advances that understanding in a fashion distinct from the other social sciences, philosophy, and literature. Yet our shared values do not prevent our criticizing one another, sometimes in biting, self-righteous terms. To what ends are such criticisms directed? Fundamentally, I think they supersede careerism, one-upmanship, and related pettinesses. We criticize one another because we care about our work, our discipline, and – to some degree – our world. Moreover, our criticisms are self-defenses. The social sciences, like the humanities, deeply engage selves in their scholarly and ideological forays. To that extent, our skirmishes with one another reflect not only the state of the discipline but also the state of selves repeatedly asked to reexamine the worthwhileness of the models, methods, and topics they intermesh in their "work."

Unsurprisingly, then, appeals for phenomenological sociology often meet with skepticism or even resistance.[1] Frequently, sociologists interpret those appeals as criticisms that confound social philosophy and social science. Many sociologists also suspect that phenomenological sociology advocates social theory at the expense of sociological experiments and surveys. Similarly, "phenomenological sociology" evokes images of massive changes that would lead away from science. Briefly put, sociologists often experience the idea of phenomenological sociology as an assault on their sensibilities and an affront to their achievements. In no way, though, does the idea of phenomenological sociology imply such criticisms and programmatic priorities. Rather, "phenomenological sociology" affirms the intellectual and cultural significance of sociology and the discipline's possibilities for further illuminating the processes that establish a shared world.

Phenomenological sociology builds on phenomenologically informed insights into the practices institutionalized as sociology and into the actions constitutive of social reality. Essentially, phenomenological sociology is a double-edged heightening of extant sociological sensibilities: It involves understanding as its core process and social action as its principal focus. Neither the method a sociologist uses nor the topic of inquiry he or she selects makes a sociological study phenomenological. Rather, its phenomenological dimension derives from the style of understanding it exhibits and the focus on social action it encompasses. Phenomenological sociology elaborates the foundations of sociology and sharpens the vision of sociologists. It is not constrictive in its methods of data collection or theory construction.

The reflexive understanding of social reality

The cognitive style of sociology involves its own distinctive tension between life and thought, specifically the tension between social life and sociological thought. When phenomenologically informed, sociological consciousness grapples with that tension through practices reflectively aimed at understanding. Needless to say, the intention to understand presupposes a conception of understanding and of the activities that accomplish it. Most immediately, then, phenomenological sociology necessitates an examination of understanding and its constitution. In turn, it requires examining the subjective–objective polarity underlying the theoretical and methodological issues that divide sociologists.

To inquire into understanding means to seek understanding of understanding. Thus examinations of understanding express a commitment to reflexivity. Phenomenological sociology is sociology practiced reflexively through rigorous self-consciousness. It comprises persistent attempts to understand one's understanding in the process of constituting research designs, data, interpretations, findings, concepts, descriptions, explanations, models, and theories. The phenomenological sociologist shares with the philosopher, then, "the distinguishing trait that he possesses *inseparably* the taste for evidence and the feeling for ambiguity."[2] He or she cultivates a sense of perpetual beginnings in the face of unlimited possibilities for making evidence less incomplete and ambiguity less subterranean. The phenomenological sociologist honors the horizons of his or her experiences by forestalling the sense of closure that ordinarily comes from objectivating the outcomes of one's lived experiences as a social scientist.

Although many interpretive sociologists and philosophers of the social sciences have dissected it, the problem of understanding remains unresolved. Max Weber noted the absence of a theory of understanding but did not fill that gap.[3] Diverse as his studies were, they did not adequately describe acts of understanding. Phenomenology is philosophical *Verstehen*.[4] Husserl's work illuminated the intentionality of understanding, and his successors, particularly Schutz, have clarified the process of understanding both in daily life and in the social sciences. Frequently, Husserl referred to "meaning-conferring" acts as acts of understanding and interpretation.[5] In the context of his findings about intentionality, perception, judgment, and evidence, that equivalence provides a sound starting point for inquiring into understanding.

Schutz extended Husserl's insights by working toward a phenomenological sociology. Distinguishing acts with and without communicative intent, Schutz disclosed various meanings of the "understanding of a human act."[6] He concluded that *some interpretations of another individual are interpretations of the observer's own experiences*. Specifically,

there is, first, the interpretation that the observed person is really a human being and not an image of some kind. The observer establishes this solely by interpretation of his own perceptions of the other's body. Second, there is the interpretation of all the external phases of action, that is, of all bodily movements and their effects. Here, as well, the observer is engaging in interpretation of his own perceptions. . . . In order to understand what is occurring, he is appealing solely to his own past experience, not to what is going on in the mind of the observed person. Finally, the same things may be said of the perception of all the other person's expressive movements and all the signs which he used, provided that one is here referring to the general and objective meaning of such manifestations and not their occasional and subjective meaning.[7]

Yet "understanding the other person" implies more than interpreting one's own experiences of the other's body, movements, and use of signs. Strictly speaking, "understanding the other"

involves grasping those things of which the external manifestations are mere indications. To be sure, interpretation of such external indications and signs in terms of interpretation of one's own experiences must come first. But the interpreter will not be satisfied with this. He knows perfectly well from the total context of his own experience that . . . there is this other, inner, subjective meaning.[8]

Thus, "understanding the other person" in the strict sense leads to the other's "own meaning-contexts, to the complex ways in which his own lived experiences have been constituted polythetically and also to the monothetic glance with which he attends to them."[9]

Schutz's findings counsel observers of social reality to distinguish between interpretations of their own experiences and interpretations of their subjects' lived experiences. Sociological work includes both types of interpretive acts. Moreover, both types involve common-sense assumptions and understandings. The distinction between the two types of interpretive acts illuminates how we understand and specifies the facets of sociological experience that necessitate disciplined self-consciousness.

Initially, reflexivity demands that sociologists cultivate awareness of how common-sense assumptions enter their work. Thereafter, they must examine the implications, utility, and tenability of those assumptions.

When common-sense assumptions are uncritically admitted into the apparatus of a science, they have a way of taking their revenge. This may appear through equivocations creeping into its basic concepts and thereby working an adverse effect on research. Or it may occur through a failure to see that apparently diverse phenomena are really of the same type, a failure generated by not having penetrated beyond the appearances to the roots of the phenomena in question. If this danger hangs over every science, its threat to sociology is particularly acute. For sociology's task is to make a scientific study of social phenomena. Now, if social phenomena are constituted in part by common-sense concepts, it is clear that it will not do for sociology to abstain from a scientific examination of these "self-evident" ideas.[10]

Although common-sense assumptions pervade sociological practice, sociologists can curtail their role through methodical attention to terms and definitions, on the one hand, and the idealizations that underlie them, on the other hand.

In the common-sense world, words are given as references to what-is-(taken-as-)real. When everyday terms infiltrate sociological discourse – and that seems necessarily often – they introduce conceptions of reality that demand clarification. Phenomenologically, a serious error results from treating an abstractum as if it were the "thing" of interest.[11] The reflective, rigorous use of terms requires seeing that they represent both "untanglings and entanglements."[12] Thus understanding how we understand means recognizing that empirical investigations illustrate, not overcome, the limitations of vocabulary.[13] Phenomenological approaches to concept formation invoke a "style of solicitation" aimed at the dense meaning inherent in lived experience.[14] A phenomenological sociologist habitually asks whose experiences are being interpreted – one's own or others' – and whose vocabulary – whose "reality" – informs the interpretive scheme in use.

Similarly, a phenomenological sociologist attends to the idealizations that underlie any nontranscendental perspective he or she adopts. As Schutz and others have indicated, scientific activity presupposes the disinterested attitude that fundamentally modifies the common-sense outlook. The disinterested observer shifts the center of his or her world from self to some other "null point," for example, alienated workers, urbanites, criminals. Although the researcher investigates the life-world of others,

the scientist, who is *also* a human being among human beings in this single and uniform life-world and whose scientific work is in itself a working-together with Others in it, constantly refers and is obliged to refer in his scientific work to his own experience of the life-world. But . . . the disinterested observer has to a certain extent departed from the living stream of intentionalities. *Together with the sub-stitution of another null point for the framework of orientation, every meaning-reference which was self-evident for the naive person, in reference to his own I, has now undergone a fundamental specific modification.* It remains for each social and cultural science to develop the type of such modification proper to it, that is, *to work out its particular methods.* In other words, each of these sciences must give the equation of transformation according to which the phenomena of the life-world become transformed by a process of idealization.[15]

The idealizations that undergird sociology need astute attention, particularly directed toward the typifications they incorporate and the modifications of common-sense experience they accomplish. Prereflectively using the ideal-izations necessary for investigating some (type of) thing obscures the com-plexity of the investigation and makes the thing itself less accessible.

Reflexive concern with terms, definitions, and idealizations necessitates concern with perspective. As Weber indicated, knowing is perspectival.[16] Some point of view conditions every inquiry. Phenomenological sociology attends to perspective by insisting, as Polanyi and Porsch have, that we recognize our own inescapable role in determining the boundaries as well as the content and rigor of our scientific knowledge.[17] We cannot understand knowledge apart from our situations and lived experiences; our interpretive schemes are situationally conditioned.[18] Properly conducted, a sociological study avoids confounding perspectival findings with the lived experiences they comment on. Sociologists should, in other terms, acknowledge their "transcoding" from one perspective to another.[19] They need to examine how they build up insights into their own and others' lived experiences. They need, in short, to make their own perspectives objects of inquiry.

Like other scientists, sociologists appear sensitive to the close connection between perspective and findings. We query one another as to how data were gathered, what kinds of biases underlie our concepts and methods, and how our data and our theoretical constructs relate. Our formal and informal discourse with one another presupposes the relevance of such questions. Moreover, our awareness that various sociological perspectives compete with one another and that each comprises distinctive presuppositions, concerns, and methods also suggests we are attuned to the perspectival quality of knowing and understanding. Yet that awareness informs only selected aspects of our work, mostly affecting our critical stances toward examinations of the extant conceptualizations, methods, and findings relevant to our own research problems; our descriptions of sample selection, ques-tionnaire construction, experimental control, and other methodological matters; and our judgments about the direction future research should take. Outside those general areas, however, our sensitivity to perspective seems to peter out. For example, when we discuss what we have "found" and what it means, we become presumptuous in tone and implications, appearing to dismiss the cautions we specify in prefacing and concluding our research reports. At some juncture, the tension between social life and sociological thought subsides and we act *as if* that tension is, after all, negligible for purposes at hand. And that "as-if" is prereflective. Rarely, if ever, does one find a sociologist who, preparing to discuss his or her findings, says explicitly: "All those theoretical and methodological problems aside . . ."; or: "Let us now imagine that the foregoing problems are unimportant. . . ." Sociologists routinely imply that posture, however. We leap from discussions of theoretical and methodological limitations to facile interpretations of our findings. All too easily one cognitive style substitutes for another. In other terms, we pay our respects to the complexity of lived experiences and then talk about those experiences as if we know what they *really* are. Discussions of self-esteem, identity, attitudes, alienation, and self-concept, for example, usually exhibit such a disjuncture. The progression from discussing the limitations of data derived from a narrow scale measuring (operationally defined) "self-esteem" to discussing self-esteem in a global, mundane sense is a commonplace type of accomplishment among sociologists.

Max Black argues that all models are "heuristic fictions."[20] And Robert Nisbet reminds us that

we do not see "death," "decadence," "degeneration," or "sickness." We do not see "genesis," "growth," "unfolding," or "development." Not in cultures and societies. All of these words have immediate and unchallengeable relevance to the organic world. . . . There they are literal and empirical in meaning. But applied to social and cultural phenomena these words are not literal. They are metaphoric.[21]

Nisbet's remarks are cautionary, not critical. He goes on to note that

metaphor is indispensable – indispensable in language, poetry, philosophy, and even science. But, clearly, metaphor is also dangerous. It is dangerous when from the initial encapsulating and iconic vision of something distant, or unknowable in standard terms of analysis, there begin to be drawn corollaries of ever more literal and empirical signification.[22]

More recently, Brown has argued that an aesthetic perspective on sociological knowledge, a "poetic for sociology," bares the contradictions in our discipline.[23] Phenomenological findings elaborate Brown's viewpoint, partly by showing how the fictive (or "as-if") infuses all human experience. Phenomenology provides techniques for disclosing the roots of the factual in the fictive. Thus phenomenological commitment harbors respect for the fictive. In sociological terms, that commitment means rejecting an unduly large gap between what we observe and measure, on the one hand, and what we say, on the other hand. That wide gap is a self-defeating but routine outcome of sociological work. We habitually shuttle between interpretations of our own lived experiences as researchers and interpretations of others' lived experiences without acknowledging the large gap we create through the terms, definitions, and idealizations that mark us as "competent sociologists."

Sociologists can cultivate a wider sense of perspective. First, we need to recognize that every effort to understand anticipates meaning.[24] The protentions of our lived experiences inform the determinations we make in the course of inquiry. Examining those protentions and their constitution clarifies our efforts to understand. In phenomenological terms, intentional analyses elucidate our lived experiences as disinterested observers by revealing the sources of current relevances. Thus phenomenological method offers grounds for reflexively controlling the extrascientific interests that shape our conceptualizations, methods, and interpretations. Second, we gain by scrutinizing our assertions as responses to questions.[25] Since we answer questions with a sense of their "motivational background,"[26] recognizing the full scope of our questioning illuminates our relevances and, indirectly, their biographical and situational conditioning. And recognizing our topical, interpretative, and motivational relevances helps us recognize what we have objectivated in our perspective on a given object of inquiry. Although we need not share those recognitions in sociological discourse, they should nonetheless inform that discourse.

Finally, we can intensify our sense of perspective by appreciating the rules we prereflectively apply when making judgments about equivalence, difference, and similarity among objects of inquiry.[27] Since those rules are essentially types, insights into typification are necessary for sharpening one's sense of perspective. For example, sociologists often refer to tendencies, including statistical patterns, trends, and ambivalences we discern in mundane action. But the *type* of pattern, trend, or ambivalence we commonly label a *tendency* is, at root, bidirectional: "Any tendency to do something is by the same token a tendency *not* to do it."[28] Alertness to the double-edged nature of types – the abstraction of like elements and the suppression of the atypical elements among a class of objects – enhances sense of perspective. It opens one's mind to the possibility that criminals might not belong together, after all. The typical then becomes our line of access to the atypical. Sociological practice demands that access inasmuch as it aims toward understanding. In other terms,

what we have to explain is the trend toward order which is the overwhelming de-
liverance of experience. What we have also to explain is the frustration of order,
and the absence of necessity in any particular form of order.[29]

Insights into typification clarify, for example, the relationship between a
"consensus perspective" and a "conflict perspective" on social reality.
Phenomenologically approached, the two perspectives demand one another
not as logical complements but as elements of a single interpretive scheme
bifurcated by what each set of terms, definitions, and idealizations *takes*
as typical and atypical.

Phenomenologically, then, to understand how we understand demands
rigorous reflexivity. In a sense, we must see ourselves seeing in order to
develop a sociology as experientially sound as it is scientifically credible.
Thus we must make our words, definitions, idealizations, and perspectives
objects of investigation alongside whatever types of social action concern
us in our studies. The reflexivity necessary to phenomenological sociology
is not, however, solipsistic. It is "epistemic self-consciousness"[30] phenomenologically established and clarified. Although such reflexivity does
not itself reveal the conditions that make social science possible, it does
heighten our understanding of what access to the purely social entails.[31]

When it is phenomenologically based, reflexivity necessarily promotes
attention to constitution. It leads toward the sorts of insights that constitutional
analyses fulfill. To understand understanding, in fact, requires radical reflection on its constitution. Phenomenologically, reflexivity involves reflectively grasping the genesis of understanding in reflective and prereflective
acts of consciousness. Sociologically, reflexivity necessitates attention not
only to terms, definitions, and idealizations but also to the intentional activities
that objectivate them as meaningful tools for studying social reality.

Because of its connection with constitution, reflexivity also elicits attention
to the subjective–objective polarity, a presupposition that underlies theoretical
and methodological debates among social scientists. Every social-scientific
logic of inquiry represents a set of judgments about *the* problem of the
social sciences: How can we treat subjective phenomena in objective terms
or, alternatively, how is it possible to establish objectively verifiable theories
of subjective meaning-structures?[32] In phenomenological terms, that problem
concerns constituting objective results about subjective activities and their
consequences without distorting the social "things themselves" that ultimately
rest on the lived experiences of common-sense people. Rigorous awareness
of one's words, idealizations, and perspectives is one thing; radical reflection
on their constitution is another, though related, matter; and inquiry into
how those meant-as-objective sedimentations relate to taken-as-subjective

realities represents another project, though it resonates with the first two concerns. All three concerns are central to phenomenological sociology.

Alfred Schutz's works confronted the subjective–objective polarity in the social sciences. Schutz delineated its dimensions and established some principles necessary to its solution. Although considerable work on that problem remains, Schutz's findings lessen the burdens we face in clarifying the possibilities and limits of sociology.

Schutz's formulation of *the* methodological problem of the social sciences presupposes several principles central to his studies. He held that the subject matter of the social sciences demands a kind of understanding distinct from that of the natural sciences. Specifically, we cannot adequately understand "social things," including human acts, by referring only to other things or facts.[33]

I do not understand a tool without knowing the purpose for which it was designed, a sign or symbol without knowing what it stands for in the mind of the person who uses it, an institution without understanding what it means for the individuals who orient their behavior with regard to its existence.[34]

What a cultural object is or *what* given types of actors routinely do necessitates attention to motives, projects, situations, and subjective meanings. Books, mascara, sweat suits, rose gardens, and the common cold cannot be defined in natural-scientific terms; human beings constitute *what* they are by lodging those objects in a common world. Such objects demand a different kind of understanding from that necessary for understanding molecular structures, radioisotopes, or brain lateralization. A second principle is that we achieve degrees of understanding. Meaning-conferral of any sort constitutes some measure of understanding. Absolute understanding, however, "would presuppose the full identity of my stream of thought with that of the alter ego, and that would mean an identity of both our selves."[35] The problem of understanding in the social sciences involves determining what constitutes *adequate* understanding for the purposes at hand, that is, for objectively treating subjectively meaningful phenomena. A third principle is that only the actor

knows the span of his plans and projects. He alone knows their horizons and, therefore, the elements constituting the unity of his acts. He alone, therefore, is qualified to "break down" his own action system into genuine "unit acts."[36]

Sociologists' *only* access to social structure is actors' actions and talk.[37] No alternative sources of data exist for social scientists; people must act or speak before sociologists can move toward understanding social reality in some way and to some degree. This principle applies equally to survey researchers, ethnographers, and experimenters, among others.

Given those three principles, *the* methodological problem Schutz described is inescapable. As scientists, we must adopt a methodology that maximizes objectivity; as social scientists, we must neither neglect nor distort the subjective activities that create our subject matter. In no way did Schutz's delineation of the options for achieving *social science* advocate, as some might suppose, specific methods. For example, Schutz expressed no preference for intensive case studies or careful ethnographies. From the outset, he accepted Weber's position "that all scientific explanations of the social world *can*, and for certain purposes *must*, refer to the subjective meaning of the actions of human beings from which social reality originates."[38] We *always can* and *sometimes must* refer to subjects' activities and their interpretations of those activities by considering projects, life plans, available means, relevances, situations, and knowledge on hand, among other things.[39] Schutz did not hold that every sociological interpretation must explicitly consider the common-sense activities constitutive of the object of inquiry. What he consistently implied was that when our purposes do not necessitate such considerations, we must nonetheless maintain the reflexive awareness described earlier and restrict our discourse accordingly. In addition, he did insist that *adequate* understanding of social reality necessitates attention to subjects' activities and motives.[40]

Schutz's analysis of *Verstehen* prefaces his principal points as to how social scientists can and often do accomplish objective results about subjective activities. Schutz noted that

> both defenders and critics of the process of *Verstehen* maintain, and with good reason, that *Verstehen* is "subjective." Unfortunately, however, this term is used by each party in a different sense. The critics of understanding call it subjective, because they hold that understanding the motives of another man's action depends upon the private, uncontrollable, and unverifiable intuition of the observer or refers to his private value system. The social scientists, such as Max Weber, however, call *Verstehen* subjective because its goal is to find out what the actor "means" in his action, in contrast to the meaning which this action has for the actor's partner or a neutral observer.[41]

Schutz indicated that social scientists fail to distinguish among *Verstehen* as the "experiential form of common-sense knowledge of human affairs," as an (unsolved) epistemological problem, and as a social-scientific method.[42] He noted that *Verstehen* is an experiential form whereby common-sense individuals know their world and carry out their daily affairs.[43] It gives rise to common-sense constructs and interpretations. In everyday life we have merely a *chance* to understand the Other's action sufficiently for our purpose at hand; . . . to increase this chance we have to search for the meaning the action has for the actor. Thus, the postulate of the "subjective interpretation of meaning," as the unfortunate term goes, is not a particularity of Max Weber's sociology or of the methodology of the social sciences in general but a principle of constructing course-of-action types in common-sense experience.[44]

The types common-sense individuals thus constitute establish the reality of everyday life and condition mundane activities.

To understand that reality and those activities, social scientists must base their constructs on common-sense ones using social-scientific methods. "Thus, the exploration of the general principles according to which man in daily life organizes his experiences, and especially those of the social world, is the first task of the methodology of the social sciences."[45] By investigating experience, meaning, the self, intentionality, and so on, phenomenologists disclose what makes meaningful, coherent experience possible. Their findings also suggest that among social scientists *Verstehen* guides the search for the principles organizing mundane experience. As social scientists use it, *Verstehen*

is a conceptual clarification of the interpretive understanding descriptively involved in the affairs of common-sense men in daily life. . . . *Verstehen* is not concerned at any level with providing empirical criteria for determining the validity of hypotheses; as a philosophically directed method it is concerned rather with the conceptual framework within which social reality may be comprehended.[46]

Verstehen thus figures prominently in social science, both as the common-sense experiential form that constitutes social reality and as a systematic approach to understanding that reality.

That *Verstehen* underlies different levels of interpretation and understanding means that the mundane actor and the scientific observer interpret others' actions in related, though distinct, ways. Schutz's delineation of those two levels of understanding integrates the Husserlian principles he adopted, the insights into the social life-world he developed, and the faith in rationality he maintained. His treatment of *the* problem of the social sciences is, together with his analysis of social action, the capstone of his work. Here I can but point to its basic principles.[47]

Schutz emphasized that as observers of others' activities the social scientist and the mundane actor do have much in common. Both necessarily lack direct access to the intentionality and meaning of others' actions. Further, both necessarily experience within biographically and socially conditioned situations. Moreover, both necessarily use interpretive schemes constituted through typification. Yet the two types of observers do interpret others' actions distinctively. The common-sense actor's lived experiences of Other are elements of the world of daily life, which presupposes a reciprocity of perspectives; the social-scientific observer's lived experiences of Other are elements of the world of (social) science, which presupposes the "rationality" of Other and a specific corpus of scientific knowledge. In addition, each of the two types of observers has a distinctive system of relevances that determines the fullness of content, degree of coherence, and amount of reflection typically associated with their observations and interpretations. The world of daily life comprises the starting points of the world of science, but the sets of meaning-compatible experiences that constitute each world differ profoundly. The theory of ideal types illuminates the boundary between those two worlds.

Theoretical constructs called ideal types make a world of social science possible. They are essential to the constitution of the objects of sociological consciousness. Ideal types undergird sociological attention to the meaning of the social phenomena constituted through human acts. Properly constructed and verified, they are necessary for social-scientifically disclosing the social world as a "structure of intelligible intentional meaning."[48] The construction, verification, and application of ideal types, however, expresses the social scientist's meaning-context and interpretive scheme. Ideal types "vary and shift in accordance with the observer's point of view, the questions he is asking, and the total context of his experience."[49] Nonetheless, as a science of social worlds, sociology requires an "overarching a priori framework that is not identical with any one given social world and yet is constituted so that . . . all social phenomena occurring in concrete social worlds can be empirically investigated." Phenomenological studies lead to universal ideal types that sociologists can then develop through interpretive procedures.[50]

Many, probably most, social scientists recognize that social phenomena like prices, female labor-force participation, population growth, and crime rates do rest on the meaningful activities of human beings. They believe, however, that they need not examine those subjective activities in order to describe and explain what interests them. They believe, then, that social scientists may restrict their attention to what the social world means to them, ignoring the question of its meaning for mundane actors. Schutz concedes that that viewpoint can lead to "real scientific work" that bypasses the problem of subjectivity.[51] Such work treats the facts of daily life without concerning itself directly with people's experiences of daily life. It considers the *objective meaning* of the products of human actions, namely, the already constituted meaning-context of the object of inquiry. It disregards the actual constitution of that object and its meaning. Objective meaning consists, then, of a meaning-context social scientists constitute by applying their own relevances to an object of inquiry and fitting it into the stream of their experiences. Thus studying objective meaning *abstracts* a human product "from every subjective flow of experiences and every subjective meaning-context that could exist in such a flow."[52] Phenomenological sociologists have no quarrel with that general approach in and of itself. They oppose, rather, the varieties of "objectivity" and quantification that substitute the researcher's viewpoint for that of subjects' *without acknowledging that substitution and taking its consequences into account.*[53]

Yet the subjective meaning-context *can* always be considered. "We can always go back to that 'forgotten man' of the social sciences, to the actor in the social world whose doing and feeling lie at the bottom of the whole system."[54] The impulse to do so pervades sociological work, most obviously in the leaps made when sociologists move from discussing methods to interpreting data.

Most fallacies in the social sciences can be reduced to a mergence of subjective and objective points of view which, unnoticed by the scientists, arose while transgressing from one level to the other in the progress of the scientific work. These are the dangers of mixing up the subjective and objective points of view in the concrete work of the social scientist. But a theory of social action must retain the subjective point of view to its fullest degree, if such a theory is not to lose its basic foundations, namely its reference to the social world of everyday life and experience. Safeguarding the subjective point of view is the only, but a sufficient, guarantee that social reality will not be replaced by a fictional non-existing world constructed by some scientific observer.[55]

In short, the subjective point of view offers the only *adequate* means of describing social activities and their outcomes.[56] In other terms, sooner or later and in one fashion or other sociologists must treat the common-sense meaning and experiential import of their objects of inquiry. Phenomenological sociology advocates undertaking that project *sooner* and doing so in a systematic, philosophically grounded *fashion*. Phenomenological sociology responds to an impulse that infiltrates all sociological work. It directs that impulse without narrowing the range of sociological techniques that express it.

The subjective point of view treats human products as evidence of the subjective experiences of the individuals who constituted them. The *subjective meaning* of a product concerns

the meaning-context within which the product stands or stood in the mind of the producer. To know the subjective meaning of the product means that we are able to run over in our minds in simultaneity or quasi-simultaneity the polythetic Acts which constituted the experience of the producer.[57]

Thus concern with subjective meaning necessitates attention to a particular person or group the observer has experienced, mediately or immediately; objective meaning is independent of particular persons. Between the understanding of subjective meaning and the understanding of objective meaning lie gradations of understanding related to the worlds of direct social experience of consociates and indirect social experiences of contemporaries, predecessors, and successors.[58]

In everyday life, the subjective interpretation of meaning involves understanding the motives underlying an *observed course of action*. It presupposes, in other terms, *course-of-action* types, ideal types of the expressive process itself or its products. Moving from a course-of-action type to the typical motives of an actor establishes a *personal type*. Thus the personal ideal type refers to a (type of) person who has expressed himself or herself in a course of action whose manifest elements or results the observer takes as signs of the expressive process itself. In seeking to understand Other's action through ideal types, then, two alternatives are available. One can take the finished act as a starting point, determine what type of action produced it, and establish what type of person must have acted so. This poses the problems of determining which aspects of a completed act are typical and how a personal ideal type is constituted from a course-of-action type. Alternatively, and less fundamentally, one can tentatively begin with a personal ideal type and deduce specific actions from it. Ultimately, though, course-of-action types precede personal ideal types.

In the process of understanding a given performance via an ideal type, the interpreter must start with his own perceptions of someone else's manifest act. His goal is to discover the in-order-to or because-motives (whichever is convenient) behind that act. He does this by interpreting the act within an objective context of meaning in the sense that the same motive is assigned to any act that repeatedly achieves the same end through the same means. This motive is postulated as constant for the act regardless of who performs the act or what his subjective experiences are at the time. For a personal ideal type, therefore, there is one and only one typical motive for a typical act. . . . Ideal-typical understanding, then, characteristically deduces the in-order-to and because-motives of a manifest act by identifying the constantly achieved goal of that act. Since the act is by definition both repeatable and typical, so is the in-order-to motive. The next step is to postulate an agent behind the action, a person who, with a typical modification of attention, typically intends this typical act – in short, a personal ideal type.

The conscious processes of the personal ideal types are, therefore, logical constructions. They are deduced from the manifest act and are pictured as temporally prior to that act, in other words, in the pluperfect tense. The manifest act is then seen as the regular and repeatable result of these inferred conscious processes. It should be noted that the conscious processes themselves are conceived in a simplified and tailored form. They are lacking all the empty protentions and expectations that accompany real conscious experiences.[59]

The observer's point of view, conditioned situationally and biographically, determines the personal ideal type, then. *"It is a function of the very question it seeks to answer."*[60] It depends on the objective meaning context of its construction and involves "translation" into subjective terms and then personification. Thus the personal ideal type "is *by definition* one who acts in such and such a way and has such and such experiences."[61] In constructing their interpretive schemes, then, sociologists create "puppets."[62] But sociologists do not construct ideal types randomly; the corpus of scientific knowledge and the purpose at hand, understanding social action, limit their arbitrary nature. Through ideal types

the social scientist arrives at a model of the social world or, better, at a reconstruction of it. It contains all relevant elements of the social event chosen as a typical one by the scientist for further examination. It is a model which complies perfectly with the postulate of the subjective point of view. For from the outset the puppet type is imagined as having the same specific knowledge of the situation – including means and conditions – which a real actor would have in the real social world. From the outset the subjective motives of a real actor performing a typical act are implanted as constant elements of the specious consciousness of the personal ideal type. It is the purpose of the personal ideal type to play the role an actor in the social world would have to adopt in order to perform the typical act. Since the type is constructed in such a way that it performs exclusively typical acts, the objective and subjective elements in the formation of unit acts coincide.[63]

The *objective* understanding of *subjectively* meaningful action through ideal types requires adherence to three postulates. The *postulate of logical consistency* requires that any system of constructs be compatible with the requirements of formal logic. The *postulate of subjective interpretation* requires that scientists consider what typical knowledge they must attribute to individuals in those models meant to account for observed facts as the result of intentional acts. The *postulate of adequacy* requires that scientific models of human action be constructed so that if an actor in the life-world conformed to its specifications, what he or she did would be understandable to that individual and other common-sense individuals. Compliance with those postulates distinguishes social-scientific from common-sense constructs, permits referring all kinds of action to actors' subjective meanings, and guarantees consistency between social-scientific and common-sense constructs regarding social reality.[64] Together with reflexive attention to the nature and constitution of understanding, adherence to those postulates would create sociological models that pinpoint the typicalities undergirding a shared world and respect the integrity of individuals' lived experiences. Thereby sociology would appear less presumptuous and more accomplished.

Sociological understanding and social action

The reflexivity essential to phenomenological sociology reveals that sociologists distinguish among different aspects and levels of lived experience, not between experience as such and something else.[65] We approach a *constituted* social world, experienced as real and meaningful. The objects we investigate presuppose human activities like believing, communicating, perceiving, judging, loving, learning, fighting, and dreaming; they presuppose, in short, intentionality. Phenomenologically, intentionality in no way implies a solipsistic sphere. Rather, it implies embodiment in a world prereflectively given at any moment in and through "my situation." Any such situation originates intersubjectively: We *are* born of mothers. Consciousness, intersubjectivity, and situation necessarily intertwine, then. Among sociologists, the concept that points to their interconnection is "social action." Thus phenomenological sociology adopts social action as its major focus. Its goal is to illuminate social action through reflexive practices oriented toward understanding.

"Social action" is a highly general ideal type. Among the attributes that figure prominently in its conceptualization is rationality or action with known intermediate goals. A rational actor begins to plan or project action by choosing a goal; he or she understands that goal attainment necessitates certain means. The means selected become intermediate goals. Rationally oriented, the actor projects action as already completed; "the planned act bears the temporal character of pastness."[66] When action begins, the goal is desired and protended. At least implicitly, sociological models of action usually encompass these elements, perhaps because of the necessity of positing such rationality in order to cite choices, preferences, goals, and motives as bases for human action.[67] Yet rational models of action are not meant to treat irrational behavior as if it were rational. Schutz's *postulate of rationality* requires that a rational model of rational human action must specify course-of-action and personal types so that a mundane actor would engage in the typified action if he or she had full, clear knowledge of all, and no more than, the elements the model designates as relevant to the action. Also, the actor would have to adopt the best means assumed available for achieving the goal defined by the model.[68] Always, though, the social scientist must remember that "rationality" is a construct with specific purposes. In the world of daily life, actors are only partially rational. In fact, a "paradox of rationality" informs the common-sense world: The more standardized the pattern of action, the less actors scrutinize its elements. The idea of rationality has its full significance only in rational models of rational action.[69]

In the social sciences, the problem of rationality raises questions about the stock of knowledge typically available to typical actors. "Rationality" presupposes an epistemic position for the mundane actor who is choosing, projecting, and enacting courses of action.[70] Objectivated in the social stock of knowledge of every life-world are recipes offering typical solutions to typical problems among typical actors. The chances of deriving desired, standardized outcomes by using standardized recipes are objective; they apply to each actor whose conduct corresponds sufficiently to that of the anonymous type the recipe specifies or presupposes.[71] But not all actors acquire the "same" stock of knowledge. Different versions of the social stock of knowledge are at work in the different strata of the stratification system. Those different versions shape actors' assessments of self and others.[72] The unequal distribution of knowledge involves partitioning knowledge, establishing relatively autonomous spheres where individuals acquire, apply, and transmit "special" knowledge. In a complex life-world, the mundane actor cannot – and typically senses that he or she cannot – survey the entire social stock of knowledge.[73] Yet knowledge about the social distribution of knowledge remains socially relevant.[74] Like all other knowledge, it affects an actor's power.[75] Constructs of rationality lead quite directly, then, to the matters of knowledge, inequality, and power. Correlatively, they force a careful distinction between a typical actor's stock of knowledge on hand and a typical actor's stock of knowledge at hand in a specific type of situation. The farther an investigation takes us from the *basic elements* of the stock of knowledge of the typical actor, the more we need to examine the effects of inequality and power on the actor's chances to achieve desired, standardized outcomes by applying standardized recipes. In short, most of the time "rational action" demands attention to inequality and power as well as knowledge.

The understanding of social action demands, too, a theory of motives based on a subjective point of view.[76] Motive and action essentially relate: A motive specifies what an action is, is going to be, or was. In-order-to and because-motives found human action. Thus accounting for *systems* of in-order-to and because-motives is vital to a mature sociology,[77] even though the constitution of such systems is complex. Over time, actors' interests shift, necessitating concepts that allow for fluidity but overcome the indeterminacy of notions like "ultimate values." Since motives are biographically and socially conditioned and expressed in specific situations, investigating them means attending to the past and future as well as a concrete present. Such attention alone sustains the recognition that

the system of motives is for the actor a given one only at a certain moment of his existence. It necessarily changes by the pure transition of inner time, . . . if for no other reason that in and by this transition new experiences emerge, further ones enter the foreground of interest, whereas still others fade into the background of attention, or are entirely forgotten.

This continual shift of interest, of relevance, and of attention is very complicated, but it is open to further detailed description. Perhaps this is a task for philosophy or psychology. But social theory is vitally interested in one basic fact: the system of motives . . . is above all a function of the human mind *in time*. . . . All really subjective description must refer to this fact, which . . . is hardly compatible with the conception of ultimate values or ultimate ends, or with a normativity which can only be temporarily complied with.[78]

Thus approached, a theory of motives anticipates a theory of social change. As an object of lived experience, "change" is constituted, actively or passively. And as a sociological construct, "social change" first concerns how human activities modify elements of social structure. Whatever factors are thought necessary for explaining a given change – technological, economic, social-psychological, and so on – refer in some way to the intentional activities of human beings, some reflective and others prereflective. Social change emanates from both action and conduct; motives (subsuming interests, relevances, and goals) inform both varieties of human activity. Accounting for actors' systems of motives is a sociological task of no small significance: It portrays social change as an accomplishment constituted out of the past and the present of a group whose members variously sustain and modify a shared world through their activities. Purposes at hand can, in sum, alter as well as maintain the ingredients of a shared world. In this sense, interests rather than power as such found stability and change.[79]

Intentionality, situation, intersubjectivity, knowledge, inequality, power, and motives are essential to an adequate treatment of rational action. Yet they cannot account for such action. Only attention to choice, projecting, and practical reasoning exposes the interrelationships among those elements. But the notions of choice and decision remain unclarified.[80] Though preliminary, Schutz's comments on choice, decision, freedom, and voluntary action pinpoint the issues social scientists must address in order to refine their models of rational action.[81] Schutz insisted that modern social science presupposes that "the conduct of man has to be explained *as if* occurring in the form of choosing among problematic possibilities."[82] To the extent that social scientists imply that postulate but fail to elaborate it in their interpretive schemes, their models limp. Moreover, to the extent that they neglect either the "openness" or the "predetermination" of situations,[83] their schemes remain inordinately removed from the lived experiences they reconstruct. Finally, accounting for rational action necessitates differentiating between fancying and projecting.[84]

In any scheme concerning choice, volition or "will" figures centrally, though often implicitly. In voluntaristic action theory, statements about recurrent actions imply that they derive from repeated *decisions* rather than from necessity.[85] Social scientists analyze recurrent types of action in terms of the constituent elements of the action itself *and* the volition of typical actors. The explanation of the type of action itself – for example, raising one's hand – assumes a profound difference between explaining an arm's rising and explaining the raising of an arm;[86] the latter presupposes volition. Human action is by definition free; it contrasts with fixed or mechanical responses. The *possibility* of action presupposes the *will* of an agent.[87] Although acts of practical intent or willing represent a distinctive type of intentionality, they nonetheless confirm the general findings about intentionality.[88] Significantly, they force attention, perhaps more than any other element of action, to the emotions. As Husserl indicated, emotional and volitional processes presuppose intentionality, but "all cultural objects, all values, all goods, all works can be experienced, understood, and made objects *as such* only through the participation of emotional and volitional consciousness."[89] Phenomenologically, the commonplace dichotomy between feeling and thought obfuscates the structural features of each; feeling is a way of meaning essentially related to cognitive formulations.[90] Yet social scientists neglect the emotions in their models of actors, action, and interaction. They largely focus on the instrumental-rational-voluntary at the expense of the emotional-imaginary-involuntary aspects of action.[91] In sociological reconstructions, the praxic heavily overshadows the pathic features of lived experience.

Recent efforts to incorporate the emotions into the sociological realm are important, though preliminary. The sociological relevance of the emotions is fairly obvious: The topics of socialization, social solidarity, social control, and conflict alone establish that relevance.[92] Some emotions might be conceptualized as "role-taking emotions" that presuppose putting one's self in another's place and adopting his or her perspective.[93] In more general terms, emotions relate in anticipatory and consequent ways to social interaction.[94] But the language pertinent to the emotions and willing is not, and perhaps cannot be, readily absorbed into the language of the theoretical attitude. All the same, whatever is rational about affect and volition rests on their expressibility.[95] To that extent, both features of human action can be approached through rational models of human action. Indeed, attention to the emotions and willing leads toward understanding that any model of human action presupposes a theory of expression and communication.

The idea of phenomenological sociology appeals for attention to all these fundamental features of human experience and action. It obviously appeals, too, for moving to the center of sociological discourse the topics of meaning, self, objectivation, experience, taken-for-grantedness, and essentially related matters. "Social action" conjoins those concerns. It is the root source of the questions and answers defining the idea of phenomenological sociology.

Space permits only briefly illustrating how the idea of phenomenological sociology might actually translate into practice. Such an illustration would require inordinate space were I to use an ethnomethodological example. Because of all that the typical ethnomethodological report neglects, I would end up virtually repeating much that I have just surveyed. Therefore, I return to the work of Kai T. Erikson, this time focusing on a study that postdates *Wayward Puritans*. Since they are ethnomethodologically relevant, both of Erikson's studies illustrate how a phenomenologically sensitive study differs from ethnomethodological studies of the same topics. In *Wayward Puritans* Erikson focused on deviance, a topic of variable but significant interest to ethnomethodologists; in *Everything in Its Path* he examined a disaster that created the kinds of incongruities ethnomethodologists often produce through breaching experiments. Moreover, both studies imply the problem of modern cultural crises and thus present themselves as fitting cases. With respect to *Everything in Its Path*, I will summarize its major points in phenomenological terms and then indicate where the phenomenological framework might have enhanced that study.

Everything in Its Path describes the flood that destroyed community in Buffalo Creek, West Virginia, in 1972. As in *Wayward Puritans*, Erikson's general concern lies with the subjective meaning of specific past events: "The purpose of this report is to try to convey what the Buffalo Creek flood meant to the people who lived through it and how it touched the course of their lives."[96] Because events are unique, understanding their subjective meaning demands knowing "something about who [their participants] were and where they came from, how they organized their lives and what they asked of the future. In this case, we need to locate the people of Buffalo Creek in the larger sweep of history and on the wider social and cultural map . . . " (p. 48). Immediate situations and the types that appear to govern them, in other terms, are inadequate bases for determining subjective meanings. Those data require a broader context for their valid interpretation. In order to understand the experiences people had during the flood and its aftermath, Erikson had to turn, then, to Appalachian social history, the types of biographies correlated with it, and the lifestyles that resulted. As in *Wayward Puritans*, Erikson's goals sensitized him to the limitations of predominant sociological perspectives and to the differences between the theoretical and natural attitudes.

Erikson confronted an event that seemed "much larger than the professional lens" sociology provided him. Moreover, traditional sociological methods seemed to impede his examination of discrete events in the "flow of human experience." He found himself reversing the typical course of sociological research by focusing on a catastrophic event: "The aim of any science . . . must be to move from particular observations to general findings, but there are times when the need for generalizations must yield to the urgency of passing events . . . " (p. 12). Throughout his report, Erikson negotiates a course between the particularities of the Buffalo Creek flood and the typified elements that connect it with other human disasters (pp. 247–248). That negotiation illuminated the theoretical attitude. Again, the close connection between that attitude and imagination surfaced. Recognizing his incapacity to comprehend the horrors of the flood itself, Erikson methodically applied his imagination by trying to reconstruct those parts of the event that "touch the senses" (p. 186) and, therefore, more or less transcend relative-natural worldviews. Similarly, Erikson confronted both the need for and the hazards of metaphors in imaginative reconstructions aimed at tapping subjective meaning (pp. 193–194). Finally, he imaginatively explored the fruitfulness of defining events as disasters if they induce trauma rather than using common-sense understandings to detect disasters and then citing trauma as one of their consequences. Erikson's explorations on that point imply the utility of the phenomenological method of free variation. Although his comments are careful and his insights imaginative, one senses that the method of free variation might have led to more refined insights and provided Erikson grounds for developing those insights in more pointed terms. He might thereby have burst the limits of his theoretical attitude and at the same time more precisely illustrated the differences between that attitude and the natural attitude.

Throughout his report, Erikson implicitly comments on the natural attitude, particularly the process of taking for granted it comprises and the familiarity it thus permits. Erikson views the Buffalo Creek survivors as victims "torn out of familiar neighborhoods" and frozen into a condition of extreme dislocation in trailer camps provided by the Department of Housing and Urban Development (p. 47). Those victims had once experienced communality as "part of the natural order of things": "It is just there, the envelope in which they live, and it is taken entirely for granted" (p. 187). Though difficult to describe in sociological abstractions, their communality was clearly a "state of mind"; it was a "quiet set of understandings that became absorbed into the atmosphere and are thus a part of the natural order" (p. 189).

Buffalo Creek communality built up over the generations and reflects the culture of Appalachia itself, where a distinctive style of living remained intact for about 130 years. That style assigned the family an extreme importance and the individual a wide measure of privacy within the pervasive communality that softened the harsh conditions Appalachians faced (pp. 53–59). Yet the culture of old Appalachia drew together all sorts of contradictions and strains (pp. 62, 71–72). Erikson refuses, however, to portray contradictions as a defining feature of Appalachian culture per se; they infuse every culture:

The identifying motifs of a culture are not just the core values to which people pay tribute but also the lines of point and counterpoint along which they diverge. That is, the term "culture" refers not only to the customary ways in which a people induce conformity in behavior and outlook but the customary ways in which they organize diversity. In this view, every human culture can be visualized, if only in part, as a kind of theater in which contrary tendencies are played out. (p. 82)

Thus one understands culture by watching the way people cope with the ambiguities their life-world subsumes (p. 250). Yet one must guard against attributing an undue amount of ambiguity to a specific culture, since the natural attitude itself, ungoverned by the strictures of formal logic, guarantees that every life-world proffers considerable ambiguity as the underside of its directives. At times, Erikson appears to assign culture and environment the leverage that belongs in part to the natural attitude. For example, he maintains that "the mountains evoke an immediacy of experience, a resort to action as opposed to reflection, a respect for feeling and sensation . . . " (p. 60), all ingredients of common-sense experience that the natural attitude comprises. Although some habitats may nurture or even exaggerate those features of mundane life, they do not by themselves originate them.

Again, language holds clues about specific life-worlds, including both the possibilities they bear and the actualities they support. Language offers the tools whereby individuals "edit reality" so that it becomes manageable and its perils are largely masked (p. 240). Significantly, the people of Buffalo Creek are "uncomfortable in those corners of the universe where words and symbols have replaced everyday experiences as the coin of intelligence" (p. 128). Although words cannot replace everyday experience, since they in fact make it possible, Erikson's observation is nonetheless important. In many respects, the people of Buffalo Creek acted with a paucity of linguistic resources. After the flood their experiences of disorientation, difficult to express under any circumstances, remained profoundly inexpressible because of their limited vocabulary. "Once one has said that one feels 'strange' and 'out of place,' one has almost exhausted the available vocabulary" (p. 211). Although the survivors did express their feelings in other ways, their experiences remained inchoate because the vocabulary that served them adequately in their taken-for-granted world was inadequate to the task of constituting another world on the basis of rubble and unfamiliarity. Unable to constitute coherent experience, the survivors literally stood alone, outside the boundaries of a shared, familiar world and with little hope of constituting such a world together. Unsurprisingly, their inner time-consciousness often warped: "Survivors often answer factual questions about time – their own age or their children's grade in school – as if history had indeed stopped on the date of the flood" (p. 211). In fact, for the survivors history had stopped, since their streams of experiences were unconnected to a set of subjectively meaningful types for ordering and integrating their experiences. In short, circumstances overwhelmed the survivors with a mass of incongruities.

The focus of *Everything in Its Path*, then, was a group of people dislodged from a familiar world, needing to reconstruct the types that had given shape and continuity to their experiences but lacking the retentions necessary for that mammoth task. More than *Wayward Puritans*, the topic of this study is a fertile one for in-depth phenomenological treatment, which space does not permit me. In Buffalo Creek, Erikson faced a set of subjects struggling to constitute familiarity out of the depths of strangeness; phenomenological findings about inner time-consciousness, longitudinal intentionality, typification, the stock of knowledge at hand, familiarity, language, identity, and objectivity provide for sharply disclosing the perplexing complexity of their situation. At the same time, the use of those findings in such a situation would reveal, as breaching experiments aim to, the idealizations that undergird a world people have the privilege of taking for granted.

My brief excursion into Erikson's studies illustrates, though only in general terms, what a philosophically grounded sociology means in practical terms. A phenomenological basis, specifically, means greater depth and clarity. It means greater analytical space in which to move and thus enlarged capacities to illuminate sociological objects of inquiry. It means, finally, renewed opportunities to fulfill the cultural responsibilities of the social sciences while developing a more rigorous, refined discipline.

Cultural crisis and the ideal
of phenomenological sociology

The most important lesson inherent in the idea of phenomenological sociology is that the fulfillment of sociology as a social *science* and the fulfillment of its cultural responsibilities are complementary enterprises. C. Wright Mills, among others, saw that, but most sociologists deem the two goals antagonistic or avoid the question of their relationship. In fact, the absence of explicit discussions of sociology's cultural promise derives, it seems, from assuming that that matter confounds activities properly associated with science, on the one hand, and the humanities, on the other hand. Moreover, sociologists are wont to assume that whatever cultural promise sociology bears is latent in the discipline and is best left so in the interest of the value-free pursuit of scientific knowledge about social reality.

The idea of phenomenological sociology challenges those notions. It insists that astute philosophical and empirical attention to social reality reveals that the social taken-for-real is given through – and only through – the activities of human beings in a world they prereflectively accept as real and shared. What we study as sociologists are the origins, consequences, meaning, structure, and dynamics of the sedimentations of human activities. Inescapably, we confront a subject matter that cannot be conceived apart from human activities. Thorough, rigorous investigations of that subject matter necessarily advance sociology as a science, illuminate the diverse achievements of common sense, and, therefore, expose the grounds of sociology itself as a social *and* scientific undertaking.

No science of social reality can advance using idealizations that virtually equate social reality with what is measurable, readily operationalized, and directly observable. Such a science would be a science of something other than social reality, perhaps a science of social matter-and-motion. Clearly we do not intend our discipline with that narrowness, though some of our commonplace activities evoke images along those lines. A science of social reality demands terms, definitions, idealizations, perspectives, and methods of data collection that consistently address, though in varying degrees, the diverse human activities that constitute our subject matter. The absence of such devices seriously incapacitates sociology as a science of social worlds.

Wider, more reflexive attention to the full spectrum of social reality would also disclose common sense as the consistent source of rich, credible achievements that originate science, philosophy, art, and all other worlds often contrasted with the world of daily life. The scientific illumination of social reality as a complex achievement of "ordinary," common-sense people cannot help but remediate the Crisis of Common Sense currently infecting mundane experience. To disclose the consistent potency of common sense and the beginnings of philosophy and social science (among other things) it contains is to check its contemporary denigration, at least among sociologists and their students.

The progression of sociology as a science and its positive illumination of common sense expose its reflexive relationship to its subject matter. Sociology is a set of instances of what it studies. Although the types of activities it comprises represent a specific partition of the common-sense world, sociology is nonetheless a social enterprise that addresses the social world that lodges it. Moreover, to some extent and in diverse ways the activities of sociologists, like those of all participants in the social world, help to constitute that world. What we say, how we say, and even why we say – as teachers, researchers, consultants, and culture critics – helps to make *our* world. And for phenomenological sociologists *our* world relentlessly invites rigorous attention and informed respect. *Our* world, too, reminds us that we sociologists participate in a common effort but, in addition, take on the responsibility of stepping back and elucidating that effort. In the stepping back lies a promise of return, an acknowledgment of the privilege accorded us to honor ourselves and others with the most precious of human accomplishments, understanding. Our privilege includes, in short, the opportunity to contribute to the restoration of faith in Reason.

Notes

Preface

1 Peter Berger, *Invitation to Sociology: A Humanistic Perspective*, New York, Anchor Books, 1963.

Introduction

1 Donald Vandenberg, *Being and Education: An Essay in Existentialist Phenomenology*, Englewood Cliffs, N.J., Prentice-Hall, 1971, p. 29.
2 In a letter to E. Parl Welch, Husserl asked that his philosophy *not* be referred to as a system; see Herbert Spiegelberg, "Husserl's Way into Phenomenology for Americans: A Letter and its Sequel," in F. Kersten and R. Zaner, eds., *Phenomenology: Continuation and Criticism*, The Hague, Nijhoff, 1973, pp. 179, 183.
3 Maurice Natanson, "Phenomenology as a Rigorous Science," *International Philosophical Quarterly* 7 (March 1967), 10.
4 Maurice Natanson, "A Study in Philosophy and the Social Sciences," in Maurice Natanson, ed., *Philosophy of the Social Sciences*, New York, Random House, 1963, p. 273.
5 Gaston Berger, *The Cogito in Husserl's Philosophy*, trans. Kathleen McLaughlin, Evanston, Ill., Northwestern University Press, 1972, p. 12.
6 James M. Edie, "Introduction," in *Cogito in Husserl's Philosophy*, p. ix.
7 Roderick M. Chisholm, "Editor's Introduction," in Roderick M. Chisholm, ed., *Realism and the Background of Phenomenology*, Glencoe, Ill., Free Press, 1960, p. 22; Nathaniel Lawrence and Daniel O'Connor, "The Primary Phenomenon: Human Existence," in Nathaniel Lawrence and Daniel O'Connor, eds., *Readings in Existential Phenomenology*, Englewood Cliffs, N.J., Prentice-Hall, 1967, p. 1; Joseph J. Kockelmans, "Theoretical Problems in Phenomenological Psychology," in Maurice Natanson, ed., *Phenomenology and the Social Sciences*, Evanston, Ill., Northwestern University Press, 1973, p. 245. For an overview of existentialist phenomenology, see Stephan Strasser, "Phenomenologies and Psychologies," in Lawrence and O'Connor, *Existential Phenomenology*, pp. 342–345.
8 Craib has demonstrated how Sartrean existentialism applies to sociological data interpretation, conceptualization, and explanatory efforts. See Ian Craib, *Existentialism and Sociology: A Study of Jean-Paul Sartre*, Cambridge, Cambridge University Press, 1976. For more general discussions see Edward A. Tiryakian, *Sociologism and Existentialism: Two Perspectives on the Individual and Society*, Englewood Cliffs, N.J., Prentice-Hall, 1962; Jack D. Douglas and John M. Johnson, eds., *Existential Sociology*, Cambridge, Cambridge University Press, 1977.
9 Natanson, "Phenomenology as a Rigorous Science," 16–17.
10 Lest Chapters 2 through 4 seem to imply an interpretive scheme, "beginning" merits further attention. "Beginning," according to Maurice Natanson, means "invading [Husserl's]

163

position and seizing it from within"; Natanson, *Edmund Husserl: Philosopher of Infinite Tasks*, Evanston, Ill., Northwestern University Press, 1973, p. 75. In the phenomenological findings surveyed in Chapters 2 through 4, then, beginners find *clues* for systematically investigating human experience. Those clues provide the preliminaries for undertaking one's own beginning.

1. The struggle toward critical unity in sociology

1 I intend something distinct from the incongruity between attitudes and behavior, sentiments and acts, or "what we say" and "what we do"; for a discussion of that problem, see Irwin Deutscher, *What We Say/What We Do: Sentiments and Acts*, Glenview, Ill., Scott, Foresman, 1973. I am referring to a gap between what an individual knows and what he or she can meaningfully do (or plan to do) on that basis.
2 Richard Sennett and Jonathan Cobb, *The Hidden Injuries of Class*, New York, Vintage Books, 1973, p. 191.
3 Robert Nisbet offers one of the most detailed expositions of the crisis of legitimacy; see his *Twilight of Authority*, New York, Oxford University Press, 1975. For complementary judgments based on different frames of reference, see Daniel J. Boorstin, *Democracy and its Discontents: Reflections on Everyday America*, New York, Random House, 1971; Claus Mueller, *The Politics of Communication: A Study in the Political Sociology of Language, Socialization, and Legitimation*, New York, Oxford University Press, 1975; Theodore Roszak, *Unfinished Animal: The Aquarian Frontier and the Evolution of Consciousness*, New York, Harper Colophon Books, 1977; and Philip Slater, *The Pursuit of Loneliness: American Culture at the Breaking Point*, Boston, Beacon Press, 1971.
4 Karl Marx, *Writings of the Young Marx on Philosophy and Society*, ed. and trans. Lloyd D. Easton and Kurt H. Guddat, Garden City, N.Y., Anchor, 1967, p. 214.
5 *Writings of the Young Marx*, p. 402; my italics.
6 Karl Marx, *Early Writings*, trans. and ed. T. B. Bottomore, New York, McGraw-Hill, 1964, p. 164.
7 *Writings of the Young Marx*, p. 72.
8 *Writings of the Young Marx*, p. 157.
9 *Writings of the Young Marx*, p. 401. The implication here corresponds to Sapir's contention that formulations that fail to meet the test of individuals' experiences have only transitory or technical authority. See Edward Sapir, *Culture, Language and Personality*, Berkeley, University of California Press, 1956, p. 178.
10 *Writings of the Young Marx*, p. 186.
11 *Writings of the Young Marx*, pp. 183, 185.
12 Max Weber, *The Theory of Social and Economic Organization*, trans. A. M. Henderson and Talcott Parsons, New York, Free Press, 1964, pp. 337, 339.
13 Max Weber, *From Max Weber: Essays in Sociology*, trans. and ed. H. H. Gerth and C. Wright Mills, New York, Oxford University Press, 1958, p. 233.
14 *Social and Economic Organization*, p. 339.
15 See Reinhard Bendix, *Max Weber: An Intellectual Portrait*, Garden City, N.Y., Anchor Books, 1962, pp. 285–328.
16 *Social and Economic Organization*, p. 338.
17 *Social and Economic Organization*, pp. 337, 339.
18 *From Max Weber*, pp. 140–141; 149. In other terms, people need a theory of everyday meanings that accounts for their real coherence; see Michael Polanyi and Harry Prosch, *Meaning*, Chicago, University of Chicago Press, 1975, p. 68.

19 Karl Mannheim, "American Sociology," in Maurice Stein and Arthur Vidich, eds., *Sociology on Trial*, Englewood Cliffs, N.J., Prentice-Hall, 1963, pp. 3–11.

20 Robert S. Lynd, *Knowledge for What? The Place of Social Science in American Culture*, New York, Grove Press, 1964, p. 181.

21 *Knowledge for What?*, p. 129.

22 C. Wright Mills, *The Sociological Imagination*, New York, Oxford University Press, 1959, p. 5; my italics.

23 *Sociological Imagination*, pp. 168–169.

24 *Sociological Imagination*, p. 34.

25 Early works in this area include Robert W. Friedrichs, *A Sociology of Sociology*, New York, Free Press, 1970; Larry T. Reynolds and Janice M. Reynolds, eds., *The Sociology of Sociology: Analysis of the Thought, Research, and Ethical Folkways of Sociology and its Practitioners*, New York, McKay, 1970.

26 See, for example, Peter Berger, *Invitation to Sociology: A Humanistic Perspective*, Garden City, N.Y., Anchor, 1973, Ch. 8; J. David Colfax and Jack L. Roach, eds., *Radical Sociology*, New York, Basic Books, 1971.

27 During this period concern with reason, rationality, and common sense *were* manifest in discussions of ideology, bias, and other topics related to the sociology of knowledge.

28 Alvin W. Gouldner, *The Coming Crisis of Western Sociology*, New York, Equinox Books, 1970, pp. 493–510.

29 Alvin W. Gouldner, *For Sociology: Renewal and Critique in Sociology Today*, New York, Basic Books, 1973, pp. 100–101.

30 *For Sociology*, p. 111.

31 *For Sociology*, p. 113.

32 Lewis A. Coser, "Presidential Address: Two Methods in Search of a Substance," *American Sociological Review* 40 (December 1975), 691.

33 Anthony Giddens, "Classical Social Theory and the Origins of Modern Sociology," *American Journal of Sociology* 81 (January 1976), 703.

34 Alfred McClung Lee, *Sociology for Whom?* New York, Oxford University Press, 1978.

35 Maurice Natanson, *Edmund Husserl: Philosopher of Infinite Tasks*, Evanston, Ill., Northwestern University Press, 1973, pp. 144, 161.

36 Eugene T. Gendlin, "Experiential Phenomenology," in Maurice Natanson, ed., *Phenomenology and the Social Sciences*, Evanston, Ill., Northwestern University Press, 1973, p. 287.

37 John E. Smith, "The Experience of the Holy and the Idea of God," in James M. Edie, ed., *Phenomenology in America*, Chicago, Quadrangle, 1967, p. 295; my italics.

38 Quentin Lauer, *Phenomenology: Its Genesis and Prospect*, New York, Harper Torchbooks, 1965, p. 77.

39 Maurice Natanson, *Literature, Philosophy, and the Social Sciences*, The Hague, Nijhoff, 1962, p. 9.

40 Natanson, *Husserl*, p. 16.

41 Felix Kaufmann, "Phenomenology and Logical Empiricism," in Marvin Farber, ed., *Philosophical Essays in Honor of Edmund Husserl*, New York, Greenwood Press, 1968, p. 131.

42 Edmund Husserl, *Phenomenology and the Crisis of Philosophy*, trans. Quentin Lauer, New York, Harper Torchbooks, 1965, p. 185.

43 Marvin Farber, *The Aims of Phenomenology: The Motives, Methods, and Impact of Husserl's Thought*, New York, Harper Torchbooks, 1966, p. 122; Maurice Natanson, "Phenomenology from the Natural Standpoint: A Reply to Van Meter Ames," *Philosophy and Phenomenological Research* XVII (December 1956), 243. Husserl's phenomenology attempts, then,

to consummate empiricism. See Ludwig Landgrebe, "The Phenomenological Concept of Experience," trans. Donn C. Welton, *Philosophy and Phenomenological Research* 34 (September 1973), 4.

44 Natanson, *Husserl*, p. 33.

45 Husserl, *Phenomenology and the Crisis of Philosophy*, p. 145.

46 Edmund Husserl, *The Crisis of European Sciences and Transcendental Phenomenology*, trans. David Carr, Evanston, Ill., Northwestern University Press, 1970; Natanson, *Husserl*, p. 143; Gian-Carlo Rota, "Edmund Husserl and the Reform of Logic," in David Carr and Edward S. Casey, eds., *Explorations in Phenomenology*, The Hague, Nijhoff, 1973, p. 301; cf. Stephan Strasser, *Phenomenology and the Human Sciences*, Pittsburgh, Duquesne University Press, 1963, p. 69.

47 Robert Sokolowski, *Husserlian Meditations: How Words Present Things*, Evanston, Ill., Northwestern University Press, 1974, p. 268.

48 Edmund Husserl, "Phenomenology," in Roderick Chisholm, ed., *Realism and the Background of Phenomenology*, trans. C. V. Solomon, Glencoe, Ill., Free Press, 1960, p. 127. For Husserl, a philosopher "was a self-thinker, a man who sought to give an ultimate account for all his thoughts and convictions, beginning with the basic problems of science . . . but extending to all the problems of human life, and a man for whom every uncontrollable and unproven conviction must appear as a loss of his own inner self-confidence." See Hans-Georg Gadamer, *Philosophical Hermeneutics*, trans. and ed. David E. Linge, Berkeley, University of California Press, 1976, p. 188.

49 Natanson, *Husserl*, p. 17.

50 Maurice Natanson, "Philosophy and Psychiatry," in Maurice Natanson, ed., *Psychiatry and Philosophy*, New York, Springer-Verlag, 1969, p. 86.

51 Kai T. Erikson, *Wayward Puritans: A Study in the Sociology of Deviance*, New York, Wiley, 1966, p. vi. Page references in the remainder of the chapter refer to this study.

2. Consciousness and constitution

1 Edmund Husserl, *Phenomenology and the Crisis of Philosophy*, trans. Quentin Lauer, New York, Harper Torchbooks, 1965, p. 89.

2 Edmund Husserl, *Cartesian Meditations: An Introduction to Phenomenology*, trans. Dorion Cairns, The Hague, Nijhoff, 1970, p. 59.

3 Aron Gurwitsch, *Studies in Phenomenology and Psychology*, Evanston, Ill., Northwestern University Press, 1966, p. 118.

4 Harmon M. Chapman, "Realism and Phenomenology," in John Wild, ed., *The Return to Reason*, Chicago, Regnery, 1953, p. 6.

5 Quentin Lauer, *Phenomenology: Its Genesis and Prospect*, New York, Harper Torchbooks, 1965, p. 5. Luijpen has articulated the same principles: "We cannot escape the simple truth that without human consciousness there *is* no world"; "without man there *is* nothing, since being always implies being-for-man." See William A. Luijpen, *Phenomenology and Humanism: A Primer in Existential Phenomenology*, Pittsburgh, Duquesne University Press, 1966, pp. 33, 35.

6 Edmund Husserl, *The Phenomenology of Internal Time-Consciousness*, ed. Martin Heidegger, trans. James S. Churchill, Bloomington, Indiana University Press, 1964, p. 28.

7 Aron Gurwitsch, "Some Fundamental Principles of Constitutive Phenomenology," in Lester Embree, ed., *Phenomenology and the Theory of Science*, Evanston, Ill., Northwestern University Press, 1974, p. 203.

8 Lauer, *Phenomenology*, p. 7.

9 Edmund Husserl, *Ideas: General Introduction to Pure Phenomenology*, trans. W. R. Boyce Gibson, New York, Collier, 1972, pp. 222, 373.

10 Husserl used "intention" in a broader and narrower sense. In the broader sense intentionality means that all consciousness is "consciousness of"; in the narrower sense it means that some acts of consciousness point toward their "fulfillment" in additional acts of consciousness (e.g., acts of thinking, doubting). For a discussion of Husserl's distinction, see J. N. Mohanty, *Edmund Husserl's Theory of Meaning*, The Hague, Nijhoff, 1969, pp. 45ff. Husserl's distinction indicates that not all intentional experience is qualitatively indistinguishable except by virtue of unique intentional objects.

11 Gerd Brand, "Intentionality, Reduction, and Intentional Analysis in Husserl's Later Manuscripts," in Joseph J. Kockelmans, ed., *Phenomenology*, Garden City, N.Y., Anchor Books, 1967, pp. 197–198.

12 Lauer, *Phenomenology*, p. 93.

13 Husserl, *Cartesian Meditations*, pp. 40, 36.

14 Gurwitsch, *Studies in Phenomenology*, pp. 332–334.

15 Edmund Husserl, *Experience and Judgment*, rev. and ed. Ludwig Landgrebe, trans. James S. Churchill and Karl Ameriks, Evanston, Ill., Northwestern University Press, 1973, p. 165.

16 Husserl, *Cartesian Meditations*, p. 45; also see Helmet Kuhn, "The Phenomenological Concept of 'Horizon,' " in Marvin Farber, ed., *Philosophical Essays in Memory of Edmund Husserl*, New York, Greenwood Press, 1968, p. 112; V. J. McGill, "Evidence in Husserl's Phenomenology," in F. Kersten and R. Zaner, eds., *Phenomenology: Continuation and Criticism*, The Hague, Nijhoff, 1973, p. 151.

17 Husserl, *Experience and Judgment*, pp. 360–361.

18 Husserl used "explicative contemplation" and "relational contemplation" to refer to those acts of consciousness concerning the initially given object and those going beyond it, respectively; see Husserl, *Experience and Judgment*, p. 149.

19 Maurice Natanson, *Edmund Husserl: Philosopher of Infinite Tasks*, Evanston, Ill., Northwestern University Press, 1973, p. 205.

20 Husserl, *Experience and Judgment*, p. 162; Kuhn, "Phenomenological Concept," p. 114. Also see Ernst Cassirer, *The Philosophy of Symbolic Forms, Volume Three: The Phenomenology of Knowledge*, trans. Peter Manheim, New Haven, Conn., Yale University Press, 1957, p. 167.

21 Husserl, *Experience and Judgment*, p. 254.

22 Robert Sokolowski, *The Formation of Husserl's Concept of Constitution*, The Hague, Nijhoff, 1970, p. 179; cf. Donald S. Lee, "The Construction of Empirical Concepts," *Philosophy and Phenomenological Research* 27 (December 1966), 188.

23 Husserl, *Experience and Judgment*, pp. 122, 124, 127, 331.

24 *Experience and Judgment*, p. 37.

25 *Experience and Judgment*, p. 38.

26 *Experience and Judgment*, p. 38.

27 Erwin W. Straus, "Psychiatry and Philosophy," in Maurice Natanson, ed., *Psychiatry and Philosophy*, New York, Springer-Verlag, 1969, p. 80.

28 Maurice Natanson, "Philosophy and Psychiatry," in Natanson, *Psychiatry and Philosophy*, p. 96. Whitehead has remarked that "one characteristic of the primary mode of conscious experience is its fusion of a large generality with an insistent particularity"; Alfred North Whitehead, *Modes of Thought*, New York, Free Press, 1968, p. 4; also see Aron Gurwitsch, "Perceptual Coherence as the Foundation of the Judgment of Predication," in Kersten and Zaner, eds., *Phenomenology*, p. 65.

29 Natanson, "Philosophy and Psychiatry," p. 97; cf. Husserl, *Experience and Judgment*, p. 332.
30 Herbert Spiegelberg, *The Phenomenological Movement*, vol. 1, The Hague, Nijhoff, 1960, p. 146; also see Gaston Berger, *The Cogito in Husserl's Philosophy*, trans. Kathleen McLaughlin, Evanston, Ill., Northwestern University Press, 1972, pp. 44–49; Joseph J. Kockelmans, *A First Introduction to Husserl's Phenomenology*, Pittsburgh, Duquesne University Press, 1967, pp. 201–202; J. N. Mohanty, "The 'Object' in Husserl's Phenomenology," *Philosophy and Phenomenological Research* 14 (March 1954), 348; Natanson, *Husserl*, pp. 93–94; Nathan Rotenstreich, "Ambiguities of Husserl's Notion of Constitution," in Dale Riepe, ed., *Phenomenology and Natural Existence*, Albany, State University of New York Press, 1973, pp. 151–170.
31 Husserl, *Phenomenology of Internal Time-Consciousness*, p. 152.
32 *Phenomenology of Internal Time-Consciousness*, pp. 152–153.
33 *Phenomenology of Internal Time-Consciousness*, pp. 106–108.
34 I thank Gilbert Schultz for offering the notion of intersection to describe the unity of transverse and longitudinal intentionality.
35 Husserl, *Ideas*, pp. 348–349.
36 Walter Biemel, "The Decisive Phases in the Development of Husserl's Philosophy," in R. O. Elveton, ed. and trans., *The Phenomenology of Husserl*, Chicago, Quadrangle, 1970, p. 158.
37 Husserl, *Ideas*, p. 391.
38 Husserl, *Cartesian Meditations*, p. 42.
39 Aron Gurwitsch, *The Field of Consciousness*, Pittsburgh, Duquesne University Press, 1964, p. 184.
40 Richard M. Zaner, *The Way of Phenomenology: Criticism as a Philosophical Discipline*, New York, Pegasus, 1970, p. 173; also see deMuralt, *The Idea of Phenomenology: Husserlian Exemplarism*, trans. Gary L. Breckon, Evanston, Ill., Northwestern University Press, 1974, p. 216.
41 For a detailed commentary on this standpoint, see Robert Sokolowski, *Husserlian Meditations: How Words Present Things*, Evanston, Ill., Northwestern University Press, 1974.
42 Phenomenologically, "origin" and its derivatives does not refer to temporal, historical, or chronological conditions. Rather, it concerns the conditions that make sense a possibility. The question of origins concerns the acts that must be experienced to account for the object as given, not acts actually experienced. See Aron Gurwitsch, "Some Fundamental Principles of Constitutive Phenomenology," in Embree, ed., *Phenomenology*, p. 194.
43 Speigelberg, *Phenomenological Movement*, vol. 1, p. 147.
44 Husserl, *Cartesian Meditations*, p. 77.
45 *Cartesian Meditations*, p. 77.
46 *Cartesian Meditations*, p. 37.
47 *Cartesian Meditations*, p. 40.
48 *Cartesian Meditations*, p. 46.
49 Sokolowski, *Husserl's Concept of Constitution*, p. 53. cf. Berger, *Cogito in Husserl's Philosophy*, p. 74; Alfred Schutz, *The Phenomenology of the Social World*, trans. George Walsh and Frederick Lehnert, Evanston, Ill., Northwestern University Press, 1967, p. 35.
50 Kockelmans, *First Introduction to Husserl's Phenomenology*, p. 223.
51 Lauer, "Introduction," in Husserl, *Phenomenology and the Crisis of Philosophy*, p. 55.
52 Quentin Lauer, "The Other Explained Intentionally," in Kockelmans, ed., *Phenomenology*, p. 168.

3. Experience, meaning, and the self

1 Lothar Eley, "Afterword to Husserl, *Experience and Judgment:* Phenomenology and Philosophy of Language," in Edmund Husserl, *Experience and Judgment: Investigations in a Genealogy of Logic*, Evanston, Ill., Northwestern University Press, 1973, p. 415.

2 Husserl, *Experience and Judgment*, p. 27.

3 *Experience and Judgment*, pp. 27–29.

4 Herbert Spiegelberg, *Doing Phenomenology: Essays on and in Phenomenology*, The Hague, Nijhoff, 1975, pp. 180–181.

5 Richard M. Zaner, *The Problem of Embodiment: Some Contributions to a Phenomenology of the Body*, The Hague, Nijhoff, 1971, p. 54.

6 Edmund Husserl, *Ideas: General Introduction to Pure Phenomenology*, trans. W. R. Boyce Gibson, New York, Collier, 1972, pp. 104–105, 109.

7 Husserl, *Experience and Judgment*, pp. 54–56.

8 William A. Sadler, Jr., *Existence & Love: A New Approach in Existential Phenomenology*, New York, Scribner, 1969, p. 35.

9 Donald S. Lee, "The Construction of Empirical Concepts," *Philosophy and Phenomenological Research* 27 (December 1966), 187.

10 Cf. Maurice Natanson, "Philosophy and Psychiatry," in Maurice Natanson, ed., *Psychiatry and Philosophy*, New York, Springer-Verlag, 1969, p. 90.

11 Sing-Nan Fen, "Situation as an Existential Unit of Experience," *Philosophy and Phenomenological Research* II (June 1951), 556; Paul Meadows, "The Dialectic of the Situation: Some Notes on Situational Psychology," *Philosophy and Phenomenological Research* 5 (March 1945), 356; cf. Alfred Schutz, *Reflections on the Problem of Relevance*, ed. and ann. Richard M. Zaner, New Haven, Conn., Yale University Press, 1970, pp. 135, 167. Spurling notes that, unlike "role," "situation" provides for both the commonality and individuality of concrete people; see Laurie Spurling, *Phenomenology and the Social World: The Philosophy of Merleau-Ponty and its Relation to the Social Sciences*, Boston, Routledge & Kegan Paul, 1977, p. 88.

12 Schutz, *Relevance*, p. 167.

13 Alfred Schutz and Thomas Luckmann, *The Structures of the Life-World*, trans. Richard M. Zaner and H. Tristram Engelhardt, Jr., Evanston, Ill., Northwestern University Press, 1973, pp. 23–24.

14 Schutz, *Relevance*, p. 133.

15 Alfred Schutz, *The Phenomenology of the Social World*, trans. George Walsh and Frederick Lehnert, Evanston, Ill., Northwestern University Press, 1967, p. 19.

16 James M. Edie, "Transcendental Phenomenology and Existentialism," *Philosophy and Phenomenological Research* 25 (September 1964), 62; Spiegelberg, *Doing Phenomenology*, p. 178.

17 Husserl, *Experience and Judgment*, p. 52.

18 Maurice Natanson, "Phenomenology as a Rigorous Science," *International Philosophical Quarterly* 7 (March 1967), 11.

19 W. H. Werkmeister, "On 'Describing a World,' " *Philosophy and Phenomenological Research* II (March 1951), 321; cf. Maurice Natanson, "Alienation and Social Role," *Social Research* 33 (Autumn 1966), 379.

20 Robert Sokolowski, *The Formation of Husserl's Concept of Constitution*, The Hague, Nijhoff, 1970, p. 161.

21 Here I adapt Natanson's idea that communication is essentially doomed to repeated interruptions and might be regarded as an "interruption between interruptions"; see Natanson, "Philosophy and Psychiatry," p. 102.

22 Sokolowski, *Husserl's Concept of Constitution*, p. 91.

23 Marvin Farber, "Experience and Transcendence: A Chapter in Recent Phenomenology and Existentialism," *Philosophy and Phenomenological Research* 12 (September 1951), 1.

24 Edmund Husserl, *Cartesian Meditations: An Introduction to Phenomenology*, trans. Dorion Cairns, The Hague, Nijhoff, 1970, p. 15.

25 Husserl, *Experience and Judgment*, p. 36.

26 Maurice Natanson, *Edmund Husserl: Philosopher of Infinite Tasks*, Evanston, Ill., Northwestern University Press, 1973, p. 25.

27 Maurice Natanson, *Phenomenology, Role, and Reason: Essays on the Coherence and Deformation of Social Reality*, Springfield, Ill., Thomas, 1974, p. 282.

28 Philip Pettit, *On the Idea of Phenomenology*, Dublin, Scepter, 1969, p. 59.

29 Husserl, *Experience and Judgment*, p. 276.

30 *Experience and Judgment*, p. 81.

31 Schutz, *Phenomenology of the Social World*, pp. 45, 75.

32 *Phenomenology of the Social World*, p. 82; my italics.

33 *Phenomenology of the Social World*, p. 84.

34 Schutz and Luckmann, *Structures*, p. 122.

35 Natanson, *Phenomenology, Role, and Reason*, p. 103.

36 Husserl, *Experience and Judgment*, p. 122.

37 Schutz and Luckmann, *Structures*, p. 232.

38 Schutz, *Relevance*, p. 27.

39 Cf. Schutz and Luckmann, *Structures*, p. 229.

40 See Maurice Natanson, "The Problem of Anonymity in the Thought of Alfred Schutz," in Joseph Bien, ed., *Phenomenology and the Social Sciences*, The Hague, Nijhoff, 1978, p. 67; Schutz and Luckmann, *Structures*, p. 237.

41 Natanson, *Husserl*, p. 140.

42 Husserl, *Experience and Judgment*, p. 331.

43 Maurice Natanson, "The Phenomenology of Alfred Schutz," *Inquiry* 9 (1966), 150.

44 Husserl, *Experience and Judgment*, p. 124.

45 Natanson, *Husserl*, p. 118; my italics.

46 Schutz, *Relevance*, p. 57.

47 *Relevance*, p. 57. Schutz and Luckmann's "personal type" and "functionary type" differentiate types according to concreteness and anonymity. The former derives from direct or indirect experiences of another person and has relatively full content; the latter concerns kinds of behavior and is highly anonymous, because its object is a social collectivity. See Schutz and Luckmann, *Structures*, pp. 80–83.

48 Natanson, *The Journeying Self*, Reading, Mass., Addison-Wesley, 1970, p. 107.

49 For a discussion of typicality and prediction see Schutz and Luckmann, *Structures*, pp. 238–241.

50 Schutz, *Relevance*, pp. 57–58.

51 Schutz and Luckmann, *Structures*, p. 231.

52 Familiarity is sufficient when an object of experience "can be 'concretely' determined with the aid of typifications at hand in the stock of knowledge, in order to deal with the plan-determined necessities of the situation." See *Structures*, p. 146.

53 *Structures*, p. 140.

54 *Structures*, pp. 7, 30.

55 Natanson, *Journeying Self*, p. 129; see also his "Problem of Anonymity," pp. 65–66.

56 Husserl, *Experience and Judgment*, p. 342.

57 Here I depart somewhat from Schutz but coincide, I think, with Husserl's thinking; cf. Schutz, *Relevance*, pp. 28–29.

58 Husserl, *Experience and Judgment*, pp. 340, 63.
59 Schutz and Luckmann, *Structures*, pp. 131–134.
60 Husserl, *Experience and Judgment*, pp. 72–73.
61 *Experience and Judgment*, p. 370.
62 Husserl, *Cartesian Meditations*, p. 33. This formulation suggests that meaning is a phenomenological preoccupation. In fact, phenomenological analyses are always to some extent meaning-analyses and Husserl's own first concern might be considered meaning. See Marvin Farber, "First Philosophy and the Problem of the World," *Philosophy and Phenomenological Research* 23 (March 1963), 330; E. Parl Welch, *Edmund Husserl's Phenomenology*, Los Angeles, The University of Southern California Press, 1939, p. 10.
63 James M. Edie, "Expression and Metaphor," *Philosophy and Phenomenological Research* 23 (June 1963), 544.
64 Paul Ricoeur, *Fallible Man: Philosophy of the Will*, trans. Charles Kelbley, Chicago, Regnery, 1965, p. 44; Isabel Stearns, "The Grounds of Knowledge," *Philosophy and Phenomenological Research* 2 (March 1942), 362–363.
65 Schutz, *Relevance*, p. 88.
66 Schutz, *Phenomenology of the Social World*, pp. 51–52.
67 Maurice Natanson, "Introduction," in Alfred Schutz, *Collected Papers I: The Problem of Social Reality*, ed. Maurice Natanson, The Hague, Nijhoff, 1973, p. xxxix.
68 Schutz, *Phenomenology of the Social World*, p. 70; also see p. 85.
69 *Phenomenology of the Social World*, p. 108; Schutz, *Relevance*, p. 82.
70 Husserl, *Ideas*, p. 140.
71 Husserl, *Cartesian Meditations*, p. 68. Here "constituted" should be read as "actively constituted" and "habituality" has some, though not exclusive, reference to "type."
72 Husserl, *Ideas*, p. 130.
73 Edith Stein, *On the Problem of Empathy*, trans. Waltraut Stein, The Hague, Nijhoff, 1964, pp. 36, 105.
74 Husserl, *Experience and Judgment*, p. 200.
75 Robert Sokolowski, *Husserlian Meditations: How Words Present Things*, Evanston, Ill., Northwestern University Press, 1974, p. 101.
76 Edie, "Transcendental Phenomenology and Existentialism," 55.
77 Quentin Lauer, *Phenomenology: Its Genesis and Prospect*, New York, Harper Torchbooks, 1965, p. 110.
78 Natanson, *Phenomenology, Role, and Reason*, p. 112.
79 Husserl, *Experience and Judgment*, p. 291.
80 Paul Ricoeur, "The Antinomy of Human Reality and the Problem of Philosophical Anthropology," in Nathaniel Lawrence and Daniel O'Connor, eds., *Readings in Existential Phenomenology*, Englewood Cliffs, N.J., Prentice-Hall, 1967, p. 401. Rabil has remarked that human beings are always "on the way." See Albert Rabil, Jr., *Merleau-Ponty: Existentialist of the Social World*, New York, Columbia University Press, 1967, p. 242.
81 Richard M. Zaner, "Awakening: Toward a Phenomenology of the Self," in F. J. Smith, ed., *Phenomenology in Perspective*, The Hague, Nijhoff, 1970, p. 171.
82 Husserl, *Experience and Judgment*, p. 66.
83 Working is "action in the outer world, based upon a project and characterized by the intention to bring about the projected state of affairs by bodily movement"; Schutz, *Collected Papers I*, pp. 212.
84 *Collected Papers I*, p. 216.
85 *Collected Papers I*, p. 212.
86 Schutz, *Phenomenology of the Social World*, p. 70.

4. The life-world

1 Edmund Husserl, *Experience and Judgment: Investigations in a Genealogy of Logic*, rev. and ed. Ludwig Landgrebe, trans. James S. Churchill and Karl Ameriks, Evanston, Ill., Northwestern University Press, 1973, p. 30.

2 Edmund Husserl, *The Crisis of European Sciences and Transcendental Phenomenology*, trans. David Carr, Evanston, Ill., Northwestern University Press, 1970, p. 48.

3 *Crisis of European Sciences*, p. 130.

4 Edmund Husserl, *Cartesian Meditations: An Introduction to Phenomenology*, trans. Dorion Carins, The Hague, Nijhoff, 1970, p. 153.

5 Calvin O. Schrag, "The Life-World and its Historical Horizon," in J. M. Edie et al., eds., *Patterns of the Life-World: Essays in Honor of John Wild*, trans. Kathleen McLaughlin, Evanston, Ill., Northwestern University Press, 1970, p. 113. The phenomenological question does not concern whether science or common sense is "superior," "higher," or "better"; Stephan Strasser, *Phenomenology and the Human Sciences*, Pittsburgh, Duquesne University Press, 1963, p. 71. The fundamental concern is their essential relationship and their common origins in the life-world; see Husserl, *Crisis of European Sciences*, pp. 379–383.

6 Husserl, *Crisis of European Sciences*, pp. 5–7.

7 Edmund Husserl, *Phenomenology and the Crisis of Philosophy*, trans. Quentin Lauer, New York, Harper Torchbooks, 1965, p. 191.

8 Maurice Natanson, *Phenomenology, Role, and Reason: Essays on the Coherence and Deformation of Social Reality*, Springfield, Ill., Thomas, 1974, p. 122.

9 Enzo Paci, "The 'Lebenswelt' as Ground and as 'Leib' in Husserl: Somatology, Psychology, Sociology" in Edie et al., eds., *Patterns of the Life-World*, p. 125.

10 Husserl, *Crisis of European Sciences*, p. 17.

11 Natanson has noted the essential with-in structure of lived experience; Maurice Natanson, "Philosophy and Psychiatry," in Maurice Natanson, ed., *Psychiatry and Philosophy*, New York, Springer-Verlag, 1969, p. 90.

12 Husserl, *Crisis of European Sciences*, pp. 104–105.

13 Husserl, *Experience and Judgment*, p. 41.

14 Alfred Schutz, *Reflections on the Problem of Relevance*, ed. and ann. Richard M. Zaner, New Haven, Conn., Yale University Press, 1970, p. 136.

15 Maurice Natanson, "Introduction," in Alfred Schutz, *Collected Papers I: The Problem of Social Reality*, ed. Maurice Natanson, The Hague, Nijhoff, 1973, p. xxvi.

16 Philip Pettit, *On the Idea of Phenomenology*, Dublin, Scepter, 1969, p. 79.

17 Husserl, *Phenomenology and the Crisis of Philosophy*, p. 150. "Life-world" is Husserl's means of conjoining sociality and intentionality; Margaret Chatterjee, "Language as Phenomenon," *Philosophy and Phenomenological Research* 30 (September 1969), 120.

18 Natanson, "Philosophy and Psychiatry," p. 95.

19 Werner Marx, "The Life-World and the Particular Sub-Worlds," in Maurice Natanson, ed., *Phenomenology and Social Reality*, The Hague, Nijhoff, 1970, p. 66. "Worlds" here is properly "sub-worlds." Regarding the appropriateness of "worlds," as implied by Husserl's studies, see Robert R. Ehman, "The Phenomenon of World," in Edie et al., eds., *Patterns of the Life-World*, pp. 85–106; Kersten, "The Life-World Revisited," *Research in Phenomenology* 1 (1971), 52; Stephan Strasser, *The Idea of Dialogal Phenomenology*, Pittsburgh, Duquesne University Press, 1969, pp. 24–26, 35–39. Also relevant is Luckmann's "small life-worlds" to refer to the multidimensional quality of contemporary mundane life; Benita Luckmann, "The Small Life-Worlds of Modern Man," in Thomas Luckmann, ed., *Phenomenology and Sociology: Selected Readings*, Har-

mondsworth, Middlesex, England, Penguin, 1978, pp. 275–290. "Finite provinces of meaning" strikes me as less problematic than terminology involving "world." Moreover, it stresses the axis of meaning in the life-world that lies at the core of phenomenological preoccupations.

20 Natanson, *Phenomenology, Role, and Reason*, p. 99.

21 Robert Sokolowski, *Husserlian Meditations: How Words Present Things*, Evanston, Ill., Northwestern University Press, 1974, p. 100.

22 Aron Gurwitsch, "Problems of the Life-World," in Natanson, ed., *Phenomenology and Social Reality*, pp. 53–54.

23 Husserl, *Experience and Judgment*, p. 50.

24 Sokolowski, *Husserlian Meditations*, p. 101.

25 Edmund Husserl, "Phenomenology," in Roderick M. Chisholm, ed., *Realism and the Background of Phenomenology*, trans. C. V. Solomon, Glencoe, Ill., Free Press, 1960, p. 124.

26 Husserl, "Phenomenology," p. 125.

27 I am aware that the stock of knowledge and social action are themselves structured through processes like socialization, objectivation, and institutionalization. However, phenomenologists treat both realities at a more fundamental level than sociologists do. The stock of knowledge includes primordial, prereflective givens that universally provide the grounds for mundane knowledge. And at the most fundamental level social action subsumes all human action insofar as the latter involves language. The stock of knowledge and social action are, first of all, realities that structure any life-world. At this level of analysis they must be regarded as structured by primordial givens that lie within the phenomenological rather than the sociological purview.

28 Alfred Schutz and Thomas Luckmann, *The Structures of the Life-World*, trans. Richard M. Zaner and H. Tristram Engelhardt, Jr., Evanston, Ill., Northwestern University Press, 1973, p. 4.

29 Husserl, *Experience and Judgment*, p. 298.

30 Edmund Husserl, *Ideas: General Introduction to Pure Phenomenology*, trans. W. R. Boyce Gibson, New York, Collier, 1972, p. 96. In other terms, "belief-in" founds "perception-of"; Giuseppina Chiara Moneta, "The Foundation of Predicative Experience and the Spontaneity of Consciousness," in Lester E. Embree, ed., *Life-World and Consciousness: Essays for Aron Gurwitsch*, Evanston, Ill., Northwestern University Press, 1972, p. 176.

31 Eugen Fink, "The Phenomenological Philosophy of Edmund Husserl and Contemporary Criticism," in *The Phenomenology of Husserl*, ed. and trans. R. O. Elveton, Chicago, Quadrangle, 1970, p. 108.

32 Rodman B. Webb, *The Presence of the Past: John Dewey and Alfred Schutz on the Genesis and Organization of Experience*, Gainesville, University Presses of Florida, 1976, p. 31.

33 Maurice Natanson, "The Phenomenology of Alfred Schutz," *Inquiry* 9 (1966), 149.

34 Alfred Schutz, *Collected Papers II: Studies in Social Theory*, ed. Arvid Brodersen, The Hague, Nijhoff, 1976, p. 231.

35 Alfred Schutz, *On Phenomenology and Social Relations*, ed. Helmut R. Wagner, Chicago, University of Chicago Press, 1970, p. 111.

36 Schutz, *Collected Papers I*, p. 326; Schutz and Luckmann, *Structures*, pp. 3–4.

37 Maurice Natanson, *Edmund Husserl: Philosopher of Infinite Tasks*, Evanston, Ill., Northwestern University Press, 1973, p. 70.

38 *Husserl*, pp. 122–123.

39 Schutz and Luckmann, *Structures*, p. 5.

40 *Structures*, pp. 59–60.

41 *Structures*, p. 94.

42 *Structures*, p. 6.

43 Edmund Husserl, *The Idea of Phenomenology*, trans. William P. Alston and George Nakhnikian, The Hague, Nijhoff, 1964, p. 15.

44 These ideas provide a basis for examining the notion of taken-for-grantedness. Earlier, I used "taken-for-granted" somewhat loosely, tending to denote what is prereflectively taken as adequately familiar. But the "adequately familiar" is so only *for now*. Thus the taken-for-granted can be intended reflectively when the course of lived experience occasions it. In addition, I noted that typification and routines generate taken-for-grantedness. Yet one is tempted to treat the fundamental elements of the stock of knowledge as taken-for-granted. They cannot, though, be reflectively intended within the life-world nor do they in toto presuppose typification and routinization. To label them as taken-for-granted alters the meaning of that phrase and suggests an experiential status the fundamental elements simply do not have; see my "Taken for Grantedness," *Current Perspectives on Social Theory: A Research Annual* 2 (1981), 133–151.

45 Schutz and Luckmann, *Structures*, pp. 103–105; Schutz, *Relevance*, p. 143.

46 *Relevance*, pp. 167–168.

47 Schutz and Luckmann, *Structures*, p. 179.

48 Schutz, *Relevance*, p. 76.

49 Schutz and Luckmann, *Structures*, p. 14.

50 *Structures*, pp. 243–244. The social stock of knowledge corresponds incompletely with the subjective stock of knowledge. It is historically and institutionally structured, depending only mediately on the essential features of subjectivity; "it cannot be directly derived from them"; *Structures*, p. 305.

51 *Structures*, p. 180.

52 *Structures*, p. 180.

53 For excellent formulations in this area, see Alfred Schutz, "Language, Language Disturbances, and the Texture of Consciousness," *Collected Papers I*, pp. 260–286; Alfred Schutz, "Symbol, Reality and Society, in *Collected Papers I*, pp. 287–356; also see Peter Berger and Thomas Luckmann, *The Social Construction of Reality: A Treatise in the Sociology of Knowledge*, Garden City, N.Y., Anchor, 1967, pp. 34–36; Schutz and Luckmann, *Structures*, pp. 278–282.

54 Berger and Luckmann, *Social Construction*, p. 38.

55 Schutz, *Collected Papers I*, p. 14; cf. Schutz, *On Phenomenology and Social Relations*, p. 117.

56 Schutz and Luckmann, *Structures*, p. 234.

57 *Structures*, p. 244.

58 *Structures*, pp. 282–284.

59 Phenomenology circumvents that loss by insisting that despite the empirical priority of objectivations particular subjective experiences nonetheless originate all objectivated constructions.

60 Husserl, *Cartesian Meditations*, pp. 152–153.

61 Quentin Lauer, *Phenomenology: Its Genesis and Prospect*, New York, Harper Torchbooks, 1965, p. 89.

62 Maurice Natanson, "Alfred Schutz on Social Reality and Social Science," in Natanson, ed., *Phenomenology and Social Reality*, p. 103.

63 Schutz, *Collected Papers II*, pp. 72–73.

64 Cf. Natanson, *Husserl*, p. 127.

65 Natanson, *Literature, Philosophy, and the Social Sciences*, p. 201.

66 Natanson, *Phenomenology, Role, and Reason*, p. 112; Alfred Schutz, "Parsons' Theory of Social Action: A Critical Review," in Richard Grathoff, ed., *The Theory of Social*

Action: The Correspondence of Alfred Schutz and Talcott Parsons, Bloomington, Indiana University Press, 1978, p. 56.
67 Maurice Natanson, "Phenomenology and the Social Sciences," in Natanson, ed., *Phenomenology and the Social Sciences*, p. 5.
68 Natanson, *Husserl*, p. 47.
69 Natanson, *Phenomenology, Role, and Reason*, p. 101.
70 *Phenomenology, Role, and Reason*, p. 101.
71 Cf. Natanson, *Husserl*, p. 127.
72 Schutz, *On Phenomenology and Social Relations*, p. 241.
73 Cf. John Ladd, "Reason and Practice," in John Wild, ed., *The Return to Reason*, Chicago, Regnery, 1953, pp. 235–258.
74 Schutz and Luckmann, *Structures*, p. 20.
75 *Structures*, pp. 23–28.
76 *Structures*, pp. 16–17.
77 *Structures*, p. 41.
78 In his earlier work, first published in 1932, Schutz conceptualized action as a subclass of behavior, the latter being "an experience of consciousness that bestows meaning through spontaneous Activity"; Alfred Schutz, *The Phenomenology of the Social World*, trans. George Walsh and Frederick Lehnert, Evanston, Ill., Northwestern University Press, 1967, pp. 55–56. Later, though, in a paper first published in 1945, Schutz adopted "conduct" rather than "behavior," a term he avoided by then "because it includes in present use also subjectively non-meaningful manifestations of spontaneity such as reflexes"; Schutz, *Collected Papers I*, p. 211. As Schutz used them, the two terms are largely interchangeable; for him "conduct" became the preferable term only as "behavior" was used more in the twentieth-century behavioristic sense.
79 Schutz, *Collected Papers I*, p. 211.
80 Schutz, *Phenomenology of the Social World*, pp. 144–146.
81 Schutz, *Collected Papers I*, p. 67.
82 Professor Maurice Natanson provided this insight in conversation on 5 August 1978.
83 Schutz, *Collected Papers I*, pp. 20, 67–68, 211–212; *Phenomenology of the Social World*, p. 57.
84 Natanson, "Introduction," p. xxiv.
85 I am indebted to Professor Maurice Natanson for this insight.
86 Schutz, *Collected Papers I*, pp. 19–20, 67.
87 Schutz, *Phenomenology of the Social World*, pp. 60–61.
88 Schutz, *Collected Papers I*, pp. 22, 69–72; *Phenomenology of the Social World*, pp. 91–94. In-order-to motives are integrated into "subjective systems of planning"; because-motives are grouped into systems related to "social personality"; Schutz, "Parsons' Theory of Social Action," p. 34.
89 Schutz, *Phenomenology of the Social World*, pp. 144–150.
90 *Phenomenology of the Social World*, p. 159. Thus the prototype of all social relationships is an "intersubjective concatenation of motives"; Schutz, "Parsons' Theory of Social Action," p. 54.
91 Schutz, *Phenomenology of the Social World*, pp. 167–172; Schutz and Luckmann, *Structures*, pp. 61–68.
92 Schutz, *Phenomenology of the Social World*, p. 179.
93 Schutz and Luckmann, *Structures*, p. 79.
94 Schutz, *Phenomenology of the Social World*, pp. 183–184.
95 *Phenomenology of the Social World*, p. 207.
96 Schutz and Luckmann, *Structures*, p. 91.

97 Schutz, *Phenomenology of the Social World*, p. 214.
98 *Phenomenology of the Social World*, pp. 135–136.
99 Schutz and Luckmann, *Structures*, pp. 36–38, 45–50.
100 I have left implicit the dynamic of knowing itself; it is *relevance*. As "obvious" subjective givens, systems of relevance determine the acquisition of knowledge and therefore the structure of habitual knowledge and specific components of that knowledge. In fact, they themselves are a component of the stock of knowledge; see Schutz and Luckmann, *Structures*, pp. 182–183. Relevance, for Schutz, results from the selective, interpretive activities inherent in experience; *Collected Papers I*, p. 5. Schutz treats "topical relevance," considered in both "intrinsic" and "imposed" forms, as the first form of relevance. The other two principal forms are "interpretive relevances" and "motivational relevances." The latter include the in-order-to relevances that emanate from an already established project and the because-relevances that concern the motivation for establishing the project itself. Schutz referred to motivational relevances as "interests" that are systematically interrelated, never isolated. Schutz detailed the interdependence of the three forms of relevance in discussions of how lived experiences, conduct, and action are constituted, how the stock of knowledge at hand is used to master actual experiences, and how experiences become sedimented as elements of the stock of knowledge. In addition, Schutz treated the social conditioning of the relevance structures. Finally, he indicated the major social-psychological and social-scientific implications of his theory of relevance, emphasizing its likely fruitfulness for understanding "value" and "intersubjective understanding" as well as social-scientific methodology. See Schutz, *Relevance*; Schutz and Luckmann, *Structures*, pp. 223–233; 252–261.

5. Phenomenological methods

1 Quentin Lauer, *Phenomenology: Its Genesis and Prospect*, New York, Harper Torchbooks, 1965, p. 137.
2 Edmund Husserl, *Phenomenology and the Crisis of Philosophy*, trans. Quentin Lauer, New York, Harper Torchbooks, 1965, p. 102.
3 In this methods-oriented context, Husserl's admonitions against presuppositions derive their fullest meaning. This context also provides a sure basis for understanding Husserl's comment about prejudice and description cited at the beginning of the Introduction.
4 Herbert Spiegelberg, *Doing Phenomenology: Essays on and in Phenomenology*, The Hague, Nijhoff, 1975, p. 187.
5 Maurice Natanson, *Literature, Philosophy, and the Social Sciences*, The Hague, Nijhoff, 1962, p. 14.
6 John O'Neill, "Introduction: Perception, Expression and History," in John O'Neill, ed., *Phenomenology, Language and Sociology: Selected Essays of Maurice Merleau-Ponty*, London, Heinemann, 1974, p. xxii.
7 Edmund Husserl, *Ideas: General Introduction to Pure Phenomenology*, trans. W. R. Boyce Gibson, New York, Collier, 1972, p. 83.
8 *Ideas*, p. 83.
9 Dorion Cairns, "An Approach to Phenomenology," in Marvin Farber, ed., *Philosophical Essays in Honor of Edmund Husserl*, New York, Greenwood Press, 1968, p. 4.
10 Eugen Fink, "What Does the Phenomenology of Edmund Husserl Want to Accomplish? (The Phenomenological Idea of Laying-a-Ground)," trans. Arthur Grugan, *Research in Phenomenology* II (1972), 26.
11 Hans P. Neisser, "The Phenomenological Approach in the Social Sciences," *Philosophy and Phenomenological Research* 20 (December 1959), 201.

12 Edmund Husserl, *The Idea of Phenomenology*, trans. William P. Alston and George Nakhnikian, The Hague, Nijhoff, 1964, p. 50.

13 Edmund Husserl, *Cartesian Meditations: An Introduction to Phenomenology*, trans. Dorion Cairns, The Hague, Nijhoff, 1970, p. 57.

14 Aron Gurwitsch, "Some Fundamental Principles of Constitutive Phenomenology," in Lester Embree, ed., *Phenomenology and the Theory of Science*, Evanston, Ill., Northwestern University Press, 1974, p. 198.

15 Edmund Husserl, "Phenomenology," in Roderick M. Chisholm, ed., *Realism and the Background of Phenomenology*, trans. C. V. Solomon, Glencoe, Ill., Free Press, 1960, p. 127.

16 For a clear, concise description of the epochē and reductions, see Lauer, *Phenomenology*, pp. 49–57. He describes six reductions that can be distinguished in Husserl's works.

17 Maurice Natanson, "Phenomenology from the Natural Standpoint: A Reply to Van Meter Ames," *Philosophy and Phenomenological Research* 17 (December 1956), 245.

18 Husserl, "Phenomenology," p. 121.

19 Edmund Husserl, "Phenomenology and Anthropology," in Chisholm, ed., *Realism*, p. 134.

20 Schutz's findings suggest a preparation for the phenomenological epochē in the "epochē of the natural attitude." In fact, "putting out of action" some doubts, beliefs, judgments, and feelings is commonplace in daily life. For example, "I do not 'forget' my friends when I am not thinking of them. They then belong to the unnoticed present horizon of my world. My love for them is living even when I am not living in it"; Edith Stein, *On the Problem of Empathy*, trans. Waltraut Stein, The Hague, Nijhoff, 1964, p. 69. Stein's example suggests a limited parallel between a naive epochē, a suspension the individual does not recognize as his or her accomplishment, and phenomenological epochē.

21 Husserl, *Ideas*, pp. 99–100.

22 *Ideas*, p. 98.

23 Lauer, *Phenomenology*, p. 49.

24 Joseph J. Kockelmans, *A First Introduction to Husserl's Phenomenology*, Pittsburgh, Duquesne University Press, 1967, pp. 161–162.

25 Maurice Natanson, *Edmund Husserl: Philosopher of Infinite Tasks*, Evanston, Ill., Northwestern University Press, 1973, p. 15.

26 Husserl, p. 57.

27 Eugen Fink, "The Phenomenological Philosophy of Edmund Husserl and Contemporary Criticism," in R. O. Elveton, ed., *The Phenomenology of Husserl*, Chicago, Quadrangle, 1970, p. 110.

28 Lauer, *Phenomenology*, p. 50.

29 Natanson, *Husserl*, p. 61; my italics.

30 *Husserl*, p. 78.

31 Husserl, *Cartesian Meditations*, p. 71.

32 Werner Marx, "The Life-World and the Particular Sub-Worlds," in Maurice Natanson, ed., *Phenomenology and Social Reality*, The Hague, Nijhoff, 1970, p. 68.

33 Spiegelberg, *Doing Phenomenology*, p. 123.

34 Edmund Husserl, *Experience and Judgment: Investigations in a Genealogy of Logic*, rev. and ed. Ludwig Landgrebe, trans. James C. Churchill and Karl Ameriks, Evanston, Ill., Northwestern University Press, 1973, pp. 347–348.

35 *Experience and Judgment*, p. 341.

36 Aron Gurwitsch, "The Phenomenological and the Psychological Approach to Consciousness," *Philosophy and Phenomenological Research* 15 (March 1955), 304.

37 Edmund Husserl, *The Crisis of European Sciences and Transcendental Phenomenology*, trans. David Carr, Evanston, Ill., Northwestern University Press, 1970, p. 186; my italics.

38 Husserl, *Crisis of European Sciences*, p. 186.

39 Aron Gurwitsch, "Problems of the Life-World," in Natanson, ed., *Phenomenology and Social Reality*, p. 44.

40 Fink, "Phenomenology of Edmund Husserl," 20.

41 Natanson, *Husserl*, pp. 74, 84.

42 Robert A. Gorman, *The Dual Vision: Alfred Schutz and the Myth of Phenomenological Social Science*, Boston, Routledge & Kegan Paul, 1977, p. 26.

43 Stein, *Empathy*, p. 4.

44 *Empathy*, p. 245.

45 Natanson, *Husserl*, p. 72.

46 Fink, "Phenomenology of Edmund Husserl," 25.

47 Natanson, *Husserl*, p. 159.

48 Here I switch to the singular form, since phenomenology has *a* method which, though analytically susceptible to procedural division, is for all practical purposes unitary.

49 Kockelmans, *First Introduction to Husserl's Phenomenology*, p. 175.

50 Farber, ed., *Essays*, p. 37.

51 Maurice Natanson, "Phenomenology as a Rigorous Science," *International Philosophical Quarterly* 7 (March 1967), 13–15.

52 Natanson, *Literature, Philosophy, and the Social Sciences*, p. 14.

53 Husserl, *Cartesian Meditations*, p. 79.

54 This is the title of Husserl's most programatically important essay. It is one of the two essays in Husserl, *Phenomenology and the Crisis of Philosophy*.

55 *Phenomenology and the Crisis of Philosophy*, p. 12.

56 *Phenomenology and the Crisis of Philosophy*, p. 57.

57 *Phenomenology and the Crisis of Philosophy*, p. 58.

58 *Phenomenology and the Crisis of Philosophy*, p. 59.

59 For an excellent summary of Husserl's theory of self-evidence, see Kockelmans, *First Introduction to Husserl's Phenomenology*, pp. 119–126.

60 Leon Shestov, "In Memory of a Great Philosopher: Edmund Husserl," *Philosophy and Phenomenological Research* 22 (June 1962), 458.

61 Husserl, *Experience and Judgment*, p. 19.

62 *Experience and Judgment*, p. 289.

63 Alfred Schutz, *Collected Papers I: The Problem of Social Reality*, ed. Maurice Natanson, The Hague, Nijhoff, 1973, p. 109.

64 Husserl, *Idea of Phenomenology*, p. 40.

65 Natanson, "Phenomenology from the Natural Standpoint," 243.

66 The criterion of adequacy is the closest phenomenological approximation of the naturalistic concept of error; Henry Winthrop, "The Constitution of Error in the Phenomenological Reduction," *Philosophy and Phenomenological Research* 9 (June 1949), 743.

67 Richard M. Zaner, "Reflections on Evidence and Criticism in the Theory of Consciousness," in D. Carr and E. Casey, eds., *Explorations in Phenomenology*, The Hague, Nijhoff, 1973, p. 207.

6. Ethnomethodology: an alternative sociology?

1 George Psathas, "Introduction," in George Psathas, ed., *Phenomenological Sociology*, New York, Wiley, 1973, pp. 2–3. Concerning Weber's relationship to the phenomenological

perspective, also see Helmut R. Wagner, "Sociologists of Phenomenological Orientations: Their Place in American Sociology," *American Sociologist* 10 (August 1975), 179.

2 Harold Garfinkel, The Perception of the Other: A Study in Social Order, PhD. diss., Harvard University, 1952, p. 24.

3 Perception of the Other, p. 31. The four postulates – of relevance, subjective interpretation, adequacy, and rationality – are available in Alfred Schutz, *Collected Papers II: Studies in Social Theory*, ed. Arvid Brodersen, The Hague, Nijhoff, 1976, pp. 84–87.

4 *Collected Papers II*, p. 45.

5 Harold Garfinkel, "A Conception of, and Experiments with, 'Trust' as a Condition of Stable, Concerted Actions," in O. J. Harvey, ed., *Motivation and Social Interaction*, New York, Ronald Press, 1963, p. 210.

6 "Conception," pp. 210–214.

7 "Conception," p. 217.

8 "Conception," p. 217.

9 "Conception," p. 218. Garfinkel has altered the thrust of Schutz's thinking on this point but does not specify that he is adapting Schutz's thinking to his own purposes.

10 "Conception," p. 238.

11 Harold Garfinkel, *Studies in Ethnomethodology*, Englewood Cliffs, N.J., Prentice-Hall, 1967, p. ix.

12 *Studies in Ethnomethodology*, p. 36.

13 *Studies in Ethnomethodology*, p. 37. Here again, Garfinkel has altered Schutz's ideas. He equates "background expectancies," seen but unnoticed, with the "attitude of daily life" and cites Schutz. He also uses "scenic attributions" with reference to Schutz's thinking and attributes "world in common and taken for granted" to him. The translation from Schutz's to Garfinkel's terminology makes it difficult to interpret the precise relation of Schutz's ideas to Garfinkel's.

14 *Studies in Ethnomethodology*, pp. 55–56.

15 Harold Garfinkel and Harvey Sacks, "On Formal Structures of Practical Actions," in J. C. McKinney and E. A. Tiryakian, eds., *Theoretical Sociology*, New York, Appleton-Century-Crofts, 1970, p. 342.

16 "On Formal Structures," p. 348.

17 Aaron V. Cicourel, "Basic and Normative Rules in the Negotiation of Status and Role," in David Sudnow, ed., *Studies in Social Interaction*, New York, Free Press, 1972, pp. 250–252. For brief comments on the relationship between Garfinkel and Cicourel and, more generally, on the intellectual and social relationships among ethnomethodologists, see Nicholas C. Mullins, *Theories and Theory Groups in Contemporary American Sociology*, New York, Harper & Row, 1973, pp. 193–194.

18 Mullins, *Theories and Theory Groups*, p. 187.

19 Garfinkel, Perception of the Other, pp. 1, 82.

20 Mullins, *Theories and Theory Groups*, p. 185.

21 Paul Filmer, "On Harold Garfinkel's Ethnomethodology," in Paul Filmer, Michael Phillipson, David Silverman, and David Walsh, *New Directions in Sociological Theory*, Cambridge, Mass., MIT Press, 1972, p. 218.

22 Richard Grathoff, "Introduction," in Richard Grathoff, ed., *The Theory of Social Action: The Correspondence of Alfred Schutz and Talcott Parsons*, Bloomington, Indiana University Press, 1978, pp. xxi–xxii.

23 Talcott Parsons, "Talcott Parsons: A 1974 Retrospective Perspective," in Grathoff, ed., *Correspondence*, p. 123.

24 Maurice Natanson, *The Social Dynamics of George H. Mead*, The Hague, Nijhoff, 1973 (originally published by Public Affairs Press, Washington, D.C., 1956).

25 Peter Dreitzel, "Introduction: Patterns of Communicative Behavior," in Peter Dreitzel, ed., *Recent Sociology No. 2: Patterns of Communicative Behavior*, New York, Macmillan, 1970, pp. vii–viii; cf. Irwin Deutscher, *What We Say/What We Do: Sentiments and Acts*, Glenview, Ill., Scott, Foresman, 1973, p. 326.

26 Doyle Paul Johnson, *Sociological Theory: Classical Founders and Contemporary Perspectives*, New York, Wiley, 1981, p. 293.

27 Randall Collins, *Conflict Sociology: Toward an Explanatory Science*, New York, Academic Press, 1975, p. 30.

28 Kenneth Leiter, *A Primer on Ethnomethodology*, New York, Oxford University Press, 1980, p. 185.

29 Jack D. Douglas, "Understanding Everyday Life," in Jack Douglas, ed., *Understanding Everyday Life*, Chicago, Aldine, 1970, p. 17; cf. Norman Denzin, "Symbolic Interactionism and Ethnomethodology," in Douglas, ed., *Understanding Everyday Life*, pp. 259–284.

30 Ruth A. Wallace and Alison Wolf, *Contemporary Sociological Theory*, Englewood Cliffs, N.J., Prentice-Hall, 1980, p. 280; cf. Johnson, *Sociological Theory*, p. 340.

31 Charles C. Lemert, "De-Centered Analysis: Ethnomethodology and Structuralism," *Theory and Society* 7 (May 1979), 298.

32 Michael Phillipson, "Phenomenological Philosophy and Sociology," in Filmer et al., *New Directions*, p. 127.

33 William W. Mayrl, "Ethnomethodology: Sociology without Society?" in F. R. Dallmayr and T. A. McCarthy, eds., *Understanding and Social Inquiry*, Notre Dame, Ind., University of Notre Dame Press, 1977, pp. 274–276. Nonetheless, as Wagner has indicated, symbolic interactionism is more closely related to the phenomenological perspective than any other approach in American sociology; see Wagner, "Sociologists," 180.

34 Monica B. Morris, *An Excursion into Creative Sociology*, New York, Columbia University Press, 1977, p. 49.

35 Aaron V. Cicourel, "Delinquency and Attribution of Responsibility," in R. A. Scott and J. D. Douglas, eds., *Theoretical Perspectives on Deviance*, New York, Basic Books, 1972, pp. 142–157; Melvin Pollner, "Sociological and Common-Sense Models of the Labeling Process," in Roy Turner, ed., *Ethnomethodology*, Baltimore, Penguin, 1974, pp. 27–40.

36 Carol A. B. Warren and John M. Johnson, "A Critique of Labeling Theory from the Phenomenological Perspective," in Scott and Douglas, eds., *Theoretical Perspectives on Deviance*, pp. 69–92.

37 Melvin Pollner, "Constitutive and Mundane Versions of Labeling Theory," *Human Studies* 1 (July 1978), 269–270.

38 Douglas, "Understanding Everyday Life," pp. 21, 35–36. Giddens argues that in Garfinkel's work the opposition between "naturalism" and the "hermeneutic circle" remain unreconciled; Anthony Giddens, *New Rules of Sociological Method: A Positive Critique of Interpretative Sociologies*, New York, Basic Books, 1976, p. 52. Ironically, Thio labels Matza a phenomenologist; see Alex Thio, "The Phenomenological Perspective of Deviance," *American Sociologist* 9 (August 1974), 146.

39 Douglas, "Understanding Everyday Life," pp. 19–20; Marvin Farber, "The Ideal of a Presuppositionless Philosophy," in Marvin Farber, ed., *Philosophical Essays in Memory of Edmund Husserl*, New York, Greenwood Press, 1968, pp. 44–64.

40 Paul Attewell, "Ethnomethodology since Garfinkel," *Theory and Society* 1 (1974), 179–182.

41 Mullins, *Theories and Theory Groups*, p. 187.

42 Leiter, *Primer on Ethnomethodology*, pp. 65–66.

43 Hugh Mehan and Houston Wood, *The Reality of Ethnomethodology*, New York, Wiley-Interscience, 1975, pp. 18, 206–207.

44 Psathas contends that Garfinkel's formulation remains the foundation of ethnomethodology; analyses of his works expose the major assumptions and dimensions of ethnomethodology. Thus expositions and interpretations of Garfinkel's work are largely applicable to ethnomethodology in general. I abide by Psathas's judgment throughout and assume that I can generalize my comments – and others' – regarding Garfinkel's work to ethnomethodology without betraying the diversity within that perspective. See George Psathas, "Approaches to the Study of the World of Everyday Life," *Human Studies* 3 (January 1980), 3.

45 Garfinkel, *Studies in Ethnomethodology*, p. 1.

46 Harold Garfinkel, in R. J. Hill and K. S. Crittenden, eds., *Proceedings of the Purdue Symposium on Ethnomethodology*, Lafayette, Ind., Purdue University, Institute for the Study of Social Change, 1968, p. 198.

47 Fred R. Dallmayr, "Phenomenology and Social Science: An Overview and Appraisal," in D. Carr and E. S. Casey, eds., *Explorations in Phenomenology*, The Hague, Nijhoff, 1973, p. 157.

48 Wesley W. Sharrock and Roy Turner, "Observation, Esoteric Knowledge, and Automobiles," *Human Studies* 3 (January 1980), 28.

49 Filmer, "On Harold Garfinkel's Ethnomethodology," pp. 206–210.

50 Psathas, "Approaches," 16.

51 David Sudnow, in Hill and Crittenden, *Proceedings*, p. 51.

52 Harold Garfinkel, "The Origins of the Term 'Ethnomethodology,' " in Turner, ed., *Ethnomethodology*, p. 18.

53 Jeff Coulter, "Beliefs and Practical Understanding," in George Psathas, ed., *Everyday Language: Studies in Ethnomethodology*, New York, Irvington, 1979, pp. 165–166.

54 Leiter, *Primer on Ethnomethodology*, pp. 15–17.

55 Psathas, "Approaches," 15.

56 Garfinkel, in Hill and Crittenden, *Proceedings*, p. 13.

57 Mayrl, "Ethnomethodology," p. 268. Morris contends that Garfinkel's interest is in the *structure* of daily life and that he has denied interest in the social construction of reality; Morris, *Creative Sociology*, p. 91.

58 Leiter, *Primer on Ethnomethodology*, pp. 21, 98.

59 Garfinkel, *Studies in Ethnomethodology*, p. viii.

60 Coulter, "Beliefs and Practical Understanding," pp. 166–167.

61 "Beliefs and Practical Understanding," pp. 168–171; Charles Goodwin, "The Interactive Construction of a Sentence in Natural Conversation," in Psathas, ed., *Everyday Language*, p. 110; J. C. Heritage and D. R. Watson, "Formulations as Conversational Objects," in *Everyday Language*, p. 153; Melvin Pollner, "Explicative Transactions: Making and Managing Meaning in Traffic Court," in *Everyday Language*, p. 235.

62 Roy Turner, "Introduction," in Turner, ed., *Ethnomethodology*, p. 11.

63 Emmanuel Schegloff and Harvey Sacks, "Opening Up Closings," in *Ethnomethodology*, p. 233.

64 John O'Neill, *Making Sense Together: An Introduction to Wild Sociology*, New York, Harper & Row, 1974, p. 20.

65 Jack D. Douglas, "Deviance and Order in a Pluralistic Society," in McKinney and Tiryakian, eds., *Theoretical Sociology*, p. 376.

66 For the most radical delineation of the necessary shifts in theory construction, see Alan F. Blum, "Positive Thinking," *Theory and Society* 1 (Fall 1974), 245–269; Alan F. Blum, *Theorizing*, London, Heinemann Educational Books, 1974. Blum, though, no longer

considers himself an ethnomethodologist; Attewell, "Ethnomethodology since Garfinkel," 208.

67 Mehan and Wood, *Reality of Ethnomethodology*, p. 225. These authors state that ethnomethodology uses the scientific idiom but aims to transcend the scientific worldview in the process.
68 *Reality of Ethnomethodology*, p. 65.
69 *Reality of Ethnomethodology*, p. 211.
70 *Reality of Ethnomethodology*, p. 44.
71 *Reality of Ethnomethodology*, p. 51. Yet in their study Hadden and Lester used interviews with musicians taken from jazz magazines; see Stuart C. Hadden and Marilyn Lester, "Talking Identity: The Production of 'Self' in Interaction," *Human Studies* 1 (October 1978), 331–356. Also noteworthy here is Zimmerman and Wieder's advocacy of a "diary: diary-interview method" that undercuts the limitations of direct observation. The "diary" is an annotated, chronological record that can serve as a basis for intensive interviews; see Don H. Zimmerman and D. Lawrence Wieder, "The Diary: Diary-Interview Method," *Urban Life* 5 (January 1977), 479–498.
72 *Reality of Ethnomethodology*, p. 5.
73 *Reality of Ethnomethodology*, pp. 11–12.
74 *Reality of Ethnomethodology*, p. 12.
75 Pollner, "Sociological and Common-Sense Models," p. 27.
76 Garfinkel and Sacks, "On Formal Structures," p. 353.
77 Garfinkel, *Studies in Ethnomethodology*, p. 103.
78 Filmer, "On Harold Garfinkel's Ethnomethodology," p. 216.
79 Thomas P. Wilson, "Normative and Interpretive Paradigms in Sociology," in Douglas, ed., *Understanding Everyday Life*, p. 59.
80 Don H. Zimmerman, "The Practicalities of Rule Use," in *Understanding Everyday Life*, p. 223.
81 Mehan and Wood, *Reality of Ethnomethodology*, p. 74.
82 Don H. Zimmerman, "Tasks and Troubles: The Practical Bases of Work Activities in a Public Assistance Organization," in Donald A. Hansen, ed., *Explorations in Sociology and Counseling*, Boston, Houghton Mifflin, 1969, p. 264.
83 Aaron V. Cicourel, *Cognitive Sociology: Language and Meaning in Social Interaction*, Baltimore, Penguin, 1973, p. 80.
84 Roy Turner, "Words, Utterances and Activities," in Turner, ed., *Ethnomethodology*, p. 197.
85 Turner, "Introduction," p. 10.
86 Mehan and Wood, *Reality of Ethnomethodology*, p. 198.
87 Cicourel, *Cognitive Sociology*, p. 45. Thus the ethnomethodological perspective implies that conventional sociologies adopt an "over-socialized" conception of human beings; Denis Gleeson and Michael Erben, "Meaning in Context: Notes toward a Cirtique of Ethnomethodology," *British Journal of Sociology* 27 (December 1976), 476.
88 Cicourel, "Basic and Normative Rules," p. 233.
89 Mehan and Wood, *Reality of Ethnomethodology*, p. 66.
90 Garfinkel, Perception of the Other, pp. 222.
91 Alfred Schutz, *Collected Papers I: The Problem of Social Reality*. ed. Maurice Natanson, The Hague, Nijhoff, 1973, p. 42.
92 Garfinkel, Perception of the Other, p. 43.
93 Blum, *Theorizing*, p. 233.
94 Harold Garfinkel, "Studies of the Routine Grounds of Everyday Activities," in Sudnow, ed., *Studies in Social Interaction*, p. 24.

95 Turner, "Introduction," p. 10.

96 Blum, *Theorizing*, p. 238.

97 Garfinkel, "Studies of the Routine Grounds," p. 30; my italics. Garfinkel also refers to members' "doing" ethnographies; Garfinkel, *Studies in Ethnomethodology*, p. 10. Wieder claims that members' "use of ethnographies" reveals appearances of order as ongoing accomplishments. He also refers to members as "folk sociologists." See D. Lawrence Wieder, *Language and Social Reality: The Case of Telling the Convict Code*, The Hague, Mouton, 1974, pp. 43, 132.

98 Don H. Zimmerman and Melvin Pollner, "The Everyday World as a Phenomenon," in Douglas, ed., *Understanding Everyday Life*, p. 82.

99 Alan F. Blum, "The Corpus of Knowledge as a Normative Order: Intellectual Critiques of the Social Order of Knowledge and the Commonsense Features of Bodies of Knowledge," in McKinney and Tiryakian, eds., *Theoretical Sociology*, p. 334.

100 Turner, "Words, Utterances and Activities," p. 204.

101 W. W. Sharrock, "On Owning Knowledge," in Turner, ed., *Ethnomethodology*, p. 46.

102 Cicourel, *Cognitive Sociology*, p. 84.

103 Jack D. Douglas, "Deviance and Respectability: The Social Construction of Moral Meanings," in Jack Douglas, ed., *Deviance and Respectability: The Social Construction of Moral Meanings*, New York, Basic Books, 1970, pp. 6–7.

104 Douglas, "Understanding Everyday Life," p. 4.

105 Zimmerman and Pollner, "Everyday World," p. 81.

106 Garfinkel, *Studies in Ethnomethodology*, pp. 99–100.

107 Blum, *Theorizing*, p. 58.

108 Turner, "Introduction," pp. 7–8.

109 Schutz, *Collected Papers II*, p. 59.

110 Filmer, "On Harold Garfinkel's Ethnomethodology," p. 216.

111 Garfinkel and Sacks, "On Formal Structures," p. 361.

112 "On Formal Structures," pp. 345–346.

113 Edward A. Tiryakian, "Structural Sociology," in McKinney and Tiryakian, eds., *Theoretical Sociology*, p. 125.

114 Peter McHugh, *Defining the Situation: The Organization of Meaning in Social Interaction*, Indianapolis, Bobbs-Merrill, 1968, p. 11.

115 Douglas, "Deviance and Respectability," p. 11.

116 "Deviance and Respectability," p. 5.

117 "Deviance and Respectability," p. 5.

118 Filmer, "On Harold Garfinkel's Ethnomethodology," p. 228.

119 Mehan and Wood, *Reality of Ethnomethodology*, p. 6; Garfinkel, in Hill and Crittenden, eds., *Proceedings*, p. 17.

120 Harvey Sacks, in Hill and Crittenden, eds., *Proceedings*, p. 200.

121 At this point I must distinguish two overlapping but distinct groupings of ethnomethodologists. "Situational ethnomethodologists" focus on contextual meanings and social interaction; language is only one of their principal concerns. "Linguistic ethnomethodologists" focus on conversation, using recorded conversations as their principal data. See Douglas, "Understanding Everyday Life," pp. 33–34. Although the two groups share the critique of traditional sociology just delineated, they tend not to share the same research focuses. The latter grouping, for example, offers a version of sociolinguistics. The presuppositions I am about to discuss are those most situational ethnomethodologists adopt. From this point the discussion focuses on their work (except where noted), since members of that grouping are likelier to cite or imply a phenomenological dimension in their work.

122 Alan F. Blum, "Sociology, Wrongdoing, and Akrasia: An Attempt to Think Greek about the Problem of Theory and Practice," in Scott and Douglas, eds., *Theoretical Perspectives on Deviance*, p. 351.

123 Ian Craib, *Existentialism and Sociology: A Study of Jean-Paul Sartre*, New York, Cambridge University Press, 1976, p. 62.

124 Douglas, "Understanding Everyday Life," p. 37.

125 James L. Heap, "Description in Ethnomethodology," *Human Studies* 3 (January 1980), 89.

126 Heritage and Watson, "Formulations," p. 136.

127 Richard A. Hilbert, "Approaching Reason's Edge: 'Nonsense' as the Final Solution to the Problem of Meaning," *Sociological Inquiry* 47, No. 1 (1977), 25.

128 The ethnomethodological conception of reflexivity might also radicalize Austin's "performatives" and "doing things with words"; see Laurie Spurling, *Phenomenology and the Social World: The Philosophy of Merleau-Ponty and its Relation to the Social Sciences*, Boston, Routledge & Kegan Paul, 1977, p. 65.

129 Garfinkel, in Hill and Crittenden, eds., *Proceedings*, pp. 207–208.

130 *Proceedings*, p. 206.

131 *Proceedings*, p. 208.

132 *Proceedings*, p. 173. Reflexivity does not imply intent. The practical procedures of interaction, which Garfinkel deems "reflexivities," are "nobody's serious business," even when affairs at hand need attention. Reflexivities are ignored and glossed, insistently so when necessary. See Garfinkel, in *Proceedings*, p. 208.

133 Garfinkel, in *Proceedings*, p. 13.

134 Craib, *Sartre*, p. 61.

135 Attewell, "Ethnomethodology since Garfinkel," 183.

136 Garfinkel, *Studies in Ethnomethodology*, p. 1; my italics.

137 Douglas, "Understanding Everyday Life," p. 37.

138 Egon Bittner, "Objectivity and Realism in Sociology," in George Psathas, ed., *Phenomenological Sociology*, New York, Wiley, 1973, p. 115.

139 Wilson, "Normative and Interpretive Paradigms," pp. 66–67.

140 Cicourel, *Cognitive Sociology*, p. 167. "Cross-modal" refers to the tendency for exchanges to instruct all the participants in the exchange, including the speaker.

141 Attewell, "Ethnomethodology since Garfinkel," 185.

142 "Ethnomethodology since Garfinkel," 185.

143 Mehan and Wood, *Reality of Ethnomethodology*, p. 90.

144 Bittner, "Objectivity and Realism," p. 116.

145 Don H. Zimmerman, "A Reply to Professor Coser," *American Sociologist* 11 (February 1976), 10.

146 Dreitzel, "Introduction," p. xv.

147 Douglas, "Deviance and Respectability," p. 13.

148 Filmer, "On Harold Garfinkel's Ethnomethodology," pp. 222–223.

149 Garfinkel and Sacks, "On Formal Structures," pp. 338, 349.

150 Mehan and Wood, *Reality of Ethnomethodology*, p. 94.

151 Garfinkel and Sacks, "On Formal Structures," p. 349.

152 Blum, "Corpus of Knowledge," p. 333.

153 See, for example, Cicourel, *Cognitive Sociology*, p. 256; Jack D. Douglas, "The Experience of the Absurd and the Problem of Social Order," in Scott and Douglas, eds., *Theoretical Perspectives on Deviance*, pp. 203, 211; Garfinkel, Perception of the Other, pp. 33–34.

154. Garfinkel, *Studies in Ethnomethodology*, p. 13.

155 *Studies in Ethnomethodology*, pp. 172–173.

156 Ray P. Cuzzort and Edith W. King, *20th Century Social Thought*, 3rd ed., New York, Holt, Rinehart and Winston, 1980, p. 325. Thus Garfinkel's conception of rationality resonates with some phenomenological findings about the differences between the natural and the theoretical attitudes, Weber's distinction between formal and substantive rationalities, and Kaplan's distinction between a logic-in-use and a reconstructed logic; see William Skidmore, *Theoretical Thinking in Sociology*, 2d ed., New York, Cambridge University Press, 1979, pp. 256–257.

157 Garfinkel and Sacks, "On Formal Structures," pp. 342, 353.

158 Garfinkel, in Hill and Crittenden, eds., *Proceedings*, p. 119.

159 *Proceedings*, p. 121. "Member" has shifted over time from Parsonian emphasis on collectivity membership to linguistic emphasis on mastery of natural language; Don H. Zimmerman, "Ethnomethodology," in Scott G. McNall, ed., *Theoretical Perspectives in Sociology*, New York, St. Martin's Press, 1979, p. 385.

160 Cicourel, "Basic and Normative Rules." Hilbert has discussed "role" from an ethnomethodological perspective; Richard A. Hilbert, " 'Role': From Functionalism to Symbolic Interactionism to Ethnomethodology," paper presented at annual meeting of American Sociological Association, New York, August 27–31, 1980.

161 Zimmerman and Pollner, "Everyday World," p. 94. On "occasioned corpus," see Leiter, *Primer on Ethnomethodology*, pp. 94ff.

162 "Everyday World," p. 99.

163 "Everyday World," p. 98.

164 "Everyday World," p. 98.

165 "Everyday World," p. 99.

166 Attewell, "Ethnomethodology since Garfinkel," 187.

167 Garfinkel, "Conception," p. 190.

168 "Conception," p. 200.

169 Pollner, "Sociological and Commonsense Models," p. 32.

170 Cicourel, *Cognitive Sociology*, p. 81.

171 Garfinkel and Sacks, "On Formal Structures," p. 356.

172 Garfinkel, "Conception," p. 30.

173 "Conception," p. 31.

174 Garfinkel and Sacks, "On Formal Structures," p. 351.

175 Matthew Speier, "The Everyday World of the Child," in Douglas, ed., *Understanding Everyday Life*, p. 189.

176 Turner, "Introduction," p. 11.

177 Douglas, "Understanding Everyday Life," p. 16.

178 Mehan and Wood, *Reality of Ethnomethodology*, p. 71.

179 Garfinkel, in Hill and Crittenden, eds., *Proceedings*, p. 199.

180 Blum, *Theorizing*, p. 3.

181 *Theorizing*, p. 19.

182 David Walsh, "Sociology and the Social World," in Filmer et al., eds., *New Directions*, p. 31.

183 Garfinkel, Perception of the Other, p. 201.

184 Mehan and Wood, *Reality of Ethnomethodology*, p. 223.

185 Garfinkel, in Hill and Crittenden, eds., *Proceedings*, p. 135.

186 *Proceedings*, p. 135.

187 Mullins, *Theories and Theory Groups*, pp. 191–192.

188 Garfinkel, Perception of the Other, pp. 92, 24.

189 Perception of the Other, p. 24.

190 Blum, *Theorizing*, p. 222.

191 *Theorizing*, pp. 223, 225.
192 Garfinkel, in Hill and Crittenden, eds., *Proceedings*, p. 129; cf. Garfinkel, *Studies in Ethnomethodology*, pp. 77–78.
193 Garfinkel, *Studies in Ethnomethodology*, p. 78.
194 Stuart C. Hadden and Marilyn Lester, "Talking Identity: The Production of 'Self' in Interaction," *Human Studies* 1 (October 1978), 335.
195 Filmer, "On Harold Garfinkel's Ethnomethodology," p. 227.
196 Mehan and Wood, *Reality of Ethnomethodology*, pp. 118–119.
197 Psathas, "Approaches," p. 11.
198 Douglas, "Understanding Everyday Life," p. 9.
199 Sudnow, in Hill and Crittenden, eds., *Proceedings*, p. 44.
200 Garfinkel, in *Proceedings*, p. 171.
201 Garfinkel, *Proceedings*, pp. 173–174.
202 Matthew Speier, "Some Conversational Problems for Interactional Analysis," in Sudnow, ed., *Studies in Social Interaction*, p. 398.
203 Roy Turner, "Some Formal Properties of Therapy Talk," in *Studies in Social Interaction*, p. 368.
204 Cicourel, *Cognitive Sociology*, p. 111.
205 Garfinkel, "Conception," p. 187.
206 Garfinkel, Perception of the Other, p. 203.
207 Douglas, "Understanding Everyday Life," pp. 34–35.
208 Mehan and Wood, *Reality of Ethnomethodology*, p. 204.
209 Mayrl, "Ethnomethodology," p. 266. On ethnomethodological description, see Heap, "Description."
210 Cicourel, *Cognitive Sociology*, pp. 158, 160.
211 Hill and Crittenden, eds., *Proceedings*.
212 Garfinkel, in *Proceedings*, pp. 169, 194. Similarly, Mehan and Wood argue that "I cannot justify my ethnomethodology as a pursuit of privileged knowledge; every farmer, freak, witch and alchemist has such knowledge"; see Hugh Mehan and Houston Wood, "The Morality of Ethnomethodology," *Theory and Society* 2 (Winter 1975), 509.
213 Sudnow, in Hill and Crittenden, eds., *Proceedings*, p. 70.
214 Sacks, in *Proceedings*, p. 42.
215 Marvin B. Scott, *The Racing Game*, Chicago, Aldine, 1968, pp. 5–6.
216 Sudnow, in Hill and Crittenden, eds., *Proceedings*, p. 101.
217 Garfinkel, in *Proceedings*, p. 94.
218 *Proceedings*, p. 258.
219 Here the methods of linguistic ethnomethodologists stand as a major exception.
220 Sudnow, in Hill and Crittenden, eds., *Proceedings*, pp. 102–103.
221 Garfinkel, in *Proceedings*, p. 111.
222 *Proceedings*, p. 136.
223 Garfinkel and Sacks, "On Formal Structures," p. 342.
224 Garfinkel, *Studies in Ethnomethodology*, p. vii.
225 George Psathas, "Misinterpreting Ethnomethodology," paper presented at meetings of American Sociological Association, New York, August, 1976.
226 Sudnow, in Hill and Crittenden, eds., *Proceedings*, p. 86.
227 Psathas, "Approaches," p. 14. Gidlow contends, however, that ethnomethodology is "glorified participant-observation"; see Bob Gidlow, "Ethnomethodology: A New Name for Old Practices," *British Journal of Sociology* 22 (December 1972), 399.
228 Don H. Zimmerman and D. Lawrence Wieder, "You Can't Help But Get Stoned: Notes on the Social Organization of Marijuana Smoking," *Social Problems* 25 (December 1977), 199.

229 Psathas, "Approaches," p. 6.
230 "Approaches," cf. Donelson R. Forsyth, "Scientific and Common Sense Reasoning: A Comparison," *Human Studies* 2 (April 1979), 159; Leiter, *Primer on Ethnomethodology*, p. 21.
231 See, for example, O'Neill, *Making Sense Together*, p. 97; Kenneth Stoddart, "Pinched: Notes on the Ethnographer's Location of Argot," in Turner, ed., *Ethnomethodology*, pp. 173–174.
232 Jim Schenkein, "The Radio Raiders Story," in Psathas, ed., *Everyday Language*, p. 195.
233 Mehan and Wood, *Reality of Ethnomethodology*, p. 75.
234 *Reality of Ethnomethodology*, p. 76.
235 Douglas, "Understanding Everyday Life," p.41.
236 *Reality of Ethnomethodology*, p. 76.
237 George Psathas, personal communication, July 1977.
238 Douglas, "Understanding Everyday Life," pp. 32–33.
239 Cicourel, *Cognitive Sociology*, p. 211.
240 Garfinkel, "Conception," pp. 220ff.; Garfinkel, *Studies in Ethnomethodology*, pp. 42–44.
241 Garfinkel, "Conception," pp. 223ff.
242 "Conception," pp. 225–226; Garfinkel, *Studies in Ethnomethodology*, pp. 44–49.
243 Garfinkel, *Studies in Ethnomethodology*, p. 54, 60; Garfinkel, "Conception," pp. 228–229.
244 Turner, "Some Formal Properties"; Sheldon Twer, "Tactics for Determining Persons' Resources for Depicting, Contriving, and Describing Behavioral Events," in Sudnow, ed., *Studies in Social Interaction*, pp. 329–366; David Sudnow, "Temporal Parameters of Interpersonal Observation," in *Studies in Social Interaction*, pp. 259–279; Emmanuel Schegloff, "Notes on a Conversational Practice: Formulating Place," *Studies in Social Interaction*, pp. 75–119.
245 Sudnow, "Temporal Parameters"; A. Lincoln Rayave and James N. Schenkein, "Notes on the Art of Walking," in Turner, ed., *Ethnomethodology*, pp. 265–274; Marilyn Lester, "The Interactional Generation of Newsworthiness: Ideology as Accomplishment," paper presented at annual meeting of American Sociological Association, Chicago, September 1977; Garfinkel, *Studies in Ethnomethodology*, pp. 116–118; Don H. Zimmerman and Candace West, "Doing Gender," paper presented at annual meeting of American Sociological Association, Chicago, September 1977.
246 Albert Adato, " 'Occasionality' as a Constituent Feature of the Known-in-Common Character of Topics," *Human Studies* 3 (January 1980), 47–64; Albert Adato, "Unanticipated Topic Continuations," *Human Studies* 2 (April 1979), 171–186; Hilbert, "Approaching Reason's Edge"; Ken Liberman, "Ambiguity and Gratuitous Concurrence in Inter-Cultural Communication," *Human Studies* 3 (January 1980), 65–85; Pollner, "Explicative Transactions"; Schenkein, "The Radio Raiders Story"; Sharrock and Turner, "Observation."
247 Zimmerman and Wieder, "You Can't Help"; Robert P. Gephart, Jr., "Status Degradation and Organizational Succession: An Ethnomethodological Approach," *Administrative Science Quarterly* 23 (December 1978), 553–581; Candace West and Don H. Zimmerman, "Woman's Place in Everyday Talk: Reflections on Parent-Child Interaction," *Social Problems* 24 (June 1977), 521–529; Mick A. Atkinson, "Some Practical Uses of 'A Natural Lifetime,' " *Human Studies* 3 (January 1980), 33–46; Harvey Sacks, "Hotrodder: A Revolutionary Category," in Psathas, ed., *Everyday Language*, pp. 7–14.
248 David Silverman, "Methodology and Meaning," in Filmer et al., eds., *New Directions*, p. 193.
249 Garfinkel, in Hill and Crittenden, eds., *Proceedings*, p. 113.

250 Douglas, "Deviance and Order," p. 377.
251 Cicourel, *Cognitive Sociology*, p. 100.
252 *Cognitive Sociology*, p. 140.
253 *Cognitive Sociology*, p. 112.
254 Douglas, "Deviance and Order," p. 386.
255 Douglas, "Understanding Everyday Life," p. 41.
256 Cicourel, "Basic and Normative Rules," p. 244.
257 Cicourel, *Cognitive Sociology*, p. 122.
258 McHugh, *Defining the Situation*, p. 37.
259 *Defining the Situation*, p. 62.
260 Garfinkel, *Studies in Ethnomethodology*, p. 114.
261 McHugh, *Defining the Situation*; Cicourel, *Cognitive Sociology*, pp. 51–58; 81; 168–169; Peter Winch, *The Ideal of a Social Science and Its Relation to Philosophy*, London, Routledge & Kegan Paul, 1970, p. 58. For ethnomethodologists, though,

>   Norms, rules, motives, and social types are . . . not . . . causal agents. They are glosses, devices that people use to render the factual character of social sense and actions observable as such. They are aids to perception used to convert raw behavior into social action and to portray that social action as factual to oneself and others. . . . Instead of being followed or complied with, they are used as sense-making aids to report and observe people's behavior.

See Leiter, *Primer on Ethnomethodology*, p. 192.
262 Mayrl, "Ethnomethodology," p. 265.
263 McHugh, *Defining the Situation*, p. 14.
264 *Defining the Situation*, p. 50.
265 Egon Bittner, "The Concept of Organization," in Turner, ed., *Ethnomethodology*, p. 77.
266 McHugh, *Defining the Situation*, p. 14.
267 Cicourel, *Cognitive Sociology*, p. 100.
268 James Heap, "Reconceiving the Social," *Canadian Review of Sociology and Anthropology* 13 (August 1976), 272–273.
269 Pollner, "Explicative Transactions," p. 253.
270 "Explicative Transactions," p. 141.
271 David Silverman, "Introductory Comments," in Filmer et al., eds., *New Directions*, p. 11.
272 Psathas, "Approaches," p. 4.
273 Mehan and Wood, *Reality of Ethnomethodology*, pp. 8–27.
274 *Reality of Ethnomethodology*, pp. 13–14.
275 Harvey Sacks, "On the Analysability of Stories by Children," in Turner, ed., *Ethnomethodology*, p. 218.
276 Mayrl, "Ethnomethodology," p. 269.
277 Garfinkel, *Studies in Ethnomethodology*, p. 110.
278 Don H. Zimmerman, "The Practicalities of Rule Use," in Douglas, ed., *Understanding Everyday Life*, p. 237.
279 Psathas, "Study of Everyday Structures," p. 3.
280 "Study of Everyday Structures," p. 5.
281 Garfinkel, in Hill and Crittenden, eds., *Proceedings*, p. 47.
282 Walsh, "Sociology and the Social World," p. 21.
283 Zimmerman, "Practicalities of Rule Use," p. 238.
284 "Practicalities of Rule Use," p. 225.
285 Filmer, "On Harold Garfinkel's Ethnomethodology," p. 224.
286 Cicourel, *Cognitive Sociology*, p. 58.
287 *Cognitive Sociology*, p. 52.
288 Psathas, "Study of Everyday Structures," p. 8.
289 Thomas M. Kando, *Social Interaction*, St. Louis, Mosby, 1977, p. 149.
290 Garfinkel, *Studies in Ethnomethodology*, p. 77.

291 Garfinkel, "Conception," p. 188. The presuppositions of reflexivity and indexicality make *emergence* a hallmark of the ethnomethodological conception of social structure and members' sense of social structure. Nonetheless members use their sense of social structure as a tacit resource; see Leiter, *Primer on Ethnomethodology*, pp. 104–105.
292 Turner, "Words, Utterances and Activities," p. 327.
293 Wilson, "Normative and Interpretive Paradigms," p. 78.
294 Garfinkel, *Studies in Ethnomethodology*, p. 77; "Conception," p. 188.
295 Schegloff and Sacks, "Opening Up Closings," p. 234.
296 See, for example, McHugh, *Defining the Situation*, p. 20; Deborah Schiffrin, "Opening Encounters," *American Sociological Review* 42 (October 1977), 680; Turner, "Introduction," p. 11.
297 John Law and Peter Lodge, "Structure as Process and Environmental Constraint," *Theory and Society* 5 (May 1978), 382.
298 Psathas, "Approaches," pp. 7–8.
299 Cicourel, *Cognitive Sociology*, p. 46.
300 Cicourel, "Basic and Normative Rules," p. 244.
301 "Basic and Normative Rules," pp. 249–250.

7. Ethnomethodology: a phenomenological sociology?

1 Harold Garfinkel, in R. J. Hill and K. S. Crittenden, eds., *Proceedings of the Purdue Symposium on Ethnomethodology*, Lafayette, Ind., Institute for the Study of Social Change, Purdue University, 1968, p. 114.
2 Zimmerman, for example, argues that "phenomenological" does not apply across the board to ethnomethodology; it blurs the distinction between intellectual roots and intellectual content. He points out that ethnomethodologists have altered Schutz's ideas. Don H. Zimmerman, "Ethnomethodology," in Scott G. McNall, ed., *Theoretical Perspectives in Sociology*, New York, St. Martin's Press, 1979, p. 384.
3 Thomas M. Kando, *Social Interaction*, St. Louis, Mosby, 1977, p. 6; Ian Craib, *Existentialism and Sociology: A Study of Jean-Paul Sartre*, New York, Cambridge University Press, 1976, p. 59; Fred R. Dallmayr and Thomas A. McCarthy, "Introduction: The Crisis of Understanding," in F. R. Dallmayr and T. A. McCarthy, eds., *Understanding and Social Inquiry*, Notre Dame, Ind., University of Notre Dame Press, 1977, p. 10; John O'Neill, *Sociology as a Skin Trade: Essays Toward a Reflexive Sociology*, New York, Harper Torchbooks, 1972, p. 212; Monica B. Morris, *An Excursion into Creative Sociology*, New York, Columbia University Press, 1977, p. 9; William W. Mayrl, "Ethnomethodology: Sociology without Society?" in Dallmayr and McCarthy, eds., *Understanding and Social Inquiry*, pp. 267, 276.
4 James L. Heap and Phillip A. Roth, "On Phenomenological Sociology," in Alan Wells, ed., *Contemporary Sociological Theories*, Santa Monica, Calif., Goodyear, 1978, p. 288. Elsewhere Heap calls ethnomethodology a "phenomenological empiricism"; see James L. Heap, "Description in Ethnomethodology," *Human Studies* 3 (January 1980), 87. Collins uses "social phenomenology" and "ethnomethodology" interchangeably, although he notes that phenomenological (or cognitive) sociologists would not all accept any single label; see Randall Collins, *Conflict Sociology: Toward an Explanatory Science*, New York, Academic Press, 1975, pp. 8–10, 108.
5 Zimmerman, "Ethnomethodology," p. 383; Laurie Spurling, *Phenomenology and the Social World: The Philosophy of Merleau-Ponty and its Relation to the Social Sciences*, Boston, Routledge & Kegan Paul, 1977, p. 72. Leiter stresses only two of Husserl's works in discussing his influence on ethnomethodology, *Cartesian Meditations* and *Phenomenology and the Crisis of Philosophy*. Leiter's position suggests a partial, selective influence; Kenneth Leiter, *A Primer on Ethnomethodology*, New York, Oxford University Press,

1980, p. 39. Wagner points out that no single "school" of phenomenological sociology exists. Rather, orientations variously related to phenomenology have developed, including ethnomethodology, existential sociology, and Schutzian phenomenology; Helmut R. Wagner, "Sociologists of Phenomenological Orientations: Their Place in American Sociology," *American Sociologist* 10 (August 1975), 180.

6 Irwin Deutscher, *What We Say/What We Do: Sentiments and Acts*, Glenview, Ill., Scott, Foresman, 1973, p. 325.

7 Maurice Natanson, "The Phenomenology of Alfred Schutz," *Inquiry* 9 (1966), 147–155; "Alfred Schutz on Social Reality and Social Science," *Social Research* 35 (Summer 1968), 218–244; "Phenomenology and Typification: A Study in the Philosophy of Alfred Schutz," *Social Research* 37 (Spring 1970), 1–22; "Introduction," in Alfred Schutz, *Collected Papers I: The Problem of Social Reality*, ed. Maurice Natanson, The Hague, Nijhoff, 1973, pp. xxv–xlvii; Peter L. Berger and Thomas Luckmann, *The Social Construction of Reality: A Treatise in the Sociology of Knowledge*, Garden City, N.Y., Anchor, 1967.

8 Fred R. Dallmayr, "Phenomenology and Social Science: An Overview and Appraisal," in D. Carr and E. Casey, eds., *Explorations in Phenomenology*, The Hague, Nijhoff, 1973, p. 157; Craib, *Sartre*, p. 59; Hugh Mehan and Houston Wood, *The Reality of Ethnomethodology*, New York, Wiley-Interscience, 1975, p. 31; Scott McNall and James C. M. Johnson, "The New Conservatives: Ethnomethodologists, Phenomenologists, and Symbolic Interactionists," *Insurgent Sociologist* V (Summer 1975), 54, 55; Deutscher, *What We Say*, p. 325; Peter Dreitzel, "Introduction: Patterns of Communicative Behavior," in Peter Dreitzel, ed., *Recent Sociology No. 2: Patterns of Communicative Behavior*, New York, Macmillan, 1970, vii–viii; John C. McKinney, "Sociological Theory and the Process of Typification," in J. C. McKinney and E. A. Tiryakian, eds., *Theoretical Sociology*, New York, Appleton-Century-Crofts, 1970, p. 225; Zygmunt Bauman, *Hermeneutics and Social Science*, New York, Columbia University Press, 1978, p. 188; Morris, *Creative Sociology*, p. vii; Margaret M. Poloma, *Contemporary Sociological Theory*, New York, Macmillan, 1979, p. 181.

9 Anthony Giddens, *New Rules of Sociological Method: A Positive Critique of Interpretative Sociologies*, New York, Basic Books, 1976, p. 36; Jack D. Douglas, "Appendix: The Origins of Existential Sociology," in J. Douglas and J. Johnson, eds., *Existential Sociology*, New York, Cambridge University Press, 1977, p. 293. Charles C. Lemert, "De-Centered Analysis: Ethnomethodology and Structuralism," *Theory and Society* 7 (May 1979), 290; Stephen Mennell, *Sociological Theory: Uses and Unities*, New York, Praeger, 1974, p. 58.

10 Cited by Jeff Coulter, "Decontextualized Meanings: Current Approaches to Verstehende Investigations," in Marcello Truzzi, ed., *Verstehen: Subjective Understanding in the Social Sciences*, Reading, Mass., Addison-Wesley, 1974, p. 142. Coulter himself argues, though, that "if the brain cannot properly be the recipient or 'subject' of specific mental predicates or a range of 'intentional' predicates more generally, then we should cease to conceive of the brain as an agent in its own right"; see Jeff Coulter, "The Brain as Agent," *Human Studies* 2 (October 1979), 347.

11 One ethnomethodologist, Jim Schenkein, reports, for example, "I do not know how what we call 'memory' brings either current or old 'news' into understanding, and I am not all too wise about how 'understanding' works either – especially since it is clear enough that what would pass for understanding in one circumstance might fail in another. . . . Even if questions of memory, understanding, recognition, and fascination are left unanswered, we can pick away at questions of referentiality." See Jim Schenkein, "The Radio Raiders Story," in George Psathas, ed., *Everyday Language: Studies in Ethnomethodology*, New York, Irvington, 1979, p. 201.

12 Cuzzort and King arrive at a similar conclusion; they compare Garfinkel's approach to that of a physicist. See Ray P. Cuzzort and Edith W. King, *20th Century Social Thought*, 3d ed., New York, Holt, Rinehart and Winston, 1980, p. 313.

13 Alfred Schutz, *Collected Papers III: Studies in Social Theory*, ed. Arvid Brodersen, The Hague, Nijhoff, 1976, p. 69.

14 Alfred Schutz and Thomas Luckmann, *The Structures of the Life-World*, trans. Richard M. Zaner and H. Tristram Engelhardt, Jr., Evanston, Ill., Northwestern University Press, 1973, p. 116.

15 Schutz, p. 9.

16 *Collected Papers III*, p. 76.

17 Maurice Natanson, *The Journeying Self: A Study in Philosophy and Social Role*, Reading, Mass., Addison-Wesley, 1970, p. 27.

18 *Journeying Self*, p. 5.

19 Cicourel's work deviates from that pattern. As Skidmore has noted, "There is continuity in everyday interaction because of what Cicourel calls the *retrospective-prospective sense of occurrence*." See William Skidmore, *Theoretical Thinking in Sociology*, 2d ed., New York, Cambridge University Press, 1979, p. 251. Moreover, Heritage and Watson point out that "in Garfinkel and Sacks' terms, then, the status of formulations as 'proper glosses' may be adjudged by members through a retrospective consultation of, and a reliance upon, 'accountable texts' furnished in the conversation in progress"; see J. C. Heritage and D. R. Watson, "Formulations as Conversational Objects," in Psathas, ed., *Everyday Language*, p. 128. Such notions as these merit a central place in the ethnomethodological framework. Their development is crucial to the long-term success of ethnomethodology as a formal sociology of everyday life.

20 Schutz and Luckmann, *Structures*, pp. 115–116.

21 "Subjectivity" refers here to the intrinsic relation of experience to consciousness and of action and understanding to the essential structure of awareness; see Maurice Natanson, "History, Historicity, and the Alchemistry of Time," *Chicago Review* 15 (Summer 1961), 81.

22 Coulter, "Decontextualized Meanings," p. 143.

23 Schutz and Luckmann, *Structures*, pp. 16–17.

24 Natanson, *Journeying Self*, p. 117.

25 *Journeying Self*, p. 13.

26 Hadden and Lester are among the few ethnomethodologists who have studied identity and self. Their method and analysis, however, allow for only a narrow conception of the self. See Stuart C. Hadden and Marilyn Lester, "Talking Identity: The Production of 'Self' in Interaction," *Human Studies* 1 (October 1978), 331–356. It remains extremely questionable, then, whether ethnomethodologists "put the individual at the center of sociological analysis," as Skidmore has argued; see Skidmore, *Theoretical Thinking*, p. 255.

27 Natanson, *Journeying Self*, p. 7.

28 *Journeying Self*, p. 6.

29 Maurice Natanson, *Phenomenology, Role, and Reason: Essays on the Coherence and Deformation of Social Reality*, Springfield, Ill., Thomas, 1974, p. vii.

30 *Phenomenology, Role, and Reason*, p. 112.

31 *Phenomenology, Role, and Reason*, p. 201.

32 *Phenomenology, Role, and Reason*, p. 211.

33 *Phenomenology, Role, and Reason*, p. 214.

34 George Psathas, "The Study of Everyday Structures and the Ethnomethodological Paradigm," paper presented at colloquium "Alfred Schutz und die idee des Alltags in den Sozialwis-

senschaften," University of Konstanz, June 23–27, 1974, 9; a revised version appeared as "Approaches to the Study of Everyday Life," *Human Studies* 3 (January 1980), 1–17.

35 Alfred Schutz, *On Phenomenology and Social Relations*, ed. Helmut R. Wagner, Chicago, University of Chicago Press, 1970, p. 241; *Collected Papers I*, pp. 11; 61; Schutz and Luckmann, *Structures*, pp. 297, 300.

36 Howard Brotz, "Theory and Practice: Ethnomethodology versus Humane Ethnography," *Jewish Journal of Sociology* 16 (December 1974), 229.

37 Mennell, *Sociological Theories*, p. 54.

38 Natanson, *Journeying Self*, p. 7.

39 Lemert, "De-Centered Analysis."

40 Philip Pettit, *The Concept of Structuralism: A Critical Analysis*, Berkeley, University of California Press, 1977, pp. i–ii, 38–39, 68–69. Also see David Goddard, "On Structuralism and Sociology," *American Sociologist* 11 (May 1976), 123–133; G. Russell Carpenter, "On Structuralism and the Sociological Domain: Comment on Goddard," *American Sociologist* 11 (May 1976), 133–137; David Goddard, "Reply to Carpenter," *American Sociologist* 11 (May 1976), 137–139.

41 Natanson, *Journeying Self*, p. 105.

42 Maurice Natanson, "Alienation and Social Role," *Social Research* 33 (Autumn 1966), 380.

43 Natanson, "Alfred Schutz on Social Reality," 105.

44 "Alfred Schutz on Social Reality," p. 107.

45 Natanson, "Alienation and Social Role," 377.

46 "Alienation and Social Role," p. 376.

47 Beng-Huat Chua, "Delineating a Marxist Interest in Ethnomethodology," *American Sociologist* 12 (February 1977), 25.

48 James Heap, "Reconceiving the Social," *Canadian Review of Sociology and Anthropology* 13 (August 1976), 272.

49 Psathas, "Study of Everyday Structures," 4.

50 "Study of Everyday Structures," p. 12.

51 Kenneth Stoddart, "Pinched: Notes on the Ethnographer's Location of Argot," in Roy Turner, ed., *Ethnomethodology*, Baltimore, Penguin, 1974, pp. 173–174.

52 Don H. Zimmerman and Melvin Pollner, "The Everyday World as a Phenomenon," in Jack D. Douglas, ed., *Understanding Everyday Life*, Chicago, Aldine, 1970, p. 98.

53 Harold Garfinkel and Harvey Sacks, "On Formal Structures of Practical Actions," in McKinney and Tiryakian, *Theoretical Sociology*, pp. 345–346.

54 "On Formal Structures," p. 357; Zimmerman and Pollner, "Everyday World," p. 95.

55 Harold Garfinkel, The Perception of the Other: A Study in Social Order, PhD. diss., Harvard University, 1952, p. 109.

56 Perception of the Other, p. 110. Bauman also detects a phenomenological dimension in Parsons's thought; Bauman, *Hermeneutics and Social Science*, pp. 131–146. Roche intimates that that may be so; Maurice Roche, *Phenomenology, Language and the Social Sciences*, Boston, Routledge & Kegan Paul, 1973, pp. 15, 32.

57 *If* one were forced to place Schutz on one or the other side of the fence Garfinkel constructs, his proper location would be the "can" side. However, the problem is artificial. Schutz did not straddle that fence, let alone restrict his attention in the manner Garfinkel suggests. Schutz consistently concerned himself with how mundane actors both can and do believe, even act, on the basis of knowledge derived from firsthand experience.

58 Paul Filmer, "On Harold Garfinkel's Ethnomethodology," in Paul Filmer, Michael Phillipson, David Silverman, and David Walsh, eds., *New Directions in Sociological Theory*, Cambridge, Mass., MIT Press, 1972, pp. 217–218.

59 "On Harold Garfinkel's Ethnomethodology," p. 220.
60 "On Harold Garfinkel's Ethnomethodology," pp. 218–219.
61 "On Harold Garfinkel's Ethnomethodology," p. 221.
62 "On Harold Garfinkel's Ethnomethodology," p. 217.
63 Harold Garfinkel, *Studies in Ethnomethodology*, Englewood Cliffs, N.J., Prentice-Hall, 1967, pp. 57, 76; footnotes. These footnotes were cited by Filmer, who expresses indebtedness to Frank Pierce for pointing out the Parsonian usage of "member" in Garfinkel's work; Filmer, "On Harold Garfinkel's Ethnomethodology," p. 217.
64 Maurice Natanson, "Foreword," in *The Theory of Social Action: The Correspondence of Alfred Schutz and Talcott Parsons*, ed. Richard Grathoff, Bloomington, Indiana University Press, 1978, p. xiv.
65 "Foreword," pp. xiv-xv.

8. The idea of phenomenological sociology

1 Armstrong has surveyed such reactions to phenomenological sociology and ethnomethodology. He centers his analysis with the neologism "phenomenologophobia," an aversive reaction that departs from "normal scholarship not only by its intensity but also by its inattention to detail"; see Edward G. Armstrong, "Phenomenologophobia," *Human Studies* 2 (January 1979), 63–75.
2 Maurice Merleau-Ponty, *In Praise of Philosophy*, trans. John Wild and James M. Edie, Evanston, Ill., Northwestern University Press, 1963, p. 4.
3 Thomas Burger, *Max Weber's Theory of Concept Formation: History, Laws, and Ideal Types*, Durham, N.C., Duke University Press, 1976, p. 107.
4 Maurice Natanson, "A Study in Philosophy and the Social Sciences," in Maurice Natanson, ed., *Philosophy of the Social Sciences*, New York, Random House, 1963, pp. 283, 284. Also see Laurie Spurling, *Phenomenology and the Social World: The Philosophy of Merleau-Ponty and its Relation to the Social Sciences*, Boston, Routledge & Kegan Paul, 1977, p. 146.
5 Jitendranath N. Mohanty, "Husserl's Theory of Meaning," in F. A. Elliston and P. McCormick, eds., *Husserl: Expositions and Appraisals*, Notre Dame, Ind., University of Notre Dame Press, 1977, pp. 29–30. Weber's conception of understanding is similar. He conceived understanding as "having" meaningful "contents" on any "level" of consciousness; "interpretation" is having such contents in judgment form. See Burger, *Max Weber's Theory*, p. 111.
6 Alfred Schutz, *The Phenomenology of the Social World*, trans. George Walsh and Frederick Lehnert, Evanston, Ill., Northwestern University Press, 1967, pp. 110–112. Giddens has noted that Weber's distinction between "action" and "social action" separates acts without and acts with communicative content; Anthony Giddens, *New Rules of Sociological Method: A Positive Critique of Interpretative Sociologies*, New York, Basic Books, 1976, p. 118.
7 Schutz, *Phenomenology of the Social World*, pp. 112–113.
8 *Phenomenology of the Social World*, p. 113.
9 *Phenomenology of the Social World*, p. 113.
10 *Phenomenology of the Social World*, p. 9.
11 Cf. Robert Sokolowski, *Husserlian Meditations: How Words Present Things*, Evanston, Ill., Northwestern University Press, 1974, p. 14. Burke notes that many "observations" are implications of terminology; Kenneth Burke, *Language as Symbolic Action: Essays on Life, Literature, and Method*, Berkeley, University of California Press, 1966, p. viii.
12 Cf. *Husserlian Meditations*.

13 Kenneth Burke, *A Grammar of Motives*, Berkeley, University of California Press, 1969, p. 314.
14 David Michael Levin, *Reason and Evidence in Husserl's Phenomenology*, Evanston, Ill., Northwestern University Press, 1970, p. 167.
15 Alfred Schutz, *Collected Papers I: The Problem of Social Reality*, ed. Maurice Natanson, The Hague, Nijhoff, 1973, pp. 137–138.
16 Max Weber, *The Methodology of the Social Sciences*, trans. and ed. Edward A. Shils and Henry A. Finch, Glencoe, Ill., Free Press, 1949, p. 81.
17 Michael Polanyi and Harry Prosch, *Meaning*, Chicago, University of Chicago Press, 1975, p. 29.
18 Alfred Schutz and Thomas Luckmann, *The Structures of the Life-World*, trans. Richard M. Zaner and H. Tristram Engelhardt, Jr., Evanston, Ill., Northwestern University Press, 1973, p. 207. For example, the typical situation of social scientists today might lead them toward greater concern with science than with understanding humankind. See Edward Sapir, *Culture, Language and Personality*, Berkeley, University of California Press, 1956, p. 182; also p. 173.
19 Richard H. Brown, *A Poetic for Sociology: Toward a Logic of Discovery for the Human Sciences*, Cambridge, Cambridge University Press, 1978, p. 47.
20 Max Black, *Models and Metaphors: Studies in Language and Philosophy*, Ithaca, N.Y., Cornell University Press, 1962.
21 Robert A. Nisbet, *Social Change and History: Aspects of the Western Theory of Development*, New York, Oxford University Press, 1970, pp. 3–4.
22 *Social Change and History*, p. 6; cf. Stanford W. Gregory, Jr., " 'Social Resonance' as Demonstrated in Conversation," paper presented at annual meeting of American Sociological Association, New York, August 27–31, 1980.
23 Brown, *Poetic for Sociology*.
24 Hans-Georg Gadamer, *Philosophical Hermeneutics*, trans. and ed. David E. Linge, Berkeley, University of California Press, 1976, p. 101.
25 *Philosophical Hermeneutics*, p. 11.
26 *Philosophical Hermeneutics*, p. 67.
27 Peter Winch, *The Idea of a Social Science and Its Relation to Philosophy*, London, Routledge & Kegan Paul, 1970, p. 27.
28 Burke, *Grammar of Motives*, p. 32.
29 Alfred North Whitehead, *Modes of Thought*, New York, Free Press, 1968, p. 88.
30 Cf. Brown, *Poetic for Sociology*, p. 234.
31 Kersten regards the study of "access to the social purely as such" as the philosophical foundation of the social sciences; Frederick I. Kersten, "The Constancy Hypothesis in the Social Sciences," in Lester E. Embree, ed., *Life-World and Consciousness: Essays for Aron Gurwitsch*, Evanston, Ill., Northwestern University Press, 1972, p. 556.
32 Alfred Schutz, "Parsons' Theory of Social Action: A Critical Review," in Richard Grathoff, ed., *The Theory of Social Action: The Correspondence of Alfred Schutz and Talcott Parsons*, Bloomington, Indiana University Press, 1978, p. 36; *Collected Papers I*, p. 62.
33 Schutz, "Parsons' Theory of Social Action," p. 52.
34 Schutz, *Collected Papers I*, pp. 10–11.
35 Schutz, "Parsons' Theory of Social Action," p. 52.
36 "Parsons' Theory of Social Action," p. 41.
37 Maurice Roche, *Phenomenology, Language and the Social Sciences*, Boston, Routledge & Kegan Paul, 1973, p. 314.
38 Schutz, *Collected Papers I*, p. 62. More recent, phenomenologically relevant analyses of *Verstehen* include James L. Heap, "Verstehen, Language, and Warrants," *Sociological*

Quarterly 18 (Spring 1977), 177–184; Arthur S. Parsons, "Interpretive Sociology: The Theoretical Significance of *Verstehen* in the Constitution of Social Reality," *Human Studies* I (April 1978), 111–137.

39 *Collected Papers I*, p. 35.
40 Schutz, "Parsons' Theory of Social Action," pp. 10, 44, 52.
41 Schutz, *Collected Papers I*, pp. 56–57.
42 *Collected Papers I*, p. 57.
43 *Collected Papers I*, p. 56.
44 *Collected Papers I*, pp. 24–25.
45 *Collected Papers I*, p. 59.
46 Natanson, "Study in Philosophy," pp. 280–281.
47 Although Schutz addressed this problem in most of his work, the core of his treatment of the philosophical foundations and problems of the social sciences appears in *Phenomenology of the Social World* and in Parts I and II of *Collected Papers I*.
48 Schutz, *Phenomenology of the Social World*, p. 7.
49 *Phenomenology of the Social World*, p. 192. Yet the application of any idealization submits our subject matter to a "preestablished matrix"; see Hellmut R. Wagner, "Between Ideal Type and Surrender: Field Research as Asymmetrical Relation," *Human Studies* 1 (April 1978), 155. Necessarily, then, some of the meaning social phenomena have for individuals in the social world is omitted. Thus social science has meaning only within certain limits. It leaves room for other approaches to the social world, including the common-sense approach. See Joseph J. Kockelmans, "Reflections on Social Theory," *Human Studies* 1 (January 1978), 7.
50 Kockelmans, "Reflections," 9, 14. Like Schutz, Kockelmans stresses that the application of ideal types makes the content of social, historical experiences more intelligible than it was in the relevant lived experiences. All sociology *reconstructs*, then. At the same time, however, it leaves human experiences to some degree obscure and confused; "Reflections," p. 13.
51 Schutz, "Parsons' Theory of Social Action," pp. 46–47.
52 Schutz, *Phenomenology of the Social World*, p. 135.
53 Cf. Kenneth Leiter, *A Primer on Ethnomethodology*, New York, Oxford University Press, 1980, p. 22. Phenomenologically, then, "Hard figures and percentages . . . do not represent 'hard facts' but the reduction of 'soft facts' to simplistic expressions for a price: the neglect of the fluidities and subtleties that characterize the subjective units of the investigation"; Helmut R. Wagner, "Sociologists of Phenomenological Orientations: Their Place in American Sociology," *American Sociologist* 10 (August 1975), 181. Phenomenological sociologists do recognize, though, that sometimes that price is reasonable, even attractive. They only insist that the price be consistently recognized throughout the process of paying it.
54 Schutz, "Parsons' Theory of Social Action," p. 48.
55 "Parsons' Theory of Social Action," pp. 49–50.
56 "Parsons' Theory of Social Action," p. 44.
57 Schutz, *Phenomenology of the Social World*, p. 133.
58 *Phenomenology of the Social World*, p. 136.
59 *Phenomenology of the Social World*, pp. 188–189.
60 *Phenomenology of the Social World*, p. 190.
61 *Phenomenology of the Social World*, p. 190.
62 Schutz, "Parsons' Theory of Social Action," p. 58.
63 "Parsons' Theory of Social Action," p. 59. Since those "puppets" perform in specific finite provinces of meaning, ideal types should refer to the types of social action typical within specific provinces. Schutz's studies of ideal types and finite provinces of meaning,

taken together, offer grounds for reliably imputing subjective meaning and motivation; see William C. Gay, "Probability in the Social Sciences: A Critique of Weber and Schutz," *Human Studies* 1 (January 1978), 30–31.

64 Schutz, *Collected Papers I*, pp. 43–44.

65 Cf. John Kultgen, "Intentionality and the Publicity of the Perceptual World," *Philosophy and Phenomenological Research* 33 (June 1973), 503.

66 Schutz, *Phenomenology of the Social World*, p. 61.

67 Ruth Macklin, "Reasons vs. Causes in Explanation of Action," *Philosophy and Phenomenological Research* 33 (September 1972), 86.

68 Schutz, *Collected Papers I*, pp. 44–45.

69 *Collected Papers I*, pp. 33, 42.

70 Alfred Schutz, "Choice and the Social Sciences," in Embree, ed., *Life-World and Consciousness*, pp. 578, 586.

71 Alfred Schutz, *On Phenomenology and Social Relations*, ed. Helmut R. Wagner, Chicago, University of Chicago Press, 1970, p. 91.

72 Schutz and Luckmann, *Structures*, p. 326.

73 *Structures*, p. 315.

74 *Structures*, p. 321.

75 *Structures*, p. 315.

76 Schutz, "Parsons' Theory of Action," p. 32.

77 "Parsons' Theory of Action," p. 137; footnote.

78 "Parsons' Theory of Action," p. 35.

79 Cf. Giddens, *New Rules of Sociological Method*, p. 112. In broader terms, Schutz indicated that "our practical interest alone, as it arises in a certain situation of our life and as it will be modified by the change in the situation which is just on the point of occurring, is the only relevant principle in the building up of the perspective structure in which our social world appears to us in daily life." Alfred Schutz, *Collected Papers II: Studies in Social Theory*, ed. Arvid Brodersen, The Hague, Nijhoff, 1976, p. 72.

80 Schutz, "Choice and the Social Sciences," p. 565.

81 See Schutz, *Collected Papers I*, pp. 83–84; *Phenomenology of the Social World*, pp. 66–68.

82 Schutz, *Collected Papers I*, p. 83.

83 Schutz and Luckmann, *Structures*, p. 114.

84 Concerning the differences between these two activities, see Schutz, *Collected Papers I*, pp. 72–73.

85 Burger, *Weber's Theory of Concept Formation*, p. 171.

86 Arthur C. Danto, "Complex Events," *Philosophy and Phenomenological Research* 30 (September 1969), 73, 75.

87 Burke, *Language as Symbolic Action*, p. 436.

88 For an elaboration of this point see Paul Ricoeur, *Husserl: An Analysis of His Phenomenology*, trans. Edward G. Ballard and Lester E. Embree, Evanston, Ill., Northwestern University Press, 1967, pp. 213–233; also see Alexander Pfander, *Phenomenology of Willing and Motivation*, Evanston, Ill., Northwestern University Press, 1967, pp. 20–23.

89 Edmund Husserl, "Husserl's Inaugural Lecture at Freiburg im Breisgau (1917)," in Embree, ed., *Life-World and Consciousness*, p. 8.

90 Maurice Natanson, "The Claims of Immediacy," in M. Natanson and H. W. Johnstone, Jr., eds., *Philosophy, Rhetoric, and Argumentation*, University Park, Pennsylvania State University Press, 1965, p. 16.

91 The dimensions contrasted here are from Joseph P. Fell III, *Emotion in the Thought of Sartre*, New York, Columbia University Press, 1965, p. 104; Lester E. Embree, "Toward a Phenomenology of Theoria," in Embree, ed., *Life-World and Consciousness*, p. 195.

92 Susan Shott, "The Sociology of Emotion: Some Starting Points," in Scott G. McNall, ed., *Theoretical Perspectives in Sociology*, New York, St. Martin's Press, 1979, pp. 451– 452.

93 Susan Shott, "Emotion and Social Life: A Symbolic Interactionist Analysis," *American Journal of Sociology* 84 (May 1979), 1323.

94 Theodore D. Kemper, *A Social Interactional Theory of Emotions*, New York, Wiley-Interscience, 1978, p. 49.

95 Garth Gillan, "The Noematics of Reason," *Philosophy and Phenomenological Research* 32 (June 1972), 525, 528.

96 Kai T. Erikson, *Everything in Its Path: Destruction of Community in the Buffalo Creek Flood*, New York, Simon and Schuster, 1976, p. 47. The remaining page references in the text refer to this study.

Bibliography

Adato, Albert. 1979. "Unanticipated Topic Continuations." *Human Studies* 2 (April), 171–186.

1980. " 'Occasionality' as a Constituent Feature of the Known-in-Common Character of Topics." *Human Studies* 3 (January), 47–64.

Armstrong, Edward G. 1979. "Phenomenologophobia." *Human Studies* 2 (January), 63–75.

Atkinson, Mick A. 1980. "Some Practical Uses of 'A Natural Lifetime.' " *Human Studies* 3 (January), 33–46.

Attewell, Paul. 1944. "Ethnomethodology Since Garfinkel." *Theory and Society* 1, 179–210.

Bauman, Zygmunt. 1978. *Hermeneutics and Social Science*. New York: Columbia University Press.

Bendix, Reinhard, 1962. *Max Weber: An Intellectual Portrait*. Garden City, N.Y.: Anchor Books.

1970. *Embattled Reason: Essays on Social Knowledge*. New York: Oxford University Press.

Berger, Gaston. 1972. *The Cogito in Husserl's Philosophy*. Trans. Kathleen McLaughlin. Evanston, Ill.: Northwestern University Press.

Berger, Peter L. 1963. *Invitation to Sociology: A Humanistic Perspective*. Garden City, N.Y.: Anchor Books.

Berger, Peter L., and Thomas Luckmann. 1967. *The Social Construction of Reality: A Treatise in the Sociology of Knowledge*. Garden City, N.Y.: Anchor Books.

Biemel, Walter. 1970. "The Decisive Phases in the Development of Husserl's Philosophy." In R. O. Elveton, ed. and trans., *The Phenomenology of Husserl*, pp. 148–173. Chicago: Quadrangle.

Bien, Joseph, ed. 1978. *Phenomenology and the Social Sciences*. The Hague: Nijhoff.

Bittner, Egon. 1973. "Objectivity and Realism in Sociology." In George Psathas, ed., *Phenomenological Sociology*, pp. 109–125. New York: Wiley.

1974. "The Concept of Organization." In Roy Turner, ed., *Ethnomethodology*, pp. 69–81. Baltimore: Penguin.

Blum, Alan F. 1970. "The Corpus of Knowledge as a Normative Order: Intellectual Critiques of the Social Order of Knowledge and the Commonsense Features of Bodies of Knowledge." In J. C. McKinney and E. A. Tiryakian, eds., *Theoretical Sociology*, pp. 319–336. New York: Appleton-Century-Crofts.

1972. "Sociology, Wrongdoing, and Akrasia: An Attempt to Think Greek about the Problem of Theory and Practice." In R. A. Scott and J. D. Douglas, eds., *Theoretical Perspectives on Deviance*, pp. 342–362. New York: Basic Books.

1974. "Positive Thinking." *Theory and Society* 1 (Fall), 245–269.

1974. *Theorizing*. London: Heinemann Educational Books.

Boorstin, Daniel J. 1971. *Democracy and Its Discontents: Reflections on Everyday America*. New York: Random House.

198

Brand, Gerd. 1967. "Intentionality, Reduction, and Intentional Analysis in Husserl's Later Manuscripts." In Joseph J. Kockelmans, ed., *Phenomenology*, pp. 197–217. Garden City, N.Y.: Anchor.

Brotz, Howard. 1974. "Theory and Practice: Ethnomethodology versus Humane Ethnography." *Jewish Journal of Sociology* XVI (December), 225–236.

Brown, Richard H. 1978. *A Poetic for Sociology: Toward a Logic of Discovery for the Human Sciences*. Cambridge: Cambridge University Press.

Burger, Thomas. 1976. *Max Weber's Theory of Concept Formation: History, Laws, and Ideal Types*. Durham, N.C.: Duke University Press.

Burke, Kenneth. 1966. *Language as Symbolic Action: Essays on Life, Literature, and Method*. Berkeley: University of California Press.

   1969. *A Grammar of Motives*. Berkeley: University of California Press.

   1969. *A Rhetoric of Motives*. Berkeley: University of California Press.

Cairns, Dorion. 1968. "An Approach to Phenomenology." In Marvin Farber, ed., *Philosophical Essays in Memory of Edmund Husserl*, pp. 3–18. New York: Greenwood.

Carpenter, G. Russell. 1976. "On Structuralism and Sociological Domain." *American Sociologist* 11 (May), 133–137.

Carr, David. 1977. "Husserl's Problematic Concept of the Life-World." In F. A. Elliston and P. McCormick, eds., *Husserl: Expositions and Appraisals*, pp. 202–212. Notre Dame, Ind.: University of Notre Dame Press.

Carr, David, and Edward S. Casey, eds. 1973. *Exploration in Phenomenology*. The Hague: Nijhoff.

Cassirer, Ernst. 1957. *The Philosophy of Symbolic Forms. Volume Three: The Phenomenology of Knowledge*. Trans. Ralph Manheim. New Haven: Yale University Press.

Chapman, Harmon M. 1953. "Realism and Phenomenology." In John Wild, ed., *The Return to Reason*, pp. 3–35. Chicago: Regnery. Also in Natanson, 1963, 79–115.

Chatterjee, Margaret. 1969. "Language as Phenomenon." *Philosophy and Phenomenological Research* 30 (September), 116–121.

Chisholm, Roderick M. 1960. "Editor's Introduction." In Roderick M. Chisholm, ed., *Realism and the Background of Phenomenology*, pp. 3–36. Glencoe, Ill.: Free Press.

   Ed. 1960. *Realism and the Background of Phenomenology*. Glencoe, Ill.: Free Press.

Chua, Beng-Huat. 1977. "Delineating a Marxist Interest in Ethnomethodology." *American Sociologist* 12 (February), 24–32.

Cicourel, Aaron V. 1972. "Basic and Normative Rules in the Negotiation of Status and Role." In David Sudnow, ed., *Studies in Social Interaction*, pp. 229–258. New York: Free Press.

   1972. "Delinquency and the Attribution of Responsibility." In R. A. Scott and J. D. Douglas, eds., *Theoretical Perspectives on Deviance*, pp. 142–157. New York: Basic Books.

   1973. *Cognitive Sociology: Language and Meaning in Social Interaction*. Baltimore: Penguin.

Colfax, J. David, and Jack L. Roach, eds. 1971. *Radical Sociology*. New York: Basic Books.

Collins, Randall. 1975. *Conflict Sociology: Toward an Explanatory Science*. New York: Academic Press.

Coser, Lewis A. 1975. "Presidential Address: Two Methods in Search of a Substance." *American Sociologist Review* 40 (December), 691–700.

Coulter, Jeff. 1974. "Decontextualized Meanings: Current Approaches to Verstehende Investigations." In Marcello Truzzi, ed., *Verstehen: Subjective Understanding in the Social Sciences*, pp. 135–164. Reading, Mass.: Addison-Wesley.

   1979. "Beliefs and Practical Understanding." In George Psathas, ed., *Everyday Language: Studies in Ethnomethodology*, pp. 163–186. New York: Irvington.

   1979. "The Brain as Agent." *Human Studies* 2 (October), 335–348.

Craib, Ian. 1976. *Existentialism and Sociology: A Study of Jean-Paul Sartre*. Cambridge: Cambridge University Press.

Cuzzort, Ray P., and Edith W. King. 1980. *20th Century Social Thought*, 3d ed. New York: Holt, Rinehart and Winston.

Dallmayr, Fred R. 1973. "Phenomenology and Social Science: An Overview and Appraisal." In D. Carr and E. S. Casey, eds., *Explorations in Phenomenology*, pp. 133–166. The Hague: Nijhoff.

Dallmayr, Fred R., and Thomas A. McCarthy, eds. 1977. *Understanding and Social Inquiry*. Notre Dame, Ind.: University of Notre Dame Press.

Danto, Arthur C. 1969. "Complex Events." *Philosophy and Phenomenological Research* 30 (September), 66–77.

deMuralt, Andre. 1974. *The Idea of Phenomenology: Husserlian Exemplarism*. Trans. Gary L. Breckon. Evanston, Ill.: Northwestern University Press.

Denzin, Norman K. 1970. "Symbolic Interactionism and Ethnomethodology." In Jack D. Douglas. ed., *Understanding Everyday Life*, pp. 259–284. Chicago: Aldine.

Deutscher, Irwin. 1973. *What We Say/What We Do: Sentiments and Acts*. Glenview, Ill.: Scott, Foresman.

Douglas, Jack D. 1970. "Deviance and Order in a Pluralistic Society." In J. C. McKinney and E. A. Tiryakian, eds., *Theoretical Sociology*, pp. 367–401. New York: Appleton-Century-Crofts.

    1970. *Deviance and Respectability: The Social Construction of Moral Meanings*. New York: Basic Books.

    1970. "Deviance and Respectability: The Social Construction of Moral Meanings." In Jack D. Douglas, ed., *Deviance and Respectability: The Social Construction of Moral Meanings*, pp. 3–30. New York: Basic Books.

    1970. "Understanding Everyday Life." In Jack D. Douglas, ed., *Understanding Everyday Life*, pp. 3–44. Chicago: Aldine.

    1972. "The Experience of the Absurd and the Problem of Social Order." In R. A. Scott and J. D. Douglas, eds., *Theoretical Perspectives on Deviance*, pp. 189–214. New York: Basic Books.

    1977. "Appendix: The Origins of Existential Sociology." In J. D. Douglas and R. A. Scott, eds., *Existential Sociology*, pp. 291–297. Cambridge: Cambridge University Press.

Dreitzel, Peter. 1970. "Introduction: Patterns of Communicative Behavior." In Peter Dreitzel, ed., *Recent Sociology No. 2: Patterns of Communicative Behavior*, pp. vii–xxii. New York: Macmillan.

    Ed. 1970. *Recent Sociology No. 2: Patterns of Communicative Behavior*. New York: Macmillan.

Edie, James M. 1963. "Expression and Metaphor." *Philosophy and Phenomenological Research* 23 (June), 538–561.

    1964. "Transcendental Phenomenology and Existentialism." *Philosophy and Phenomenological Research* 25 (September), 52–63.

    1967. *Phenomenology in America*. Chicago: Quadrangle.

Edie, James M., Francis H. Parker, and Calvin O. Schrag, eds. 1970. *Patterns of the Life-World: Essays in Honor of John Wild*. Evanston, Ill.: Northwestern University Press.

    1972. "Introduction." In Gaston Berger, *The Cogito in Husserl's Philosophy*, pp. ix–xxiv. Trans. Kathleen McLaughlin. Evanston, Ill.: Northwestern University Press.

Ehman, Robert R. 1970. "The Phenomenon of World." In J. M. Edie, F. H. Parker, and C. O. Schrag, eds., *Patterns of The Life-World: Essays in Honor of John Wild*, pp. 85–106. Evanston, Ill.: Northwestern University Press.

Eley, Lothar. 1973. "Afterword to Husserl, *Experience and Judgment:* Phenomenology and Philosophy of Language." In Edmund Husserl, *Experience and Judgment*, pp. 399–429. Rev. and ed. Ludwig Landgrebe; trans. James S. Churchill and Karl Ameriks. Evanston, Ill.: Northwestern University Press.

Elveton, R. O. 1970. "Introduction." In *The Phenomenology of Husserl*, pp. 3–39. Ed. and trans. R. O. Elveton. Chicago: Quadrangle.

1970. *The Phenomenology of Husserl*. Chicago: Quadrangle.

Embree, Lester E. 1972. "Toward a Phenomenology of Theoria." In Lester E. Embree, ed., *Life-World and Consciousness: Essays for Aron Gurwitsch*, pp. 191–207. Evanston, Ill.: Northwestern University Press.

1974. *Phenomenology and the Theory of Science*. Evanston, Ill.: Northwestern University Press.

Erikson, Kai T. 1966. *Wayward Puritans: A Study in the Sociology of Deviance*. New York: Wiley.

1976. *Everything in Its Path: Destruction of Community in the Buffalo Creek Flood*. New York: Simon and Schuster.

Farber, Marvin. 1951. "Experience and Transcendence: A Chapter in Recent Phenomenology and Existentialism." *Philosophy and Phenomenological Research* XII (September), 1–23.

1963. "First Philosophy and the Problem of the World." *Philosophy and Phenomenological Research* 23 (March), 315–334.

1966. *The Aims of Phenomenology: The Motives, Methods, and Impact of Husserl's Thought*. New York: Harper Torchbooks.

1968. "The Ideal of a Presuppositionless Philosophy." In Marvin Farber, ed., *Philosophical Essays in Memory of Edmund Husserl*, pp. 44–64. New York: Greenwood.

Ed. 1968. *Philosophical Essays in Memory of Edmund Husserl*. New York: Greenwood.

Fell, Joseph P., III. 1965. *Emotion in the Thought of Sartre*. New York: Columbia University Press.

Fen, Sing-Nan. 1951. "Situation as an Existential Unit of Experience." *Philosophy and Phenomenological Research* XI (June), 555–560.

Filmer, Paul. 1972. "On Harold Garfinkel's Ethnomethodology." In Paul Filmer, Michael Phillipson, David Silverman, and David Walsh, *New Directions in Sociological Theory*, pp. 203–234. Cambridge, Mass.: MIT Press.

Filmer, Paul, Michael Phillipson, David Silverman, and David Walsh. 1972. *New Directions in Sociological Theory*. London: Collier-Macmillan.

Fink, Eugen. 1970. "The Phenomenological Philosophy of Edmund Husserl and Contemporary Criticism." In R. O. Elveton, ed. and trans., *The Phenomenology of Husserl*, pp. 74–147. Chicago: Quadrangle.

1972. "What Does the Phenomenology of Edmund Husserl Want to Accomplish? (The Phenomenological Idea of Laying-a-Ground)." Trans. Arthur Grugan. *Research in Phenomenology* 11, 5–27.

Forsyth, Donelson R. 1979. "Scientific and Common Sense Reason: A Comparison." *Human Studies* 2 (April), 159–170.

Friedrichs, Robert W. 1970. *A Sociology of Sociology*. New York: Free Press.

Funke, Gerhard. 1973. "Phenomenology and History." In Maurice Natanson, ed., *Phenomenology and the Social Sciences*, Vol. 2, pp. 3–101. Evanston, Ill.: Northwestern University Press.

Gadamer, Hans-Georg. 1976. *Philosophical Hermeneutics*. Trans. and ed. David E. Linge. Berkeley: University of California Press.

Garfinkel, Harold. 1952. The Perception of the Other: A Study in Social Order. PhD. diss., Harvard University.

1963. "A Conception of, and Experiments with, 'Truth' as a Condition of Stable Concerted Actions." In O. J. Harvey, ed., *Motivation and Social Interaction*, pp. 187–238. New York: Ronald Press.

1967. *Studies in Ethnomethodology*. Englewood Cliffs, N.J.: Prentice-Hall.

1972. "Studies of the Routine Grounds of Everyday Activities." In David Sudnow, ed., *Studies in Social Interaction*, pp. 1–30. New York: Free Press.

1974. "The Origins of the Term 'Ethnomethodology.' " In Roy Turner, ed., *Ethnomethodology*, pp. 15–18. Baltimore: Penguin.

Garfinkel, Harold, and Harvey Sacks. 1970. "On Formal Structures of Practical Actions." In J. C. McKinney and E. A. Tiryakian, eds., *Theoretical Sociology*, pp. 337–366. New York: Appleton-Century-Crofts.

Gay, William C. 1978. "Probability in the Social Sciences: A Critique of Weber and Schutz." *Human Studies* 1 (January), 16–37.

Gendlin, Eugene T. 1962. *Experiencing and the Creation of Meaning*. New York: Free Press.

1973. "Experiential Phenomenology." In Maurice Natanson, ed., *Phenomenology and the Social Sciences*, pp. 281–319. Evanston, Ill.: Northwestern University Press.

Gephart, Robert P., Jr. 1978. "Status Degradation and Organizational Succession: An Ethnomethodological Approach." *Administrative Science Quarterly* 23 (December), 553–581.

Giddens, Anthony. 1976. "Classical Social Theory and the Origins of Modern Sociology." *American Journal of Sociology* 81 (January), 703–729.

1976. *New Rules of Sociological Method: A Positive Critique of Interpretive Sociologies*. New York: Basic Books.

Gidlow, Bob. 1972. "Ethnomethodology: A New Name for Old Practices." *British Journal of Sociology* 22 (December), 395–405.

Gillan, Garth. 1972. "The Noematics of Reason." *Philosophy and Phenomenological Research* 32 (June), 524–530.

Ed. 1973. *The Horizons of the Flesh: Critical Perspectives on the Thought of Merleau-Ponty*. Carbondale: Southern Illinois University Press.

1973. "In the Folds of the Flesh: Philosophy and Language." In Garth Gillan, ed., *The Horizons of the Flesh: Critical Perspectives on The Thought of Merleau-Ponty*, pp. 1–60. Carbondale: Southern Illinois University Press.

Gleeson, Denis, and Michael Erben. 1976. "Meaning in Context: Notes toward a Critique of Ethnomethodology." *British Journal of Sociology* 27 (December), 474–483.

Goddard, David. 1976. "Reply to Carpenter." *American Sociologist* 11 (May), 137–139.

1976. "On Structuralism and Sociology." *American Sociologist* 11 (May), 123–133.

Goodwin, Charles. 1980. "The Interactive Construction of a Sentence in Natural Conversation." In George Psathas, ed., *Everyday Language: Studies in Ethnomethodology*, pp. 97–121. New York: Irvington.

Gorman, Robert A. 1977. *The Dual Vision: Alfred Schutz and the Myth of Phenomenological Social Science*. Boston: Routledge & Kegan Paul.

Gouldner, Alvin W. 1970. *The Coming Crisis of Western Sociology*. New York: Equinox Books.

1973. *For Sociology: Renewal and Critique in Sociology Today*. New York: Basic Books.

Grathoff, Richard. 1978. "Introduction." In Richard Grathoff, ed., *The Theory of Social Action: The Correspondence of Alfred Schutz and Talcott Parsons*, pp. xvii–xxvi. Bloomington: Indiana University Press.

Ed. 1978. *The Theory of Social Action: The Correspondence of Afred Schutz and Talcott Parsons*. Bloomington: Indiana University Press.

Gregory, Stanford W., Jr. 1980. " 'Social Resonance' as Demonstrated in Conversation." Paper presented at annual meeting of American Sociological Association, New York, August 27–31.

Gurwitsch, Aron. 1955. "The Phenomenological and the Psychological Approach to Consciousness." *Philosophy and Phenomenological Research* XV (March), 303–319.

1964. *The Field of Consciousness*. Pittsburgh: Duquesne University Press.

1966. *Studies in Phenomenology and Psychology*. Evanston, Ill.: Northwestern University Press.

1970. "Problems of the Life-World." In Maurice Natanson, ed., *Phenomenology and Social Reality*, pp. 35–61. The Hague: Nijhoff.

1973. "Perceptual Coherence as the Foundation of the Judgment of Predication." In F. Kersten and R. Zaner, eds., *Phenomenology: Continuation and Criticism*, pp. 62–89. The Hague: Nijhoff.

1974. "The Life-World and the Phenomenological Theory of Science." In Lester Embree, ed., *Phenomenology and the Theory of Science*, pp. 3–32. Evanston, Ill.: Northwestern University Press. (Originally appeared as: "Problems of the Life-World." In Maurice Natanson, ed., *Phenomenology and Social Reality*, pp. 35–61. The Hague: Nijhoff, 1970.)

1974. "Some Fundamental Principles of Constitutive Phenomenology." In Lester Embree, ed., *Phenomenology and the Theory of Science*, pp. 190–209. Evanston, Ill.: Northwestern University Press.

Hadden, Stuart C., and Marilyn Lester. 1978. "Talking Identity: The Production of 'Self' in Interaction." *Human Studies* 1 (October), 331–356.

Hansen, Donald A., ed. 1969. *Explorations in Sociology and Counseling*. Boston: Houghton Mifflin.

Heap, James L. 1976. "Reconceiving the Social." *Canadian Review of Sociology and Anthropology* 13 (August), 271–281.

1977. "Verstehen, Language, and Warrants." *Sociological Quarterly* 18 (Spring), 177–184.

1980. "Description in Ethnomethodology." *Human Studies* 3 (January), 87–106.

Heap, James L., and Phillip A. Roth. 1978. "On Phenomenological Sociology." In Alan Wells, ed., *Contemporary Sociological Theories*, pp. 279–293. Santa Monica, Calif.: Goodyear.

Heritage, J. C., and D. R. Watson. 1980. "Formulations as Conversational Objects." In George Psathas, ed., *Everyday Language: Studies in Ethnomethodology*, pp. 123–162. New York: Irvington.

Hilbert, Richard A. 1977. "Approaching Reason's Edge: 'Nonsense' as the Final Solution to the Problem of Meaning." *Sociological Inquiry* 47, No. 1, 25–31.

1980. " 'Role': From Functionalism to Symbolic Interactionism to Ethnomethodology." Paper presented at annual meeting of American Sociological Association, New York, August 27–31.

Hill, Richard J., and Kathleen S. Crittenden, eds. 1968. *Proceedings of the Purdue Symposium on Ethnomethodology*. Lafayette, Ind.: Institute for the Study of Social Change, Purdue University.

Hinshaw, Virgil, Jr. 1958. "The Given." *Philosophy and Phenomenological Research* XVIII (March), 312–325.

Husserl, Edmund. 1960. "Phenomenology." In Roderick M. Chisholm, ed., *Realism and the Background of Phenomenology*, pp. 118–128. Trans. C. V. Solomon. Glencoe, Ill.: Free Press.

1960. "Phenomenology and Anthropology." In Roderick M. Chisholm, ed., *Realism and the Background of Phenomenology*, pp. 129–142. Trans. Richard G. Schmitt. Glencoe, Ill.: Free Press.

1964. *The Idea of Phenomenology*. Trans. William P. Alston and George Nakhnikian. The Hague: Nijhoff.

1964. *The Phenomenology of Internal Time-Consciousness*. Ed. Martin Heidegger, trans. James S. Churchill. Bloomington: Indiana University Press.

1965. *Phenomenology and the Crisis of Philosophy*. Trans. Quentin Lauer. New York: Harper Torchbooks.

1970. *Cartesian Meditations: An Introduction to Phenomenology*. Trans. Dorion Cairns. The Hague: Nijhoff.

1970. *The Crisis of European Sciences and Transcendental Phenomenology*. Trans. David Carr. Evanston, Ill.: Northwestern University Press.

1972. "Husserl's Inaugural Lecture at Freiburg im Breisqua (1917)." In Lester E. Embree, ed., *Life-World and Consciousness: Essays for Aron Gurwitsch*, pp. 3–18. Trans. Robert Welsh Jordan. Evanston, Ill.: Northwestern University Press.

1972. *Ideas*. Trans. W. R. Boyce Gibson. New York: Collier.

1973. *Experience and Judgment: Investigations in a Genealogy of Logic*. Rev. and ed. Ludwig Landgrebe; trans. James S. Churchill and Karl Ameriks. Evanston, Ill.: Northwestern University Press.

Ihde, Don. 1970. "Auditory Imagination." In F. J. Smith, ed., *Phenomenology in Perspective*, pp. 202–215. The Hague: Nijhoff.

Johnson, Doyle Paul. 1981. *Sociological Theory: Classical Founders and Contemporary Perspectives*. New York: Wiley.

Jordan, Robert Welsh. 1973. "Being and Time: Some Aspects of the Ego's Involvement in his Mental Life." In F. Kersten and R. Zaner, eds., *Phenomenology: Continuation and Criticism*, pp. 105–113. The Hague: Nijhoff.

Kando, Thomas M. 1977. *Social Interaction*. St. Louis: Mosby.

Kaufmann, Felix. 1968. "Phenomenology and Logical Empiricism." In Marvin Farber, ed., *Philosophical Essays in Memory of Edmund Husserl*, pp. 124–142. New York: Greenwood.

Kemper, Theodore D. 1978. *A Social Interactional Theory of Emotions*. New York: Wiley-Interscience.

Kersten, Fred. 1971. "The Life-World Revisited." *Research in Phenomenology* 1, 33–62.

Kersten, Frederick I. 1972. "The Constancy Hypothesis in the Social Sciences." In Lester E. Embree, ed., *Life-World and Consciousness: Essays for Aron Gurwitsch*, pp. 521–563. Evanston, Ill.: Northwestern University Press.

Kersten, Frederick I., and R. Zaner, eds. 1973. *Phenomenology: Continuation and Criticism: Essays In Memory of Dorion Cairns*. The Hague: Nijhoff.

Kockelmans, Joseph J. 1967. *A First Introduction to Husserl's Phenomenology*. Pittsburgh: Duquesne University Press.

1967. "Intentional and Constitutive Analyses." In Joseph J. Kockelmans, ed., *Phenomenology*, pp. 137–146. Garden City, N.Y.: Anchor.

Ed. 1967. *Phenomenology*. Garden City, N.Y.: Anchor.

1973. "Theoretical Problems in Phenomenological Psychology." In Maurice Natanson, ed., *Phenomenology and the Social Sciences*, pp. 225–280. Evanston, Ill.: Northwestern University Press.

1978. "Reflections on Social Theory." *Human Studies* 1 (January), 1–15.

Kuhn, Helmet. 1968. "The Phenomenological Concept of 'Horizon.' " In Marvin Farber, ed., *Philosophical Essays in Memory of Edmund Husserl*, pp. 106–123. New York: Greenwood.

Kultgen, John. 1973. "Intentionality and the Publicity of the Perceptual World." *Philosophy and Phenomenological Research* 33 (June), 503–513.

Kwant, Remy C. 1969. *Phenomenology of Expression*. Pittsburgh: Duquesne University Press.

Ladd, John. 1953. "Reason and Practice." In John Wild, ed., *The Return to Reason*, pp. 235–258. Chicago: Regnery.

Landgrebe, Ludwig. 1973. "The Phenomenological Concept of Experience." Trans. Donn C. Welton. *Philosophy and Phenomenological Research* 34 (September), 1–13.

Lauer, Quentin. 1965. "Introduction." In Edmund Husserl, *Phenomenology and the Crisis of Philosophy*, pp. 1–68. Trans. Quentin Lauer. New York: Harper Torchbooks.

　1965. *Phenomenology: Its Genesis and Prospect*. New York: Harper Torchbooks. (Originally published as: *The Triumph of Subjectivity*. New York: Fordham University Press, 1958.)

　1967. "The Other Explained Intentionally." In Joseph J. Kockelmans, ed., *Phenomenology*, pp. 167–182. Garden City, N.Y.: Anchor.

Law, John, and Peter Lodge. 1978. "Structure as Process and Environmental Constraint: A Note on Ethnomethodology." *Theory and Society* 5 (May), 373–386.

Lawrence, Nathaniel, and Daniel O'Connor. 1967. "The Primary Phenomenon: Human Existence." In N. Lawrence and D. O'Connor, eds., *Readings in Existential Phenomenology*, pp. 1–11. Englewood Cliffs, N.J.: Prentice-Hall.

　Eds. 1967. *Readings in Existential Phenomenology*. Englewood Cliffs, N.J.: Prentice-Hall.

Lee, Donald S. 1966. "The Construction of Empirical Concepts." *Philosophy and Phenomenological Research* 27 (December), 183–198.

Leiter, Kenneth. 1980. *A Primer on Ethnomethodology*. New York: Oxford University Press.

Lemert, Charles C. 1979. "De-Centered Analysis." *Theory and Society* 7 (May), 289–306.

Lester, Marilyn. 1977. "The Interactional Generation of Newsworthiness: Ideology as Accomplishment." Paper presented at annual meeting of American Sociological Association, Chicago, September.

Levin, David Michael. 1970. *Reason and Evidence in Husserl's Phenomenology*. Evanston, Ill.: Northwestern University Press.

Liberman, Ken. 1980. "Ambiguity and Gratuitous Concurrence in Inter-Cultural Communication." *Human Studies* 3 (January), 65–85.

Lingis, Alphonso F. 1972. "The Perception of Others." *Research in Phenomenology* II, 47–62.

Luckmann, Benita. 1978. "The Small Life-Worlds of Modern Man." In Thomas Luckmann, ed., *Phenomenology and Sociology: Selected Readings*, pp. 275–290. Harmondsworth, Middlesex, England: Penguin.

　Ed. 1978. *Phenomenology and Sociology: Selected Readings*. Harmondsworth, Middlesex, England: Penguin.

Luijpen, William A. 1966. *Phenomenology and Humanism: A Primer in Existentialist Phenomenology*. Pittsburgh: Duquesne University Press.

　1969. *Existential Phenomenology*. Rev. ed. Pittsburgh: Duquesne University Press.

Lynd, Robert S. 1964. *Knowledge for What? The Place of Social Science in American Culture*. New York: Grove Press.

Macklin, Ruth. 1972. "Reasons vs. Causes in Explanation of Action." *Philosophy and Phenomenological Research* 33 (September), 78–89.

Mannheim, Karl. 1963. "American Sociology." In M. Stein and A. Vidich, eds., *Sociology on Trial*, pp. 3–11. Englewood Cliffs, N.J.: Prentice-Hall.

Marcuse, Herbert. 1968. *Negations: Essays in Critical Theory*. Boston: Beacon Press.

Marx, Karl. 1964. *Karl Marx: Early Writings*. Trans. and ed. T. B. Bottomore. New York: McGraw-Hill.

1967. *Writings of the Young Marx on Philosophy and Society*. Ed. and trans. Lloyd D. Easton and Kurt H. Guddat. Garden City, N.Y.: Anchor.

Marx, Werner. 1972. "The Life-World and Gurwitsch's 'Orders of Existence.' " In Lester E. Embree, ed., *Life-World and Consciousness: Essays for Aron Gurwitsch*, pp. 445–446. Evanston, Ill.: Northwestern University Press.

Mayrl, William W. 1977. "Ethnomethodology: Sociology without Society?" In F. Dallmayr and T. McCarthy, eds., *Understanding and Social Inquiry*, pp. 262–279. Notre Dame, Ind.: University of Notre Dame Press.

McGill, V. J. 1973. "Evidence in Husserl's Phenomenology." In F. Kersten and R. Zaner, eds., *Phenomenology: Continuation and Criticism*, pp. 145–166. The Hague: Nijhoff.

McHugh, Peter. 1968. *Defining the Situation: The Organization of Meaning in Social Interaction*. Indianapolis: Bobbs-Merrill.

McKinney, John C., and Edward A. Tiryakian, eds. 1970. *Theoretical Sociology*. New York: Appleton-Century-Crofts.

McNall, Scott G., ed. 1979. *Theoretical Perspectives in Sociology*. New York: St. Martin's Press.

McNall, Scott, and James C. M. Johnson. 1975. "The New Conservatives: Ethnomethodologists, Phenomenologists, and Symbolic Interactionists." *The Insurgent Sociologist* V (Summer), 49–65.

Meadows, Paul. 1945. "The Dialectic of the Situation: Some Notes on Situational Psychology." *Philosophy and Phenomenological Research* V (March), 354–364.

Mehan, Hugh, and Houston Wood. 1975. "The Morality of Ethnomethodology." *Theory and Society* 2 (Winter), 509–530.

1975. *The Reality of Ethnomethodology*. New York: Wiley-Interscience.

Mennell, Stephen. 1974. *Sociological Theory: Uses and Unities*. New York: Praeger.

Merleau-Ponty, Maurice. 1963. *In Praise of Philosophy*. Trans. John Wild and James M. Edie. Evanston, Ill.: Northwestern University Press.

1963. *The Structure of Behavior*. Trans. Alden L. Fisher. Boston: Beacon Press.

1964. *Signs*. Trans. Richard C. McCleary. Evanston, Ill.: Northwestern University Press.

Mills, C. Wright. 1959. *The Sociological Imagination*. New York: Oxford University Press.

Mohanty, J. N. 1954. "The 'Object' in Husserl's Phenomenology." *Philosophy and Phenomenological Research* XIV (March), 343–353.

1969. *Edmund Husserl's Theory of Meaning*. The Hague: Nijhoff.

1979. "Husserl's Theory of Meaning." In F. A. Elliston and P. McCormick, eds., *Husserl: Expositions and Appraisals*, pp. 18–37. Notre Dame, Ind.: University of Notre Dame Press.

Moneta, Guiseppina Chiara. 1972. "The Foundation of Predicative Experience and the Spontaneity of Consciousness." In Lester E. Embree, ed., *Life-World and Consciousness: Essays for Aron Gurwitsch*, pp. 171–190. Evanston, Ill.: Northwestern University Press.

Morris, Monica B. 1977. *An Excursion into Creative Sociology*. New York: Columbia University Press.

Mueller, Claus. 1975. *The Politics of Communication: A Study in the Political Sociology of Language, Socialization, and Legitimation*. New York: Oxford University Press.

Mullins, Nicholas C. 1973. *Theories and Theory Groups in Contemporary American Sociology*. New York: Harper & Row.

Natanson, Maurice. 1956. "Phenomenology from the Natural Standpoint: A Reply to Van Meter Ames." *Philosophy and Phenomenological Research* XVII (December), 241–245.

1961. "History, Historicity, and the Alchemistry of Time." *Chicago Review* 15 (Summer), 76–92.

1962. *Literature, Philosophy, and the Social Sciences*. The Hague: Nijhoff.

1963. "A Study in Philosophy and the Social Sciences." In Maurice Natanson, ed., *Philosophy of the Social Sciences*, pp. 271–285. New York: Random House.

Ed. 1963. *Philosophy of the Social Sciences*. New York: Random House.

1965. "The Claims of Immediacy." In M. Natanson and H. W. Johnstone, Jr., eds., *Philosophy, Rhetoric, and Argumentation*, pp. 10–19. University Park: Pennsylvania State University Press.

1966. "Alienation and Social Role." *Social Research* 33 (Autumn), 375–388.

1966. "The Phenomenology of Alfred Schutz." *Inquiry* 9, 147–155.

1967. "Phenomenology as a Rigorous Science." *International Philosophical Quarterly* 7 (March), 5–20.

1969. "Philosophy and Psychiatry." In Maurice Natanson, ed., *Psychiatry and Philosophy*, pp. 85–110. New York: Springer-Verlag.

Ed. 1969. *Psychiatry and Philosophy*. New York: Springer-Verlag.

1970. "Alfred Schutz on Social Reality and Social Science." In Maurice Natanson, ed., *Phenomenology and Social Reality*, pp. 101–121. The Hague: Nijhoff.

1970. *The Journeying Self: A Study in Philosophy and Social Role*. Reading, Mass.: Addison-Wesley.

1970. "Phenomenology and Typification: A Study in the Philosophy of Alfred Schutz." *Social Research* 37 (Spring), 1–22.

Ed. 1970. *Phenomenology and Social Reality*. The Hague: Nijhoff.

1973. *Edmund Husserl: Philosopher of Infinite Tasks*. Evanston, Ill.: Northwestern University Press.

1973. "Introduction." In Alfred Schutz, *Collected Papers I: The Problem of Social Reality*, pp. xxv–xlvii. Ed. and introduced by Maurice Natanson. The Hague: Nijhoff.

1973. "Phenomenology and the Social Sciences." In Maurice Natanson, ed., *Phenomenology and the Social Sciences*, pp. 3–44. Evanston, Ill.: Northwestern University Press.

1973. *The Social Dynamics of George H. Mead*. The Hague: Nijhoff. (Originally published by Public Affairs Press, Washington, D.C., 1956.)

Ed. 1973. *Phenomenology and the Social Sciences*. Evanston, Ill.: Northwestern University Press.

1974. *Phenomenology, Role, and Reason: Essays on the Coherence and Deformation of Social Reality*. Springfield, Ill.: Thomas.

1978. "Foreword." In Richard Grathoff, ed., *The Theory of Social Action: The Correspondence of Alfred Schutz and Talcott Parsons*, pp. ix–xvi. Bloomington: Indiana University Press.

1978. "The Problem of Anonymity in the Thought of Alfred Schutz." In Joseph Bien, ed., *Phenomenology and the Social Sciences*, pp. 60–73. The Hague: Nijhoff.

Natanson, Maurice, and Henry W. Johnstone, eds. 1965. *Philosophy, Rhetoric, and Argumentation*. University Park: Pennsylvania State University Press.

Neisser, Hans P. 1959. "The Phenomenological Approach in the Social Sciences." *Philosophy and Phenomenological Research* 20 (December), 198–212.

Nisbet, Robert. 1975. *Twilight of Authority*. New York: Oxford University Press.

O'Neill, John. 1972. *Sociology as a Skin Trade: Essays towards a Reflexive Sociology*. New York: Harper & Row.

1974. "Introduction: Perception, Expression and History." In J. O'Neill, ed., *Phenomenology, Language and Sociology: Selected Essays of Maurice Merleau-Ponty*, pp. xi-xii. London: Heinemann.

1974. *Making Sense Together: An Introduction to Wild Sociology*. New York: Harper & Row.

Ed. 1974. *Phenomenology, Language and Sociology: Selected Essays of Maurice Merleau-Ponty*. London: Heinemann.

Orth, Ernst Wolfgang. 1973. "Phenomenology of Language as Phenomenology of Language and Logic." In Maurice Natanson, ed., *Phenomenology and the Social Sciences*, pp. 323–359. Evanston, Ill.: Northwestern University Press.

Paci, Enzo. 1970. "The 'Lebenswelt' as Ground and as 'Leib' in Husserl: Somatology, Psychology, Sociology." In J. M. Edie, F. H. Parker, and C. O. Schrag, eds., *Patterns of the Life-World: Essays in Honor of John Wild*, pp. 123–138. Evanston, Ill.: Northwestern University Press.

Parsons, Arthur S. 1978. "Interpretive Sociology: The Theoretical Significance of Verstehen in the Constitution of Social Reality." *Human Studies* 1 (April), 111–137.

Parsons, Talcott. 1978. "Talcott Parsons: A 1974 Retrospective Perspective." In Richard Grathoff, ed., *The Theory of Social Action: The Correspondence of Alfred Schutz and Talcott Parsons*, pp. 115–124. Bloomington: Indiana University Press.

Perkins, Moreland. 1953. "Intersubjectivity and Gestalt Psychology." *Philosophy and Phenomenological Research* XIII (June), 437–466.

Pettit, Philip. 1969. *On the Idea of Phenomenology*. Dublin: Scepter.

    1977. *The Concept of Structuralism: A Critical Analysis*. Berkeley: University of California Press.

Pfander, Alexander. 1967. *Phenomenology of Willing and Motivation*. Trans. Herbert Spiegelberg. Evanston, Ill.: Northwestern University Press.

Phillipson, Michael. 1972. "Phenomenological Philosophy and Sociology." In Paul Filmer, Michael Phillipson, David Silverman, and David Walsh, *New Directions in Sociological Theory*, pp. 119–163. London: Collier-Macmillan.

Polanyi, Michael, and Harry Prosch. 1975. *Meaning*. Chicago: University of Chicago Press.

Pollner, Melvin. 1974. "Sociological and Common-Senses Models of the Labelling Process." In Roy Turner, ed., *Ethnomethodology*, pp. 27–40. Baltimore: Penguin.

    1978. "Constitutive and Mundane Versions of Labeling Theory." *Human Studies* 1 (July), 269–288.

    1979. "Explicative Transactions: Making and Managing Meaning in Traffic Court." In George Psathas, ed., *Everyday Language: Studies in Ethnomethodology*, pp. 227–255. New York: Irvington.

Poloma, Margaret M. 1979. *Contemporary Sociological Theory*. New York: Macmillan.

Psathas, George. 1973. "Introduction." In George Psathas, ed., *Phenomenological Sociology*, pp. 1–21. New York: Wiley.

    Ed. 1973. *Phenomenological Sociology*. New York: Wiley.

    1974. "The Study of Everyday Structures and the Ethnomethodological Paradigm." Paper presented at colloquium, "Alfred Schutz und die idee des Alltags in den Sozialwissenschaften," University of Konstanz, June 23–27.

    1976. "Misinterpreting Ethnomethodology." Paper presented at annual meeting of American Sociological Association, New York, August.

    Ed. 1979. *Everyday Language: Studies in Ethnomethodology*. New York: Irvington.

    1980. "Approaches to the Study of the World of Everyday Life." *Human Studies* 3 (January), 3–17.

Rabil, Albert, Jr. 1967. *Merleau-Ponty: Existentialist of the Social World*. New York: Columbia University Press.

Reynolds, Larry T., and Janice M. Reynolds, eds. 1970. *The Sociology of Sociology: Analysis and Criticism of the Thought, Research, and Ethical Folkways of Sociology and its Practitioners*. New York: McKay.

Ricoeur, Paul. 1965. *Fallible Man: Philosophy of the Will*. Trans. Charles Kelbley. Chicago: Regnery.

1967. "The Antinomy of Human Reality and the Problem of Philosophical Anthropology." In N. Lawrence and D. O'Connor, eds., *Readings in Existential Phenomenology*, pp. 390–402. Englewood Cliffs, N.J.: Prentice-Hall.

1967. *Husserl: An Analysis of His Phenomenology*. Trans. Edward G. Ballard and Lester E. Embree. Evanston, Ill.: Northwestern University Press.

1967. *The Symbolism of Evil*. Trans. Emerson Buchanan. New York: Harper & Row.

Riepe, Dale, ed. 1973. *Phenomenology and Natural Existence: Essays in Honor of Marvin Farber*. Albany: State University of New York Press.

Roszak, Theodore. 1977. *Unfinished Animal: The Aquarian Frontier and the Evolution of Consciousness*. New York: Harper Colophon Books.

Rota, Gian-Carlo. 1973. "Edmund Husserl and the Reform of Logic." In D. Carr and E. S. Casey, eds., *Explorations in Phenomenology*, pp. 299–305. The Hague: Nijhoff.

Rotenstreich, Nathan. 1973. "Ambiguities of Husserl's Notion of Constitution." In Dale Riepe, ed., *Phenomenology and Natural Existence*, pp. 151–170. Albany: State University of New York Press.

Ryave, A. Lincoln, and James N. Schenkein. 1974. "Notes on the Art of Walking." In Roy Turner, ed., *Ethnomethodology*, pp. 265–274. Baltimore: Penguin.

Sacks, Harvey. 1974. "On the Analysability of Stories by Children." In Roy Turner, ed., *Ethnomethodology*, pp. 216–232. Baltimore: Penguin.

1979. "Hotrodder: A Revolutionary Category." In George Psathas, ed., *Everyday Language: Studies in Ethnomethodology*, pp. 7–14. New York: Irvington.

Sadler, William A., Jr. 1969. *Existence & Love: A New Approach in Existential Phenomenology*. New York: Scribner.

Sallis, John. 1975. "Image and Phenomenon." *Research in Phenomenology* V, 61–75.

Sapir, Edward. 1956. *Culture, Language and Personality*. Berkeley: University of California Press.

Schegloff, Emmanuel. 1972. "Notes on a Conversational Practice: Formulating Place." In David Sudnow, ed., *Studies in Social Interaction*, pp. 75–119. New York: Free Press.

Schegloff, Emmanuel, and Harvey Sacks. 1974. "Opening Up Closings." In Roy Turner, ed., *Ethnomethodology*, pp. 233–264. Baltimore: Penguin.

Schenkein, Jim. 1979. "The Radio Raiders Story." In George Psathas, ed., *Everyday Language: Studies in Ethnomethodology*, pp. 187–201. New York: Irvington.

Schiffrin, Deborah. 1977. "Opening Encounters." *American Sociological Review* 42 (October), 679–691.

Schott, Susan. 1979. "Emotion and Social Life: A Symbolic Interactionist Analysis." *American Journal of Sociology* 84 (May), 1317–1334.

1979. "The Sociology of Emotion: Some Starting Points." In Scott G. McNall, ed., *Theoretical Perspectives in Sociology*, pp. 450–462. New York: St. Martin's Press.

Schrag, Calvin O. 1970. "The Life-World and its Historical Horizon." In J. M. Edie, F. H. Parker, and C. O. Schrag, eds., *Patterns of the Life-World: Essays in Honor of John Wild*, pp. 107–122. Evanston, Ill.: Northwestern University Press.

Schutz, Alfred. 1967. *The Phenomenology of the Social World*. Trans. George Walsh and Frederick Lehnert. Evanston, Ill.: Northwestern University Press.

1970. *On Phenomenology and Social Relations*. Ed. Helmut R. Wagner. Chicago: University of Chicago Press.

1970. *Reflections on the Problem of Relevance*. Ed. and ann. Richard M. Zaner. New Haven: Yale University Press.

1972. "Choice and the Social Sciences." In Lester E. Embree, ed., *Life-World and Consciousness: Essays for Aron Gurwitsch*, pp. 565–590. Evanston, Ill.: Northwestern University Press.

1973. *Collected Papers I: The Problem of Social Reality*. Ed. Maurice Natanson. The Hague: Nijhoff.

1976. *Collected Papers II: Studies in Social Theory*. Ed. Arvid Brodersen. The Hague: Nijhoff.

1978. "Parsons' Theory of Social Action: A Critical Review." In Richard Grathoff, ed., *The Theory of Social Action: The Correspondence of Alfred Schutz and Talcott Parsons*, pp. 8–60. Bloomington: Indiana University Press.

Schutz, Alfred, and Thomas Luckmann. 1973. *The Structures of the Life-World*. Trans. Richard M. Zaner and H. Tristram Engelhardt, Jr. Evanston, Ill.: Northwestern University Press.

Scott, Marvin B. 1968. *The Racing Game*. Chicago: Aldine.

Scott, Robert A., and Jack D. Douglas, eds. 1972. *Theoretical Perspectives on Deviance*. New York: Basic Books.

Sennett, Richard, and Jonathan Cobb. 1973. *The Hidden Injuries of Class*. New York: Vintage Books.

Sharrock, W. W. 1974. "On Owning Knowledge." In Roy Turner, ed., *Ethnomethodology*, pp. 45–53. Baltimore: Penguin.

Sharrock, W. W., and Roy Turner. 1980. "Observation, Esoteric Knowledge and Automobiles." *Human Studies* 3 (January), 19–31.

Shestov, Leon. 1962. "In Memory of a Great Philosopher: Edmund Husserl." *Philosophy and Phenomenological Research* 22 (June), 449–471.

Silverman, David. 1972. "Introductory Comments." In Paul Filmer, Michael Phillipson, David Silverman, and David Walsh, *New Directions in Sociological Theory*, pp. 1–12. London: Collier-Macmillan.

1972. "Methodology and Meaning." In Paul Filmer, Michael Phillipson, David Silverman, and David Walsh, *New Directions in Sociological Theory*, pp. 183–200. London: Collier-Macmillan.

Skidmore, William. 1979. *Theoretical Thinking in Sociology*. 2d ed. New York: Cambridge University Press.

Slater, Philip. 1971. *The Pursuit of Loneliness: American Culture at the Breaking Point*. Boston: Beacon Press.

Smith, John E. 1967. "The Experience of the Holy and the Idea of God." In James M. Edie, ed., *Phenomenology in America*, pp. 295–306. Chicago: Quadrangle.

Sokolowski, Robert. 1970. *The Formation of Husserl's Concept of Constitution*. The Hague: Nijhoff.

1974. *Husserlian Meditations: How Words Present Things*. Evanston, Ill.: Northwestern University Press.

Speier, Matthew. 1970. "The Everyday World of the Child." In Jack D. Douglas, ed., *Understanding Everyday Life*, pp. 188–217. Chicago: Aldine.

1972. "Some Conversational Problems for Interactional Analysis." In David Sudnow, ed., *Studies in Social Interaction*, pp. 397–427. New York: Free Press.

Spiegelberg, Herbert. 1960. *The Phenomenological Movement*. Vol. 1. The Hague: Nijhoff.

1968. "The 'Reality-Phenomenon' and Reality." In Marvin Farber, ed., *Philosophical Essays in Memory of Edmund Husserl*, pp. 84–105. New York: Greenwood.

1973. "Husserl's Way into Phenomenology for Americans: A Letter and its Sequel." In F. Kersten and R. Zaner, eds., *Phenomenology: Continuation and Criticism*, pp. 168–191. The Hague: Nijhoff.

1975. *Doing Phenomenology: Essays On and In Phenomenology*. The Hague: Nijhoff.

Spurling, Laurie. 1977. *Phenomenology and the Social World: The Philosophy of Merleau-Ponty and Its Relation to the Social Sciences*. Boston: Routledge & Kegan Paul.

Stearns, Isabel. 1972. "The Grounds of Knowledge." *Philosophy and Phenomenological Research* II (March), 359–375.

Stein, Edith. 1964. *On the Problem of Empathy*. Trans. Waltraut Stein. The Hague: Nijhoff.

Stein, Maurice, and Arthur Vidich, eds. 1963. *Sociology on Trial*. Englewood Cliffs, N.J.: Prentice-Hall.

Stoddart, Kenneth. 1974. "Pinched: Notes on the Ethnographer's Location of Argot." In Roy Turner, ed., *Ethnomethodology*, pp. 173–179. Baltimore: Penguin.

Strasser, Stephan. 1963. *Phenomenology and the Human Sciences*. Pittsburgh: Duquesne University Press.

1967. "Phenomenologies and Psychologies." In N. Lawrence and D. O'Connor, eds., *Readings in Existential Phenomenology*, pp. 331–351. Englewood Cliffs, N.J.: Prentice-Hall.

1969. *The Idea of Dialogal Phenomenology*. Pittsburgh: Duquesne University Press.

Straus, Erwin W. 1969. "Psychiatry and Philosophy." In Maurice Natanson, ed., *Psychiatry and Philosophy*, pp. 1–83. New York: Springer-Verlag.

Sudnow, David. 1972. "Temporal Parameters of Interpersonal Observation." In David Sudnow, ed., *Studies in Social Interaction*, pp. 259–279. New York: Free Press.

Thevenaz, Pierre. 1962. *What is Phenomenology?* Ed. James M. Edie; trans. James J. Edie, Charles Courtney, and Paul Brockelman. London: Merlin Press.

Thio, Alex. 1974. "The Phenomenological Perspective of Deviance: Another Case of Class Biases." *American Sociologist* 9 (August), 146–149.

Tiryakian, Edward A. 1962. *Sociologism and Existentialism: Two Perspectives on the Individual and Society*. Englewood Cliffs, N.J.: Prentice-Hall.

1970. "Structural Sociology." In J. C. McKinney and E. A. Tiryakian, eds., *Theoretical Sociology*, pp. 111–135. New York: Appleton-Century-Crofts.

Truzzi, Marcello, ed. 1974. *Verstehen: Subjective Understanding in the Social Sciences*. Reading, Mass.: Addison-Wesley.

Turner, Jonathan H. 1974. *The Structure of Sociological Theory*. Homewood, Ill.: Dorsey.

Turner, Ralph H. 1976. "The Real Self: From Institution to Impulse." *American Journal of Sociology* 81 (March), 989–1016.

Turner, Roy. 1972. "Some Formal Properties of Therapy Talk." In David Sudnow, ed., *Studies in Social Interaction*, pp. 367–396. New York: Free Press.

1974. "Introduction." In Roy Turner, ed., *Ethnomethodology*, pp. 7–12. Baltimore: Penguin.

1974. "Words, Utterances and Activities." In Roy Turner, ed., *Ethnomethodology*, pp. 197–215. Baltimore: Penguin.

Ed. 1974. *Ethnomethodology*. Baltimore: Penguin.

Twer, Sheldon. 1972. "Tactics for Determining a Person's Resources for Depicting, Contriving, and Describing Behavioral Events." In David Sudnow, ed., *Studies in Social Interaction*, pp. 329–366. New York: Free Press.

Vandenberg, Donald. 1971. *Being and Education: An Essay in Existentialist Phenomenology*. Englewood Cliffs, N.J.: Prentice-Hall.

Van Peursen, C. A. 1970. "Life-World and Structures." In J. M. Edie, F. H. Parker, and C. O. Schrag, eds., *Patterns of the Life-World: Essays in Honor of John Wild*, pp. 139–153. Evanston, Ill.: Northwestern University Press.

Verhaar, John W. M. 1973. "Phenomenology and Present-Day Linguistics." In Maurice Natanson, ed., *Phenomenology and the Social Sciences*, pp. 361–464. Evanston, Ill.: Northwestern University Press.

Wagner, Helmut R. 1975. "Sociologists of Phenomenological Orientations: Their Place in American Sociology." *American Sociologist* 10 (August), 179–186.

1978. "Between Ideal Type and Surrender: Field Research as Asymmetrical Relation." *Human Studies* 1 (April), 153–164.

Wallace, Ruth A., and Alison Wolf. 1980. *Contemporary Sociological Theory*. Englewood Cliffs, N.J.: Prentice-Hall.

Walsh, David. 1972. "Sociology and the Social World." In Paul Filmer, Michael Phillipson, David Silverman, and David Walsh, *New Directions in Sociological Theory*, pp. 15–35. London: Collier-Macmillan.

Webb, Rodman B. 1976. *The Presence of the Past: John Dewey and Alfred Schutz on the Genesis and Organization of Experience*. Gainesville: University Presses of Florida.

Weber, Max. 1949. *The Methodology of the Social Sciences*. Trans. and ed. Edward A. Shils and Henry A. Finch. New York: Free Press.

1958. *From Max Weber: Essays in Sociology*. Trans. and ed. H. H. Gerth and C. Wright Mills. New York: Oxford University Press.

1964. *The Theory of Social and Economic Organization*. Trans. A. M. Henderson and Talcott Parsons. New York: Free Press.

Welch, E. Parl. 1939. *Edmund Husserl's Phenomenology*. Los Angeles: University of Southern California Press.

Wells, Alan. 1978. *Contemporary Sociological Theories*. Santa Monica, Calif.: Goodyear.

Werkmeister, W. H. 1951. "On 'Describing a World.' " *Philosophy and Phenomenological Research* XI (March), 303–326.

West, Candace, and Don H. Zimmerman. 1977. "Woman's Place in Everyday Talk: Reflections on Parent-Child Interaction." *Social Problems* 24 (June), 521–529.

Whitehead, Alfred North. 1968. *Modes of Thought*. New York: Free Press.

Wieder, D. Lawrence. 1974. *Language and Social Reality: The Case of Telling the Convict Code*. The Hague: Mouton.

Wild, John. 1940. "The Concept of the *Given* in Contemporary Philosophy – Its Origin and Limitations." *Philosophy and Phenomenological Research* 1 (September), 70–82.

Ed. 1953. *The Return to Reason: Essays in Realistic Philosophy*. Chicago: Regnery.

Wilson, Thomas P. 1970. "Normative and Interpretive Paradigms in Sociology." In Jack D. Douglas, ed., *Understanding Everyday Life*, pp. 57–79. Chicago: Aldine.

Zaner, Richard M. 1970. "Awakening: Towards a Phenomenology of the Self." In F. J. Smith, ed., *Phenomenology in Perspective*, pp. 171–186. The Hague: Nijhoff.

1970. *The Way of Phenomenology: Criticism as a Philosophical Discipline*. New York: Pegasus.

1971. *The Problem of Embodiment: Some Contributions to a Phenomenology of the Body*. The Hague: Nijhoff.

1972. "Reflections on Evidence and Criticism in the Theory of Consciousness." In Lester E. Embree, ed., *Life-World and Consciousness: Essays for Aron Gurwitsch*, pp. 209–230. Evanston, Ill.: Northwestern University Press.

Zimmerman, Don H. 1969. "Tasks and Troubles: The Practical Bases of Work Activities in a Public Assistance Organization." In Donald A. Hansen, ed., *Explorations in Sociology and Counseling*, pp. 237–266. Boston: Houghton Mifflin.

1970. "The Practicalities of Rule Use." In Jack D. Douglas, ed., *Understanding Everyday Life*, pp. 221–238. Chicago: Aldine.

1976. "A Reply to Professor Coser," *American Sociologist* 2 (February), 4–13.

1977. "You Can't Help But Get Stoned: Notes on the Social Organization of Marijuana Smoking." *Social Problems* 25 (December), 198–207.

1979. "Ethnomethodology." In Scott G. McNall, ed., *Theoretical Perspectives in Sociology*, pp. 381–396. New York: St. Martin's Press.

Zimmerman, Don H., and Melvin Pollner. 1970. "The Everyday World as a Phenomenon." In Jack D. Douglas, ed., *Understanding Everyday Life*, pp. 80–103. Chicago: Aldine.

Zimmerman, Don H., and Candace West. 1977. "Doing Gender." Paper presented at annual meeting of American Sociological Association, Chicago, September.

Zimmerman, Don H., and D. Lawrence Wieder. 1977. "The Diary: Diary-Interview Method." *Urban Life* 5 (January), 479–498.

Author index

Subject index

accounts, 93, 94, 95, 105
act, 61–2
action, 60, 61, 89, 193 n6; covert, 61;
ethnomethodological perspective on, 86,
130; and knowledge, 5–7; negative, 61;
overt, 61; purposive, 61; Schutz's theory
of, 60ff, 175 n78; social, 51, 59ff, 138,
153ff, 173 n27, 193 n6
adumbrations, 24, 25
anonymity, 60, 64, 75; and knowledge, 57,
124; of types, 40–1, 57
"as-if," *see* fictive
attention, 38, 43
authority, 8, 164 n3

background understandings, 86, 108, 179
n13
behavior, 60–1, 175 n78
biographically conditioned situation, *see*
situation, biographically conditioned
breaching experiments, *see* incongruity
procedures
bureaucracy, 8–9; and rationality, 8–9

certainty, 45, 47, 49, 54–5, 58, 67, 68, 77,
78
cogito, 29, 43, 44, 67, 74
common sense, 17, 57–9; *see also* Crisis of
Common Sense
communication, 102, 157, 169 n21
conduct, 60, 175 n78; covert, 60; overt, 60;
see also action
congruence of relevance systems, 53
consciousness, 22ff, 32–5; acts of, 13, 22,
23, 24, 51, 73; anonymous, 34–5; from
ethnomethodological perspective, 119ff;
and experience, 32ff; sociological, x;
stream of, 28–9, 35, 44
consociates, 64
constitution, 16, 18–9, 27ff, 145; active
and passive, 30, 43, 44;
ethnomethodological perspective on,
119, 121–2; of meaning, 43–4;
polythetic, 43, 57

constitutive expectancies, 81, 99
contemporaries, 64, 130
conversation, 93, 95, 102, 106
corpus of knowledge, 98; adequate, 96
Crisis of Common Sense, 7, 8, 10, 11, 15,
48, 57, 162
crisis of legitimacy, 6–7, 8, 164 n3
Crisis of Reason, 6–7, 8, 10, 11, 48

definition of the situation, 93, 109
deviance, 16, 18–20, 99
documentary work, 90, 94; documentary
method of interpretation, 101–2
doubt, 53; suspension of, 71

ego, 30–1, 44, 125–6; transcendental, 73,
74, 75, 127; *see also* self
eidos, *see* essence
emotions, 89, 155–6
empiricism, *see* phenomenology and
empiricism
epistemology, 13, 15, 58, 92
epochē, 70–2; among ethnomethodologists,
131–2; of the natural attitude, 132, 177
n20
essence, 71–2
et cetera assumption, 81, 111
ethnomethodological indifference, 91, 106,
132
ethnomethodology, 3–4; and common-sense
knowledge, 96, 110, 124, 128;
description in, 86, 87, 103; and
experience, 86, 89; and labeling theory,
83; and language, 83, 91, 95–6, 102,
129–30; linguistic, 84, 106, 183 n121;
and meaning, 94, 95, 108ff, 124–5;
origins, 80–2, 133–5; and
phenomenology, 80ff, 103, 105–6,
115ff, 133ff, 189 nn2, 4; and science,
86; situational, 85, 106, 183 n121; and
social reality, 85–6, 98, 99, 103, 110–2;
and social structure, 86, 95, 112ff, 133–
5; and sociology, 86ff, 98, 100; and
structuralism, 129–30; and symbolic
interactionism 82–3, 180 n33

217